CEREMONIAL OF BISHOPS

CEREMONIAL OF BISHOPS

REVISED BY DECREE OF
THE SECOND VATICAN ECUMENICAL COUNCIL
AND PUBLISHED BY AUTHORITY OF
POPE JOHN PAUL II

PREPARED BY

INTERNATIONAL COMMISSION ON ENGLISH IN THE LITURGY
A JOINT COMMISSION OF CATHOLIC BISHOPS' CONFERENCES

THE LITURGICAL PRESS
COLLEGEVILLE, MINNESOTA

1989

ACKNOWLEDGMENTS

The English translation, arrangement, and design of the *Ceremonial of Bishops* © 1989, International Committee on English in the Liturgy, Inc. (ICEL); excerpts from the English translation of the *Rite of Marriage* © 1969, ICEL; excerpts from the English translation of the *Rite of Baptism for Children* © 1969, ICEL; excerpts from the English translation of the *Rite of Funerals* © 1970, ICEL; excerpts from the English translation of the *Rite of Holy Week* © 1970, ICEL; excerpts from the English translation of the *Rite of Confirmation, Rite of Blessing of Oils, Rite of Consecrating the Chrism* © 1972, ICEL; excerpts from the English translation of *The Roman Missal* © 1973, ICEL; excerpts from the English translation of *The Liturgy of the Hours* © 1974, ICEL; excerpts from the English translation of *Holy Communion and Worship of the Eucharist outside Mass* © 1974, ICEL; excerpts from the English translation of the *Rite of Religious Profession* © 1974, ICEL; excerpts from the English translation of the *Rite of Penance* © 1974, ICEL; excerpts from the English translation of the *Rite of Blessing of an Abbot or Abbess; Rite of Consecration to a Life of Virginity* © 1975, ICEL; excerpts from the English translation of the *Rite of Confirmation*, Second Edition © 1975, ICEL; excerpts from the English translation of the *Ordination of Deacons, Priests, and Bishops* © 1975, ICEL; excerpts from the English translation of the *Institution of Readers and Acolytes; Admission to Candidacy for Ordination as Deacons and Priests* © 1976, ICEL; excerpts from the English translation of the *Dedication of a Church and an Altar* © 1978, ICEL; excerpts from the English translation of *The Roman Pontifical* © 1978, ICEL; excerpts from the English translation of *Documents on the Liturgy, 1963-1979: Conciliar, Papal, and Curial Texts* © 1982, ICEL; excerpts from the English translation of *Pastoral Care of the Sick: Rites of Anointing and Viaticum* © 1982, ICEL; excerpts from the English translation of the *Order of Christian Funerals* © 1985, ICEL; excerpts from the English translation of the *Order of Crowning an Image of the Blessed Virgin Mary* © 1986, ICEL; excerpts from the English translation of the *Rite of Christian Initiation of Adults* © 1985, ICEL; excerpts from the English translation of the *Book of Blessings* © 1987, ICEL. All rights reserved.

Printed in the United States of America.

ISBN 0-8146-1818-9

CONTENTS

Part V: SACRAMENTS

Part VI: SACRAMENTALS

CONGREGATION FOR DIVINE WORSHIP

Prot. no. CD 1300/84

DECREE

Since the revision of the liturgical books decreed by the Second Vatican Ecumenical Council is all but completed, it has been deemed necessary also to provide a thorough revision of the *Ceremonial of Bishops* and to issue it in a new form. This *Ceremonial* is intended to present the entire reformed liturgy in a suitable manner and to ensure that in celebrating the liturgy the bishop is clearly seen as "the high priest of his flock, the faithful's life in Christ in some way deriving from and depending on him" (*Sacrosanctum Concilium,* art. 41).

The purposes of the *Ceremonial* will be made more evident through attention to the pastoral and juridical norms pertaining to a bishop that have been issued by the responsible dicasteries of the Holy See.

The new *Ceremonial of Bishops* cannot be regarded as a liturgical book in the proper sense, since it is not a book for use in liturgical celebrations. But this *Ceremonial* will be helpful to bishops, to the several categories of ministers, and to masters of ceremonies, since they will all find in it the parts belonging to them in the various celebrations.

The *Ceremonial of Bishops* describes the rites carried out by a bishop in such a way that the traditions and requirements proper to each place can be retained.

The aforementioned pastoral and juridical norms issued by the Apostolic See, as well as the norms and rubrics already laid down in the liturgical books, remain in force, unless this *Ceremonial* corrects them. Additional provisions are made with the intention of achieving a liturgy for bishops that is genuine, simple, clear, dignified, and pastorally effective. These norms foster unity of spirit and avoid introducing any pointless singularity into the liturgy as celebrated by a bishop.

The Congregation for Divine Worship prepared this new *Ceremonial of Bishops* and Pope John Paul II, at an audience of 7 September 1984 granted to the undersigned Pro-Prefect and the Secretary of the Congregation, by his authority approved it and ordered its publication.

By mandate of Pope John Paul II this Congregation for Divine Worship therefore publishes the new *Ceremonial of Bishops* and decrees that it supersedes the previous *Caeremoniale Episcoporum* as soon as it is issued.

All things to the contrary notwithstanding.

Congregation for Divine Worship, on the Feast of the Triumph of the Cross, 14 September 1984.

✠ Augustin Mayer, O.S.B.
Titular Archbishop of Satrianum
Pro-Prefect

✠ Virgilio Noè
Archbishop of Voncaria
Secretary

PREFACE

I. History of the Cæremoniale Episcoporum

Pope Clement VIII in 1600 issued the *Caeremoniale Episcoporum* that has continued in use until the present time. But this was simply a new edition of an earlier work of long-standing that had been revised and emended in keeping with the spirit of the Tridentine reform.

The *Caeremoniale Episcoporum* was in fact the successor of the *Ordines Romani* that from the close of the seventh century had passed down norms for the liturgical services celebrated by the pope. One of these *Ordines*, designated as number XIII in the *Museum Italicum* of Jean Mabillon, was issued by mandate of Blessed Gregory X (1271-1276) about the year 1273, at the time of the Second Council of Lyons (1274). It did not bear the title *Caeremoniale Episcoporum*, but did contain a description of the ceremonies for the election and ordination of a pope and directives for a papal Mass and for celebrations throughout the year.

Some forty years later, somewhere between the years 1314 and 1320, an *Ordo Romanus* designated as number XIV was drawn up under the name of Cardinal James Gaetani Stefaneschi and was issued about the year 1341. This *Ordo* described the liturgy for the election and coronation of a pope and in particular the liturgies on the occasion of a general council, a canonization, and the coronation of an emperor or king.

Under Benedict XII (1334-1342) and Clement VI (1342-1352) this same work appeared in a much enlarged version and under Blessed Urban V (1362-1370) it was further supplemented by material pertaining to the death of a pope and to the status of cardinals.

Ordo Romanus XV in the numbering of Jean Mabillon, known also as the *Liber de Caeremoniis Ecclesiae Romanae*, was composed by the Patriarch Peter Ameil toward the end of the fourteenth century under Urban VI (1378-1389). Further material was added by Peter Assalbit, Bishop of Oloron, under Martin V (1417-1431). This compilation, along with manuscripts of Avignon, was used under the title *Liber Caeremoniarum Sacrae Romanae Ecclesiae* by the papal court until, by order of Innocent VIII (1484-1492), Agostino Patrizi, Bishop of Pienza and Montalcino, completed a new *Caeremoniale* in 1499. Revised by Cristoforo Marcello, Archbishop-elect of Corfu, this work was published in Venice in 1516, under the title *Rituum ecclesiasticarum sive sacrarum Caerimoniarum sanctae Romanae Ecclesiae libri tres non ante impressi*; it has remained in use for papal ceremonies until the present day.

Paris De Grassis, master of ceremonies for Julius II (1503-1513), took excerpts for the papal liturgy from the *Ordo Romanus* in the earlier *Caeremoniale* and composed a work that adapted an episcopal liturgy, that of Bologna, for use as a papal liturgy. Later, in 1564, this work was given the title *De Caeremoniis Cardinalium et Episcoporum in eorum dioecesibus libri duo.*

On 15 December 1582, Gregory XIII (1572-1585) established, under the presidency of Cardinal Gabriele Paleotti, a commission, the predecessor of the Congregation of Rites and Ceremonies, to revise the work of Paris De Grassis. Saint Charles Borromeo during a stay in Rome had suggested this revision to Gregory XIII and warmly supported it. But when the saint died in 1584, the work of the commission ceased.

On 22 January 1588 Sixtus V (1585-1590) established the Congregation for Sacred Rites and Ceremonies with the task of revising the liturgical books. Earlier, on 19 March 1586, he had ordered a large number of codexes to be brought to him from the Vatican Library, so that he himself might prepare a fresh study on the sacred rites, but the result of this project is unknown.

Finally, on 14 July 1600, Clement VIII (1592-1605) published the *Caeremoniale Episcoporum* and thus brought to completion the work of creating a ceremonial. Its composition made use of the work not only of Agostino Patrizi and Paris De Grassis, but also that of others whose names are today unknown. At the time of the preparation of this ceremonial, three men outstanding for their holiness and learning, the Venerable Cesar Baronius, Saint Robert Bellarmine, and Cardinal Silvio Antoniano, were working in the Congregation of Rites. The papal bull introducing this ceremonial refers throughout, not to a new book, but to a revision of the *Caeremoniale Episcoporum,* a work known to all.

Under Innocent X (1644-1655) an emended and revised edition of the *Caeremoniale* was published on 30 July 1650. A century later Benedict XIII (1724-1730), in keeping with his great interest in the liturgy, brought out a further edition on 7 March 1727 which clarified some obscurities and ambiguities and removed certain internal conflicts. Fifteen years later, on 25 March 1742, Benedict XIV (1740-1758), a former *Officialis* of the Congregation of Rites, produced a new edition of the *Caeremoniale,* adding a third book, on matters pertaining to the States of the Church. The work also commended the method of the school of liturgy then existing at the Gregorian Collegio Romano of the Society of Jesus.

Finally, in 1886, Leo XIII (1878-1903) ordered publication of a new *editio typica* of the *Caeremoniale Episcoporum,* which retained Book III, even though by that time it would have no use, since the States of the Church had ceased to exist or rather had been reduced to Vatican City.

Since the Second Vatican Council ordered a reform of all liturgical rites and books, a complete revision and arrangement of the *Caeremoniale Episcoporum* has proved to be needed.

II. VALUE OF THE CÆREMONIALE EPISCOPORUM

The popes who promulgated the various editions of the *Caeremoniale Epis-coporum* issued it as a book that was to be followed by all in perpetuity, but they had no intention of abolishing or abrogating ancient ceremonial practices that were in keeping with the spirit of the *Caeremoniale*. The present volume, conformed to the norms of the Second Vatican Council, takes the place of the previous ceremonial, which is henceforth to be considered entirely abrogated. As long as they are compatible with the liturgy as reformed by decree of the Second Vatican Council, the customs and traditions that each particular Church treasures as its own inheritance, to be handed on to future generations, are provided for by the directives of the present *Ceremonial*.

The greater part of the liturgical laws contained in the new *Ceremonial* have their force from the liturgical books already published. Whatever is changed in the new *Ceremonial* is to be carried out in the manner the *Ceremonial* prescribes.

Other norms in this *Ceremonial* have as their objective a liturgy of bishops that is simple, dignified, and as pastorally effective as possible, in order that the liturgy celebrated by a bishop may stand as a model for all other celebrations.

To achieve this pastoral objective more easily, the present volume has been composed in such a way that bishops and other ministers, and especially masters of ceremonies, can find in it everything necessary to make a liturgical service at which the bishop presides not a mere outward display of ceremony but rather, in keeping with the intent of the Second Vatican Council, the principal manifestation of the particular Church.

PART I

GENERAL CONSIDERATIONS

CHAPTER 1

CHARACTER AND IMPORTANCE OF A LITURGY
AT WHICH THE BISHOP PRESIDES

I. DIGNITY OF THE PARTICULAR CHURCHES

1   "The diocese forms that part of the people of God entrusted to the pastoral care of the bishop with the assistance of the presbyterate. In allegiance to its pastor and by him gathered together in the Holy Spirit through the Gospel and the eucharist, the diocese stands as a particular Church, in which Christ's one, holy, catholic, and apostolic Church is truly present and at work."[1] Indeed, Christ is present, since by his power the Church is gathered together in unity.[2] As Saint Ignatius of Antioch has truly written: "Just as where Christ Jesus is, there also is the Catholic Church, so also where the bishop is, there also should be the whole assembly of his people."[3]

2   Hence the dignity of the Church of Christ is embodied in the particular Churches. Each such Church is not simply a group of people who on their own choose to band together for some common endeavor; rather each Church is a gift that comes down from the Father of lights. Nor are the particular Churches to be regarded merely as administrative divisions of the people of God. In their own proper way they contain and manifest the nature of the universal Church, which issued from the side of Christ crucified, which lives and grows through the eucharist, which is espoused to Christ, and which, as their mother, cares for all the faithful. The particular Churches "in their own locality are the new people called by God in the Holy Spirit and in great fullness (see 1 Thessalonians 1:5)."[4]

3   But, as the Council also teaches, there is no lawful assembly of the faithful, no community of the altar except under the sacred ministry of the bishop.[5] The congregation making up the particular Church is situated and has its life in the many individual assemblies of the faithful,

---

[1] Vatican Council II, Decree on the Pastoral Office of Bishops *Christus Dominus* (hereafter, CD), no. 11: ICEL, *Documents on the Liturgy, 1963-1979: Conciliar, Papal, and Curial Texts* (hereafter, DOL; The Liturgical Press, Collegeville, Minn., 1982), 7, no. 191. See Vatican Council II, Dogmatic Constitution on the Church *Lumen gentium* (hereafter, LG), no. 23.

[2] See LG, no. 26: DOL 4, no. 146.

[3] Ignatius of Antioch, *Ad Smyrnaeos*, 8, 2: F. X. Funk, ed., *Patres apostolici*, v. 1, p. 283.

[4] LG, no. 26: DOL 4, no. 146.

[5] See LG, no. 26: DOL 4, no. 146.

17

over which the bishop places his presbyters, in order that under his authority they may sanctify and guide the portion of the Lord's flock that is assigned to them.[6]

4   Just as the universal Church is present and manifested in the particular Churches,[7] so too each particular Church contributes its own distinctive gifts to the other Churches and to the Church as a whole, "so that from their sharing of gifts with one another and their common effort in unity toward perfection, the Church achieves growth as a whole and in its particular parts."[8]

II. The Bishop as Foundation and Sign of Communion in the Particular Church

5   As Christ's vicar and representative, marked with the fullness of the sacrament of orders, the bishop leads the particular Church in communion with the pope and under his authority.[9]

"Placed there by the Holy Spirit, bishops are the successors of the apostles as shepherds of souls, . . . for Christ gave the apostles and their successors the mandate and the power to teach all nations and to sanctify and to shepherd their people in truth. By the Holy Spirit who has been given to them, therefore, bishops have been made true and authentic teachers of the faith, high priests, and pastors."[10]

6   Through the preaching of the Gospel and in the power of the Spirit the bishop calls men and women to faith or confirms them in the faith they already have, and he proclaims to them the mystery of Christ in its entirety.[11]

7   The bishop's authority regulates the orderly and effective celebration of the sacraments and through them he sanctifies the faithful. He supervises the bestowal of baptism, since it brings with it a share in the royal priesthood of Christ. He is the primary minister of confirmation, he alone confers the sacrament of holy orders, and he oversees the penitential discipline in his diocese. He regulates every lawful celebra-

---

[6] See LG, nos. 26, 28: DOL 4, nos. 146, 148. See Vatican Council II, Constitution on the Liturgy *Sacrosanctum Concilium* (hereafter, SC), art. 41: DOL 1, no. 41.

[7] See LG, no. 23.

[8] LG, no. 13.

[9] See LG, nos 26, 27: DOL 4, nos. 146-147. See CD, no. 3.

[10] CD, no. 2.

[11] See CD, no. 12: DOL 7, no. 192.

tion of the eucharist, from which the Church continually receives life and growth. He never ceases to exhort and to instruct his people to fulfill their part in the liturgy with faith and reverence, and especially in the eucharistic sacrifice.[12]

8   In the person of the bishop, with the presbyters gathered round him, the Lord Jesus Christ, the High Priest, is present in the midst of the faithful. Seated at the right hand of the Father, Christ is not absent from the gathering of his high priests. They have been chosen to feed the Lord's flock and they are Christ's ministers and the stewards of the mysteries of God.[13] Therefore, "the bishop is to be looked on as the high priest of his flock, the faithful's life in Christ in some way deriving from and depending on him."[14]

9   The bishop is "the steward of the grace of the supreme priesthood."[15] On him depend both presbyters and deacons in the exercise of their orders. Presbyters, appointed to be prudent co-workers of the order of bishops, are themselves consecrated as true priests of the New Testament; deacons serve as ministers ordained to service for the people of God in communion with the bishop and his presbyters. The bishop himself is the chief steward of the mysteries of God and the overseer, promoter, and guardian of all liturgical life in the particular Church entrusted to his care.[16] To him "is committed the office of offering to the divine majesty the worship of Christian religion and of administering it in accordance with the Lord's commandments and the Church's laws, as further specified by his particular judgment for his diocese."[17]

10   The bishop rules the particular Church entrusted to him by counsel, persuasion, and example, but also by the authority and sacred power that he received through his ordination as bishop,[18] which he uses only for the building up of his flock in truth and holiness. "The faithful should cling to the bishop as the Church clings to Jesus Christ and as Jesus Christ clings to the Father, so that through such unity there may be harmony in everything and so that everything may conspire to the glory of God."[19]

---

[12] See LG, no. 26: DOL 4, no. 146. See CD, no. 15: DOL 7, no. 194.

[13] See LG, no. 21: DOL 4, no. 145.

[14] SC, art. 41: DOL 1, no. 41.

[15] Prayer of consecration of a bishop in the Byzantine rite: *Euchologion to mega* (Rome, 1873), 139; LG, no. 26: DOL 4, no. 146.

[16] See CD, no. 15: DOL 7, no. 194.

[17] LG, no. 26: DOL 4, no. 146.

[18] See LG, no. 21: DOL 4, no. 145. See CD, no. 3.

[19] LG, no. 27.

III. Importance of a Liturgy at Which the Bishop Presides

11   The office of bishop as teacher, sanctifier, and pastor of his Church shines forth most clearly in a liturgy that he celebrates with his people.

"Therefore all should hold in great esteem the liturgical life of the diocese centered around the bishop, especially in his cathedral church; they must be convinced that the preeminent manifestation of the Church is present in the full, active participation of all God's holy people in these liturgical celebrations, especially in the same eucharist, in a single prayer, at one altar at which the bishop presides, surrounded by his college of presbyters and by his ministers."[20]

12   Hence liturgical celebrations in which the bishop presides manifest the mystery of the Church as that mystery involves Christ's presence; such celebrations, then, are not a mere display of ceremony.

These celebrations should also serve as a model for the entire diocese and be shining examples of active participation by the people. The whole gathered community should thus take part through song, dialogue, prayerful silence, and attentiveness and by sharing in the sacraments.

13   Provision should be made at appointed times and on the major dates of the liturgical year for the special manifestation of the particular Church that such a celebration means. The faithful from different areas of the diocese should be invited to gather and, as far as possible, the presbyters should join them. To encourage and make more convenient gatherings of the faithful and the presbyters, arrangement should be made for gatherings of this kind at different times in the various parts of the diocese.

14   These gatherings should be occasions for the faithful to grow in their love for the entire Church and to heighten their desire to serve the Gospel and their neighbor.

IV. The Bishop's Fulfillment of the Office of Preaching

15   Among the principal duties of a bishop the preaching of the Gospel is preeminent. The bishop as herald of the faith leads new followers to Christ. As their authentic teacher, that is, one invested with the authority of Christ, he proclaims to the people entrusted to him the truths of

---

[20] SC, art. 41: DOL 1, no. 41.

faith they are to believe and to live by. Under the light of the Holy Spirit the bishop explains the teachings of faith, bringing forth from the treasure-house of revelation new things and old. He works to make faith yield its harvest and, like the good shepherd, he is vigilant in protecting his people from the threat of error.[21]

The liturgy is one of the ways in which the bishop discharges this responsibility: he preaches the homily at celebrations of the eucharist, celebrations of the word of God and, as occasion suggests, celebrations of morning and evening prayer; also when he imparts catechesis and in his introductions, invitations, or commentary during celebrations of the sacraments and sacramentals.

16   This preaching "should draw its content mainly from scriptural and liturgical sources, being a proclamation of God's wonderful works in the history of salvation, the mystery of Christ, ever present and active within us, especially in the celebration of the liturgy."[22]

17   Since the office of preaching is proper to the bishop, so that other ordained ministers fulfill this office only in his name, he should preach the homily himself whenever he presides at a celebration of the liturgy. Unless he decides that some other way is preferable, the bishop should preach while seated at the chair, wearing the miter and holding the pastoral staff.

---

[21] See LG, no. 25.
[22] SC, art. 35, 2: DOL 1, no. 35.

CHAPTER 2

OFFICES AND MINISTRIES IN THE LITURGY OF BISHOPS

18   "Any community of the altar, under the sacred ministry of the bishop, stands out clearly as a symbol of that charity and 'unity of the Mystical Body, without which there can be no salvation.'"[23]

Thus it is very fitting that when the bishop, who is marked by the fullness of the sacrament of orders, is present at a liturgical celebration in which a congregation takes part, he personally preside. The reason for this is not to give added outward solemnity to the rite, but to make the celebration a more striking sign of the mystery of the Church.

For the same reason it is fitting that the bishop associate presbyters with himself as concelebrants.

When a bishop presides at the eucharist but is not the celebrant, he does everything in the liturgy of the word that belongs to the celebrant and he concludes the Mass with the rite of dismissal,[24] following the provisions given in nos. 176-185.

19   In every liturgical assembly, and especially one at which the bishop presides, all those present have the right and the duty to carry out their parts in the different ways corresponding to their differences in order and office. Each one, therefore, minister or layperson, should do all of, but only, those parts which pertain to that office by the nature of the rite and the principles of liturgy.[25] This way of celebration manifests the Church in its variety of orders and ministries as a body whose individual members form a unity.[26]

Presbyters

20   Even though they do not possess the fullness of priesthood that belongs to the episcopate and in the exercise of their power depend upon the bishop, presbyters are nevertheless joined to the bishop by the bond of priestly dignity.

Presbyters, prudent co-workers with the episcopal order, its aid and instrument, called to serve the people of God, constitute one college of

---

[23] LG, no. 26: DOL 4, no. 146.

[24] See Sacred Congregation of Rites (hereafter, SC Rites), Instruction *Pontificales ritus*, on the simplification of pontifical rites and insignia, 21 June 1968 (hereafter, PR), no. 24: AAS 60 (1968), p. 410; DOL 550, no. 4481.

[25] See SC, art. 28: DOL 1, no. 28.

[26] See SC, art. 26: DOL 1, no. 26.

presbyters with their bishop and, under the bishop's authority, sanctify and govern that portion of the Lord's flock entrusted to them.[27]

21   It is strongly recommended that in liturgical celebrations the bishop should have presbyters to assist him. In a eucharistic celebration presided over by the bishop, presbyters should concelebrate with him so that the mystery of the unity of the Church may be made manifest through the eucharistic celebration and so that the presbyters may be seen by the entire community to be the presbyterate of the bishop.

22   Presbyters taking part in a liturgy with the bishop should do only what belongs to the order of presbyter;[28] in the absence of deacons they may perform some of the ministries proper to the deacon, but should never wear diaconal vestments.

Deacons

23   Deacons hold the highest place among ministers and from the Church's earliest age the diaconate has been held in great honor. As men of good repute and full of wisdom,[29] they should act in such a way that, with the help of God, all may know them to be true disciples[30] of one who came, not to be served but to serve,[31] and who was among his disciples as one who serves.[32]

24   Strengthened by the gift of the Holy Spirit, deacons assist the bishop and his presbyterate in the ministry of the word, the altar, and of charity. As ministers of the altar they proclaim the gospel reading, help at the celebration of the sacrifice, and serve as eucharistic ministers.
    Deacons should therefore look on the bishop as a father and assist him as they would the Lord Jesus Christ himself, who is the eternal High Priest, present in the midst of his people.

25   In liturgical celebrations it belongs to the deacon to assist the celebrant, to minister at the altar with the book and the cup, to guide the assembly of the faithful with suitable directions, to announce the intentions of the general intercessions.

---

[27] See LG, no. 28: DOL 4, no. 148.
[28] See SC, art. 28: DOL 1, no. 28.
[29] See Acts 6:3.
[30] See John 13:35.
[31] See Matthew 20:28.
[32] See Luke 22:27.

If there is no other minister, the deacon also carries out other ministerial functions as required.[33]

When assisting at an altar that does not face the people, the deacon is always to turn toward the people when he addresses them.

26   At a liturgical celebration presided over by the bishop there should be at least three deacons, one to proclaim the gospel reading and to minister at the altar, and two to assist the bishop. If more than three deacons are present, they should divide the ministries accordingly,[34] and at least one of them should be charged with assisting the active participation of the faithful.

Acolytes

27   In the ministry of the altar acolytes have their own proper functions and should exercise these even though ministers of a higher rank may be present.

28   Acolytes receive institution so that they may help the deacon and minister to the priest. Their proper ministry is to look after the service of the altar and to assist the deacon and priest in liturgical services, especially the celebration of Mass. In addition, acolytes may serve as special ministers of the eucharist, giving holy communion in accord with the provisions of the law.

When necessary, acolytes should instruct those who serve as ministers in liturgical rites by carrying the book, the cross, candles, or the censer or by performing other similar duties. But in celebrations presided over by the bishop it is fitting that all such ministerial functions be carried out by formally instituted acolytes, and if a number are present, they should divide the ministries accordingly.[35]

29   So that they may fulfill their responsibilities more worthily, acolytes should take part in the celebration of the eucharist with ever increasing devotion, as the source of their spiritual life and the object of an ever deeper appreciation. They should seek to acquire an interior and spiritual sense of their ministry so that each day they may offer them-

---

[33] See the General Instruction of the Roman Missal, 4th ed., 1975 (hereafter, GIRM), nos. 71, 127: DOL 208, nos. 1461, 1517.

[34] See GIRM, no. 71: DOL 208, no. 1461.

[35] See Paul VI, Motu Proprio *Ministeria quaedam*, on first tonsure, minor orders, and the subdiaconate, 15 August 1972 (hereafter, MQ), no. VI: AAS 64 (1972), p. 532; DOL 340, no. 2931.

selves wholly to God and grow in sincere love for the Mystical Body of Christ, the people of God, and especially for the members who are weak and infirm.

Readers

30   In liturgical celebrations readers have their own proper function and should exercise this, even though ministers of a higher rank may be present.[36]

31   The office of reader was historically the first of the lesser ministries to emerge. This office exists in all the Churches and has never disappeared. Readers receive institution for an office proper to them: to proclaim the word of God in the liturgical assembly. Hence at Mass and in other rites of the liturgy readers proclaim the readings other than the gospel reading. When there is no cantor of the psalm present, the reader also leads the assembly in the responsorial psalm; when no deacon is present, the reader announces the intentions of the general intercessions.
    Whenever necessary, the reader should see to the preparation of any members of the faithful who may be appointed to proclaim the readings from Sacred Scripture in liturgical celebrations. But in celebrations presided over by the bishop it is fitting that readers formally instituted proclaim the readings and, if several readers are present, they should divide the readings accordingly.[37]

32   Conscious of the dignity of God's word and the importance of their office, readers should be eager to learn how best to speak and proclaim, in order that those who listen may clearly hear and understand the word of God.
    In proclaiming the word of God to others, readers should themselves receive it with docility and meditate on it with devotion so that they may bear witness to that word in their daily lives.

Psalmist or Cantor of the Psalm

33   The chants between the readings are very important liturgically and pastorally; it is therefore desirable in celebrations presided over by the

---

[36] GIRM, no. 66: DOL 208, no. 1456.

[37] See MQ, no. V: AAS 64 (1972), p. 532; DOL 340, no. 2931. See The Roman Missal, *Lectionary for Mass*, 2nd English ed., 1981 (hereafter, LM), Introduction, nos. 51-55. See General Instruction of the Liturgy of the Hours (hereafter, GILH), no. 259: DOL 426, no. 3689.

bishop, especially in the cathedral church, that there be a psalmist or cantor who has the necessary musical ability and devotion to the liturgy. The cantor of the psalm is responsible for singing, either responsorially or directly, the chants between the readings – the psalm or other biblical canticle, the gradual and *Alleluia,* or other chant – in such a way as to assist the faithful to join in the singing and to reflect on the meaning of the texts.[38]

Master of Ceremonies

34   For a liturgical celebration, especially a celebration presided over by the bishop, to be distinguished by grace, simplicity, and order, a master of ceremonies is needed to prepare and direct the celebration in close cooperation with the bishop and others responsible for planning its several parts, and especially from a pastoral standpoint.

The master of ceremonies should be well-versed in the history and nature of the liturgy and in its laws and precepts. But equally he should be well-versed in pastoral science, so that he knows how to plan liturgical celebrations in a way that encourages fruitful participation by the people and enhances the beauty of the rites.

He should seek to ensure an observance of liturgical laws that is in accord with the true spirit of such laws and with those legitimate traditions of the particular Church that have pastoral value.

35   In due time he should arrange with the cantors, assistants, ministers, and celebrants the actions to be carried out and the texts to be used, but during the celebration he should exercise the greatest discretion: he is not to speak more than is necessary, nor replace the deacons or assistants at the side of the celebrant. The master of ceremonies should carry out his responsibilities with reverence, patience, and careful attention.

36   The master of ceremonies wears either an alb or a cassock and surplice. Within a celebration a master of ceremonies who is an ordained deacon may wear a dalmatic and the other diaconal vestments.

Sacristan

37   Along with the master of ceremonies and under his direction, the sacristan sees to the preparation for a celebration with the bishop. The sacristan should carefully arrange the books needed for the proclamation of the word and for the presidential prayers; he or she should lay

---

[38] See LM, Introduction, nos. 19-20, 56.

out the vestments and have ready whatever else is needed for the celebration. He or she should see to the ringing of bells for celebrations. He or she should ensure the observance of silence and quiet in the sacristy and the vesting room. Vestments, church furnishings, and decorative objects that have been handed down from the past are not to be treated carelessly, but kept in good condition. When anything new needs to be provided, it should be chosen to meet the standards of contemporary art, but not out of a desire simply for novelty.

38   The first of all the elements belonging to the beauty of the place where the liturgy is celebrated is the spotless cleanliness of the floor and walls and of all the images and articles that will be used or seen during a service. In all the liturgical appurtenances both ostentation and shabbiness are to be avoided; instead the norms of noble simplicity, refinement, gracefulness, and artistic excellence are to be respected. The culture of the people and local tradition should guide the choice of objects and their arrangement, "on condition that they serve the places of worship and the sacred rites with the reverence and honor due to them."[39]

The adornment and decor of a church should be such as to make the church a visible sign of love and reverence toward God, and to remind the people of God of the real meaning of the feasts celebrated there and to inspire in them a sense of joy and devotion.

Choir and Musicians

39   All who have a special part in the singing and music for the liturgy—choir directors, cantors, organists, and others—should be careful to follow the provisions concerning their functions that are found in the liturgical books and other documents published by the Apostolic See.[40]

40   Musicians should constantly keep in mind those norms especially that regard the participation of the people in singing. In addition, they

---

[39] SC, art. 123: DOL 1, no. 123.

[40] See GIRM, particularly nos. 12, 19, 22, 63, 64, 272, 274, 275, 313, 324: DOL 208, nos. 1402, 1409, 1412, 1453, 1454, 1662, 1664, 1665, 1703, 1714. See *Ordo cantus Missae*, Introduction: DOL 535, nos. 4276-4302; GILH, nos. 268-284: DOL 426, nos. 3698-3714. See The Roman Ritual, the *Rite of Baptism for Children, Christian Initiation*, General Introduction, no. 33: DOL 294, no. 2282. See The Roman Ritual, *Holy Communion and Worship of the Eucharist outside Mass*, nos. 12 and 104: DOL 279, nos. 2204 and 2222. See The Roman Ritual, *Rite of Penance*, nos. 24 and 36: DOL 368, nos. 3089 and 3101. See The Roman Ritual, *Pastoral Care of the Sick: Rites of Anointing and Viaticum*, no. 38, d: DOL 411, no. 3358. See The Roman Ritual, *Order of Christian Funerals*, no. 12: DOL 416, no. 3384 (see English ed., nos. 30-33). See SC Rites, Instruction *Musicam sacram*, 5 March 1967 (hereafter, MS): AAS 69 (1967), pp. 300-320; DOL 508, nos. 4122-4190. See Sacred Congregation for Bishops, Directory on the Pastoral Ministry of Bishops (1970), no. 90, d: DOL 329, no. 2660.

should take care that the singing expresses the note of universality belonging to celebrations presided over by the bishop; hence, the faithful should be able to recite or sing together not only in the vernacular but also in Latin the parts of the Order of Mass that pertain to them.

41   From Ash Wednesday until the singing of the *Gloria* at the Easter Vigil and in celebrations for the dead, the organ and other instruments should be played only to sustain the singing.[41] An exception is made for *Laetare* Sunday (the Fourth Sunday of Lent) and for solemnities and festive days.

From the end of the *Gloria* in the Mass of the Lord's Supper on Holy Thursday until the *Gloria* at the Easter Vigil, the organ and other musical instruments should be played only to sustain the singing.

During Advent musical instruments should be played with a moderation that is in keeping with the spirit of joyful expectation characteristic of this season, but does not anticipate the fullness of joy belonging to the celebration of the nativity of the Lord.

---

[41] See MS, no. 66: AAS 69 (1967), p. 319; DOL 508, no. 4187.

CHAPTER 3

CATHEDRAL CHURCH

42   The cathedral church is the church that is the site of the bishop's cathedra or chair, the sign of his teaching office and pastoral power in the particular Church, and a sign also of the unity of believers in the faith that the bishop proclaims as shepherd of the Lord's flock.

In this church, on the more solemn liturgical days, the bishop presides at the liturgy. There also, unless pastoral considerations suggest otherwise, he consecrates the sacred chrism and confers the sacrament of holy orders.

43   The diocesan cathedral "in the majesty of its building is a symbol of the spiritual temple that is built up in souls and is resplendent with the glory of divine grace. As Saint Paul says: 'We are the temple of the living God' (2 Corinthians 6:16). The cathedral, furthermore, should be regarded as the express image of Christ's visible Church, praying, singing, and worshiping on earth. The cathedral should be regarded as the image of Christ's Mystical Body, whose members are joined together in an organism of charity that is sustained by the outpouring of God's gifts."[42]

44   With good reason, then, the cathedral church should be regarded as the center of the liturgical life of the diocese.

45   Effective measures should be taken to instill esteem and reverence for the cathedral church in the hearts of the faithful. Among such measures are the annual celebration of the dedication of the cathedral and pilgrimages in which the faithful, especially in groups of parishes or sections of the diocese, visit the cathedral in a spirit of devotion.

46   The cathedral church should be a model for the other churches of the diocese in its conformity to the directives laid down in liturgical documents and books with regard to the arrangement and adornment of churches.[43]

47   The bishop's *cathedra* or *chair* mentioned in no. 42, should be a chair that stands alone and is permanently installed. Its placement should make

---

[42] Paul VI, Apostolic Constitution *Mirificus eventus*, declaring the jubilee of 1966, 7 December 1965: AAS 57 (1965), pp. 948-949; DOL 484, no. 4054.

[43] See GIRM, nos. 253-312: DOL 208, nos. 1643-1702. See LM, Introduction, nos. 32-34. See The Roman Pontifical, *Dedication of a Church and an Altar*, ch. 2, no. 3, and ch. 4, nos. 6-11: DOL 547, no. 4371 and nos. 4403-4408. See The Roman Ritual, *Holy Communion and Worship of the Eucharist outside Mass*, General Introduction, nos. 9-11: DOL 279, nos. 2201-2203.

it clear that the bishop is presiding over the whole community of the faithful.

Depending on the design of each church, the chair should have enough steps leading up to it for the bishop to be clearly visible to the faithful.

There is to be no baldachin over the bishop's chair; but valuable works of art from the past are to be preserved with utmost care.

Apart from the cases provided for by law, only the diocesan bishop, or a bishop he permits to use it, occupies this chair.[44] Seats are to be provided in a convenient place for other bishops or prelates who may be present at a celebration, but such seats are not to be set up in the manner of a cathedra.[45]

The chair for a priest celebrant should be set up in a place separate from the site of the bishop's chair.

48   The *altar* should be constructed and adorned in accordance with the provisions of the law. It should be so placed as to be a focal point on which the attention of the whole congregation centers naturally.[46]

The altar of the cathedral church should normally be a fixed altar that has been dedicated. This altar should be freestanding to allow the ministers to walk around it easily and to permit celebration facing the people.[47] But when the cathedral has an old altar so constructed that it makes participation of the people difficult and that cannot be moved without damage to its artistic value, another fixed altar, of artistic merit and duly dedicated, should be erected. Only at this altar are liturgical celebrations to be carried out.

Flowers should not adorn the altar from Ash Wednesday until the *Gloria* at the Easter Vigil, nor in celebrations for the dead. Exceptions to this rule are *Laetare* Sunday (the Fourth Sunday of Lent), solemnities, and feasts.

49   It is recommended that the *tabernacle*, in accordance with a very ancient tradition in cathedral churches, should be located in a chapel separate from the main body of the church.[48]

---

[44] See *Codex Iuris Canonici* (*Code of Canon Law*), 1983 (hereafter, CIC), can. 463, §3. See in this *Ceremonial*, nos. 1171 and 1176.

[45] See PR, nos. 10-13: AAS 60 (1968), pp. 408-409; DOL 550, nos. 4467-4470.

[46] See GIRM, no. 262: DOL 208, no. 1652.

[47] See GIRM, no. 262: DOL 208, no. 1652.

[48] See SC Rites, Instruction *Eucharisticum mysterium*, on worship of the eucharist, 25 May 1967, no. 53: AAS 59 (1967), p. 568; DOL 179, no. 1282. See The Roman Ritual, *Holy Communion and Worship of the Eucharist outside Mass*, General Introduction, no. 9: DOL 279, no. 2201.

But when, in a particular case, there is a tabernacle on the altar at which the bishop is to celebrate, the blessed sacrament should be transferred to another fitting place.

50   The *sanctuary* or *chancel*, that is, the place where the bishop, presbyters, and ministers carry out their ministries, should be set apart from the body of the church in some way—for example, by being at a somewhat higher level or by its distinctive design and ornamentation—in such a way that even the layout of the sanctuary highlights the hierarchic offices of the ministers. The sanctuary should be sufficiently spacious for the rites to be carried out without obstruction to movement or to the view of the assembly.

Seats, benches, or stools should be provided in the sanctuary, so that concelebrants, or canons and presbyters not concelebrating but assisting in choir dress, as well as the ministers, all have their own places, and in such a way as to facilitate the exercise of their various parts in a celebration.

A minister who is not wearing a vestment, a cassock and surplice, or other lawfully approved garb may not enter the sanctuary (chancel) during a celebration.[49]

51   The cathedral church should have an *ambo* or *lectern*, constructed in keeping with liturgical norms currently in force.[50] But the bishop should address the people of God from the bishop's chair (cathedra), unless local conditions suggest otherwise.

The cantor, the commentator, or the choirmaster should not normally use the ambo or lectern, but should carry out their functions from another suitable place.

52   Even when it is not a parochial church, the cathedral should have a *baptistery*, at least for the celebration of baptism at the Easter Vigil. The baptistery should be designed and equipped in keeping with the provisions of The Roman Ritual.[51]

53   The cathedral church should have a *vesting room*, that is, a suitable place, as close as possible to the church entrance, where the bishop, concelebrants, and ministers can put on their liturgical vestments and from which the entrance procession can begin.

---

[49] See in this *Ceremonial*, nos. 65-67. See LM, Introduction, no. 54.

[50] See GIRM, no. 272: DOL 208, no. 1662. See LM, Introduction, nos. 32-34.

[51] See The Roman Ritual, *Rite of Baptism for Children, Christian Initiation*, General Introduction, no. 25: DOL 294, no. 2274.

The sacristy, which should normally be separate from the vesting room, is a room where vestments and other liturgical materials are kept. It may also serve as the place where the celebrant and the ministers prepare for a celebration on ordinary occasions.

54   If at all possible, provision should be made for a *gathering place* of the people near the cathedral church — another church, a suitable hall, a square, or a cloister — where the blessings of candles, of palms, and of fire, as well as other preparatory celebrations, may take place and from which processions to the cathedral church may begin.

CHAPTER 4

GENERAL NORMS

INTRODUCTION

55   According to the teaching of the Second Vatican Council, care must be taken to ensure that rites are marked by a noble simplicity.[52] This applies also to a liturgy in which the bishop presides, although the respect and reverence owed to a bishop are not to be disregarded. In him the Lord Jesus is present in the midst of those who believe and the faithful's life in Christ in some way depends on and derives from him.[53]

In addition, a liturgy in which the bishop presides is usually marked by the participation of those having the different orders existing in the Church and in this way the mystery of the Church is more clearly made visible. Thus celebrations with the bishop ought to be marked by love and mutual esteem between the members of the Mystical Body of Jesus Christ, so that the liturgy may truly fulfill the precept of Saint Paul: "Be first in showing honor to each other."[54]

Before describing the individual rites, it seems advisable to state some general norms that have proved valid by long use and that should be followed.

I. VESTURE AND INSIGNIA

Vesture and insignia of the bishop

56   The vestments worn by the bishop at a liturgical celebration are the same as those worn by presbyters; but, in accordance with traditional usage, it is fitting that at a solemn celebration he wear under the chasuble a dalmatic (which may always be white). This applies particularly to the celebration of ordinations, the blessing of an abbot or abbess, and the dedication of a church and an altar.

57   The pontifical insignia belonging to a bishop are: the ring, the pastoral staff, and the miter, as well as the pallium, if he is entitled to its use.

58   The *ring* is the symbol of the bishop's fidelity to and nuptial bond with the Church, his spouse, and he is to wear it always.

---

[52] See SC, art. 34: DOL 1, no. 34.
[53] See LG, no. 21: DOL 4, no. 145. See SC, art. 41: DOL 1, no. 41.
[54] Romans 12:10.

59   The bishop carries the *pastoral staff* in his own territory as a sign of his pastoral office, but any bishop who, with the consent of the diocesan bishop, solemnly celebrates may use the pastoral staff.[55] When several bishops are present at the same celebration, only the presiding bishop uses the pastoral staff.

As a rule, the bishop holds the pastoral staff, its curved head turned away from himself and toward the people: as he walks in procession, listens to the gospel reading, and gives the homily; also when receiving religious vows and promises or a profession of faith and when he bestows a blessing on persons, unless the blessing includes the laying on of hands.

60   In a liturgical service the bishop is to use only one *miter*, plain or ornate depending on the character of the celebration.[56] As a rule the bishop wears the miter: when he is seated; when he gives the homily; when he greets the people, addresses them, or gives the invitation to prayer, except when he would have to lay it aside immediately afterward; when he gives a solemn blessing to the people; when he confers a sacrament; when he is walking in procession.

The bishop does not use the miter: during the introductory rites, the opening prayer, prayer over the gifts, and prayer after communion; during the general intercessions, the eucharistic prayer, the gospel reading, hymns that are sung standing, processions in which the blessed sacrament or relics of the true cross are carried; nor does he wear the miter in the presence of the blessed sacrament exposed. The bishop need not use the miter and pastoral staff as he walks from one place to another nearby.[57]

Use of the miter in the ministration of sacraments and sacramentals should be governed by the provisions that will be given in place in this *Ceremonial*.

61   The *pectoral cross* is to be worn under the chasuble, dalmatic, or cope, but over the mozzetta.

62   A residential archbishop who has already received the *pallium* from the pope wears it outside the chasuble in the territory of his jurisdiction when he celebrates a stational Mass or another Mass celebrated with great solemnity; he wears it also for ordinations, the blessing of an abbot or

---

[55] See PR, no. 19: AAS 60 (1968), p. 410; DOL 550, no. 4476.

[56] See PR, no. 18: AAS 60 (1968), p. 410; DOL 550, no. 4475.

[57] See PR, no. 31: AAS 60 (1968), p. 411; DOL 550, no. 4488.

abbess, the consecration to a life of virginity, and the dedication of a church or an altar.

Once an archbishop has received the pallium, the archiepiscopal cross is carried when he goes to a church to celebrate any service of the liturgy.[58]

63   The *choir dress* of a bishop, both within his diocese and elsewhere, consists of: a purple cassock with purple sash of silk having silk fringes at both ends (but not tassels); a rochet of linen or similar fabric; a purple mozzetta (but without the small hood); over the mozzetta the pectoral cross, held in place by a cord of interwoven green and gold; a purple skullcap; a purple biretta with tuft.

When the purple cassock is worn, purple stockings are also worn, but are optional with the black cassock with piping.[59]

64   A purple *cappa magna*, without ermine, may be used only within the diocese and then only on the most solemn festivals.

Vesture of priests and other ministers

65   The vestment common to ministers of every rank is the alb, tied at the waist with a cincture, unless it is made to fit without a cincture. An amice should be put on first if the alb does not completely cover the minister's street clothing at the neck. A surplice may not be substituted for the alb when the chasuble or dalmatic is to be worn or when a stole is used instead of the chasuble or dalmatic.[60] When a surplice is worn, it must be worn with the cassock.

Acolytes, readers, and other ministers may wear other lawfully approved vesture in place of the vestments already mentioned.

66   Unless otherwise indicated, the chasuble, worn over the alb and stole, is the vestment proper to the presbyter who is the celebrant at Mass and other rites immediately connected with Mass.

The priest wears the stole around his neck and hanging down in front.

The cope is worn by the priest in solemn liturgical services outside Mass and in processions; in other liturgical services, in keeping with the rubrics proper to each rite.[61]

---

[58] See PR, no. 20: AAS 60 (1968), p. 410; DOL 550, no. 4477.

[59] See Secretariat of State, Instruction *Ut sive sollicite*, on the dress, titles, and insignia of cardinals, bishops, and lesser prelates, 31 March 1969, no. 4: AAS 61 (1969), p. 335; DOL 551, no. 4501.

[60] See GIRM, no. 298: DOL 208, no. 1688.

[61] See GIRM, nos. 299, 302, 303: DOL 208, nos. 1689, 1692, 1693.

Presbyters who take part in a liturgical service but not as concelebrants are to wear choir dress if they are prelates or canons,[62] cassock and surplice if they are not.

67   The dalmatic, worn over the alb and stole, is the vestment proper to the deacon. The dalmatic may be omitted either out of necessity or for less solemnity. The deacon wears the stole over his left shoulder and drawn across the chest to the right side, where it is fastened.[63]

II. Signs of Reverence in General

68   A *bow* signifies reverence and honor toward persons or toward objects that represent persons.
      There are two kinds of bows, a bow of the head and a bow of the body:

      a. a bow of the head is made at the name of Jesus, the Blessed Virgin Mary, and the saint in whose honor the Mass or the liturgy of the hours is being celebrated;

      b. a bow of the body, or deep bow, is made: to the altar if there is no tabernacle with the blessed sacrament on the altar; to the bishop, before and after incensation, as indicated in no. 91; whenever it is expressly called for by the rubrics of the various liturgical books.[64]

69   A *genuflection*, made by bending only the right knee to the ground, signifies adoration, and is therefore reserved for the blessed sacrament, whether exposed or reserved in the tabernacle, and for the holy cross from the time of the solemn adoration in the liturgical celebration of Good Friday until the beginning of the Easter Vigil.

70   Neither a genuflection nor a deep bow is made by those who are carrying articles used in a celebration, for example, the cross, candlesticks, the Book of the Gospels.

Reverence toward the blessed sacrament

71   No one who enters a church should fail to adore the blessed sacrament, either by visiting the blessed sacrament chapel or at least by genuflecting.

---

[62] See nos. 1207-1209 of this *Ceremonial*.
[63] See GIRM, nos. 300, 81, b, 302: DOL 208, nos. 1690, 1471, 1692.
[64] See GIRM, no. 234: DOL 208, no. 1624.

Similarly, those who pass before the blessed sacrament genuflect, except when they are walking in procession.

Reverence toward the altar

72   A deep bow is made to the altar by all who enter the sanctuary (chancel), leave it, or pass before the altar.

73   In addition, the celebrant and concelebrants at the beginning of Mass kiss the altar as a sign of reverence. The principal celebrant as a rule venerates the altar by kissing it before he leaves, while the other concelebrants, particularly if there are a number of them, venerate the altar by bowing.

When the bishop presides at a solemn celebration of morning or evening prayer, he kisses the altar at the beginning and, as circumstances suggest, at the end.

But if such a sign of reverence as kissing the altar is out of keeping with the traditions or the culture of the region, the conference of bishops may substitute some other sign, after informing the Apostolic See.[65]

Reverence toward the gospel

74   While the gospel reading is being proclaimed at Mass, at a celebration of the word, and at a prolonged vigil, all stand and, as a rule, face the reader.

The deacon solemnly carrying the Book of the Gospels to the ambo is preceded by the censerbearer with the censer[66] and acolytes with lighted candles.[67]

At the ambo the deacon stands facing the people and, with hands joined, says the greeting; then with his right thumb he makes the sign of the cross, first on the book at the beginning of the gospel passage that he is about to read, then on his forehead, lips, and breast, saying, A reading from the holy gospel. The bishop signs himself in the same way on

---

[65] See GIRM, nos. 208 and 232: DOL 208, nos. 1598 and 1622.

[66] See GIRM, nos. 93-95, 131: DOL 208, nos. 1483-1485, 1521. The Roman manner for the censerbearer to walk in procession is that "he walks with hands somewhat raised, he should hold the censer with the right hand, with his thumb in the ring at the top, and the middle finger holding the chain, so that the cover of the censer is somewhat raised; he holds the boat containing incense and spoon with his left hand" (*Caeremoniale Episcoporum*, ed. 1886, I, XI, 7).

[67] See GIRM, nos. 94, 131: DOL 208, nos. 1484, 1521. According to Roman practice acolytes "hold the candlesticks with their right hand, so that the acolyte walking on the right puts his left hand at the base of the candlestick and his right at the middle knob of the candlestick; the acolyte walking on the left puts his right hand at the base and his left at the middle knob of the candlestick" (*Caeremoniale Episcoporum*, ed. 1886, I, XI, 8).

forehead, lips, and breast, and all present do the same. Then, at least at a stational Mass, the deacon incenses the Book of the Gospels three times, that is, in the center, to the left, and to the right. Then he proclaims the gospel reading to its conclusion.

After the reading, the deacon takes the book to the bishop to be kissed, or the deacon himself kisses the book, unless, as mentioned in no. 73, another sign of reverence has been decided on by the conference of bishops.[68]

In the absence of a deacon, a presbyter asks for and receives a blessing from the bishop, and proclaims the gospel reading in the way just described.

75   All present also stand for the singing or recitation of the gospel canticles, the Canticles of Zechariah, of Mary, and of Simeon, and at the beginning of these canticles sign themselves with the sign of the cross.[69]

Reverence toward the bishop and other persons

76   The bishop is greeted with a deep bow by the ministers or others when they approach to assist him, when they leave after assisting him, or when they pass in front of him.[70]

77   When the bishop's chair is behind the altar, the ministers should reverence either the altar or the bishop, depending on whether they are approaching the altar or approaching the bishop; out of reverence for both, ministers should, as far as possible, avoid passing between the bishop and the altar.

78   If several bishops are present in the sanctuary (chancel), a reverence is made only to the one presiding.

79   When the bishop, vested as indicated in no. 63, proceeds to a church to celebrate some liturgical rite, he may, in accordance with local custom, be escorted publicly to the church by the canons or other presbyters and clerics in choir dress or wearing cassock and surplice, or he may be received by the clergy at the door after proceeding to the church in a less solemn way.

In both cases the bishop goes first: if he is an archbishop he is preceded by an acolyte carrying the archiepiscopal cross with the image

---

[68] See GIRM, nos. 131, 232: DOL 208, nos. 1521, 1622.

[69] See GILH, no. 266, b: DOL 426, no. 3696.

[70] See PR, no. 25: AAS 60 (1968), p. 411; DOL 550, no. 4482.

of Christ facing forward; behind the bishop follow the canons, presbyters, and clergy, two by two. At the door of the church the senior of the presbyters hands the bishop the sprinkler, unless the blessing and sprinkling of water is to replace the penitential rite. With head uncovered, the bishop sprinkles himself and those around him, then returns the sprinkler. He next goes in procession to the place of reservation of the blessed sacrament and prays there for a short time; finally he goes to the vesting room (sacristy).

The bishop may, however, go directly to the vesting room (sacristy) and be received there by the clergy.

80   In a procession the bishop who presides at a liturgical celebration always walks vested and alone, following the presbyters, but preceding his assisting ministers, who walk a little behind him.

81   When the bishop presides at a celebration or only takes part in it wearing choir dress, he has as assistants two canons in choir dress or two presbyters or deacons in cassock and surplice.

82   A head of state in official attendance at a liturgical celebration is received by the bishop, who waits in vestments at the door of the church. The bishop may offer holy water to a head of state who is a Catholic. After greeting the head of state in a manner that accords with local custom, the bishop, keeping to the left, escorts the head of state to an appointed place reserved in the church outside the sanctuary (chancel). At the end of the celebration the bishop as he leaves again greets the head of state.

83   If such is the practice, other officials holding high position in the government of a nation, region, or city are received at the door of the church in a manner that accords with local custom by an ecclesiastic dignitary, who greets them and escorts them to their appointed place. The bishop may greet such personages during the entrance procession as he goes to the altar, and as he leaves.

III. Incensation

84   The rite of incensation or thurification is a sign of reverence and of prayer, as is clear from Psalm 141 (140):2 and Revelation 8:3.

85   The substance placed in the censer should be pure sweet-scented incense alone or at least in larger proportion than any additive mixed with the incense.

86   At the stational Mass of the bishop incense should be used:

    a. during the entrance procession;

    b. at the beginning of Mass to incense the altar;

    c. at the gospel, in the procession and at the proclamation of the gospel reading;

    d. at the presentation of the gifts, to incense the gifts, the altar, the cross, the bishop, the concelebrants, and the people;

    e. at the elevation of the consecrated bread and cup after their consecration.

At other Masses incense may be used as circumstances suggest.[71]

87   Incense is also to be used as indicated in the liturgical books:

    a. in the rite of dedication of a church or altar;

    b. in the rite of the blessing of oils and consecrating the chrism, as the blessed oils and consecrated chrism are being taken away;

    c. at exposition of the blessed sacrament when the monstrance is used;

    d. at funerals.

88   In addition, incense should as a rule be used during the processions for the feast of the Presentation of the Lord, Passion Sunday (Palm Sunday), the Mass of the Lord's Supper, the Easter Vigil, the solemnity of the Body and Blood of Christ (Corpus Christi), and the solemn translation of relics and, in general, in any procession of some solemnity.

89   At the solemn celebration of morning or evening prayer the altar, the bishop, and the people may be incensed during the singing of the gospel canticle.

90   If the bishop puts incense into the censer at his chair (cathedra) or another chair, he remains seated; otherwise he puts in the incense while standing. The deacon presents the incense boat[72] and the bishop blesses the incense with the sign of the cross, saying nothing.[73]

---

[71] See GIRM, no. 235: DOL 208, no. 1625.

[72] Two acolytes may go to the bishop with the censer and boat or one acolyte carrying both, the censer with burning charcoal in the left hand and the boat with the incense and spoon in the right (see *Caeremoniale Episcoporum*, ed. 1886, I, XIII, 1).

[73] See GIRM, no. 236: DOL 208, no. 1626. From the acolyte the deacon takes the boat, half-opened and with the spoon resting in it, and offers the boat to the bishop. The bishop takes the spoon and with it three times scoops out incense, and three times puts the incense into the censer. After doing so, and having returned the spoon to the minister, the bishop with his right hand makes the sign of the cross over the incense that has been deposited in the censer (see *Caeremoniale Episcoporum*, ed. 1886, I, XXII, 1-2).

After the blessing, the deacon takes the censer from the acolyte and hands it to the bishop.[74]

91 Before and after an incensation, a profound bow is made to the person or object that is incensed, except in the case of the incensation of the altar and the gifts for the eucharistic sacrifice.[75]

92 The censer is swung back and forth three times for the incensation of: the blessed sacrament, a relic of the true cross and images of the Lord solemnly exposed, the gifts on the altar, the altar cross, the Book of the Gospels, the Easter candle, the bishop or presbyter who is celebrant, a representative of the civil authority in official attendance at a liturgical celebration, the choir and people, the body of a deceased person.
The censer is swung back and forth twice for the incensation of relics and images of the saints exposed for public veneration.

93 The altar is incensed with a series of single swings of the censer in this way:
a. if the altar is freestanding, the bishop incenses it as he walks around it;
b. if the altar is not freestanding, the bishop incenses it while walking first to the right side, then to the left.
If there is a cross on or beside the altar, he incenses it before he incenses the altar. If the cross is behind the altar, the bishop incenses it when he passes in front of it.[76]
The gifts of bread and wine are incensed before the incensation of the altar and the cross.

94 The blessed sacrament is incensed from a kneeling position.

95 Relics and images exposed for public veneration are incensed after the incensation of the altar; at Mass they are incensed only at the beginning of the celebration.

---

[74] The deacon "returns the boat to the acolyte and from him takes the censer, which he presents to the bishop, placing the top of the censer chain in the bishop's left hand and the censer itself in the bishop's right hand" (*Caeremoniale Episcoporum*, ed. 1886, I, IX, 1).

[75] The one incensing "holds the top of the censer chain in the left hand, the bottom near the censer in the right hand, so that the censer can be swung back and forth easily." "The one incensing should take care to carry out this function with grave and graceful mien, not moving head or body while swinging the censer, holding the left hand with the top of the chains near the chest and moving the right arm back and forth with a measured beat" (See *Caeremoniale Episcoporum*, ed. 1886, I, XXIII, 4 and 8).

[76] See GIRM, no. 236: DOL 208, no. 1626.

96   Whether he is at the altar or at the chair (cathedra), the bishop receives the incensation standing and without the miter, unless he is already wearing it.

Concelebrants are incensed as a body by the deacon.

Lastly, the deacon incenses the people from the place most convenient. Canons who are not concelebrating or a community assembled in choir are incensed together with the people, unless the spatial arrangement suggests otherwise.

Bishops who may be present are also incensed along with the people.

97   A bishop who presides but does not concelebrate is incensed after the celebrant or concelebrants.

Where such a practice is customary, a head of state in official attendance at a liturgical celebration is incensed after the bishop.

98   The bishop should not begin any invitation, introduction, or prayer meant to be heard by all before the rite of incensation has been completed.

IV. SIGN OF PEACE

99   After the deacon has said, Let us offer each other a sign of peace, the bishop who is celebrant gives the kiss of peace at least to the two concelebrants nearest to him, then to the first deacon.

100   Meanwhile the concelebrants and deacons and the other ministers as well as any bishops present also give each other the kiss of peace.

If a bishop presides but not as celebrant of the Mass, he offers the sign of peace to the canons or presbyters or deacons assisting him.

101   The faithful also exchange a sign of peace in the manner approved by the conference of bishops.

102   The deacon or one of the concelebrants goes to give a head of state in official attendance the sign of peace according to local custom.

103   The exchange of the sign of peace may be accompanied by the words, Peace be with you, and the response, And also with you. But other words may be used in accordance with local custom.

V. Position of the Hands

Raised and outstretched hands

104   Customarily in the Church a bishop or presbyter addresses prayers to God while standing and with hands slightly raised and outstretched.
    This practice appears already in the tradition of the Old Testament,[77] and was taken over by Christians in memory of the Lord's passion: "Not only do we raise our hands, but also hold them outstretched, so that by imitating the Lord in his passion, we bear witness to him as we pray."[78]

Outstretched hands over persons or objects

105   The bishop holds his hands outstretched over the people when he blesses them solemnly and wherever the liturgical books call for such a gesture in the celebration of the sacraments or sacramentals.

106   The bishop and the concelebrants hold their hands outstretched over the offerings in Mass at the epiclesis before the consecration.
    At the consecration, as the bishop holds the host or cup in his hands and says the words of consecration, the concelebrants say the words of institution and, if this seems appropriate, hold the right hand outstretched toward the bread and the cup.[79]

Joined hands

107   Unless the bishop is holding the pastoral staff, he keeps his hands joined:[80] when, vested, he walks in procession for the celebration of a liturgy; when he is kneeling at prayer; when he moves from altar to chair or from chair to altar; when the liturgical books prescribe joined hands.
    Similarly, concelebrants and ministers keep their hands joined when walking from place to place or when standing, unless they are holding something.

---

[77] See Exodus 9:29; Psalm 28 (27):2, 63 (62):5, 134 (133):2; Isaiah 1:15.

[78] Tertullian, *De oratione,* 14: CCL 1, 265; PL 1, 1273.

[79] See GIRM, nos. 174, a and c, 180, a and c, 184, a and c, 188, a and c: DOL 208, nos. 1564, 1570, 1574, 1578. At the epiclesis preceding the consecration the hands are to be outstretched toward and above the offerings (see *Missale Romanum,* ed. 1962, *Ritus servandus in celebratione Missae,* VIII, 4). At the consecration the palm of the right hand is held sideward (see *Notitiae,* 1, 1965, p. 143: DOL 223, no. 1810, note R8).

[80] "Hands joined" means: "Holding the palms sideward and together before the breast, with the right thumb crossed over the left" (*Caeremoniale Episcoporum,* ed. 1886, I, XIX, 1).

Other positions for the hands

108   When the bishop signs himself with the sign of the cross or when he gives a blessing,[81] he places his left hand on his breast, unless he is holding something. When he is standing at the altar and blesses the offerings or something else with his right hand, he places his left hand on the altar, unless a rubric indicates otherwise.

109   When the bishop is seated and wearing vestments, he places his palms on his knees, unless he is holding the pastoral staff.

VI. Use of Holy Water

110   It is an old and honored practice for all who enter a church to dip their hand in a font (stoup) of holy water and sign themselves with the sign of the cross as a reminder of their baptism.

111   If holy water is to be offered to the bishop as he enters the church, a senior cleric of the local Church offers it to him, presenting a sprinkler, with which the bishop sprinkles himself and those accompanying him. Then the bishop hands back the sprinkler.

112   All this is omitted if the bishop enters the church already vested, as well as on Sunday whenever the blessing and sprinkling of water replace the penitential rite.

113   The sprinkling of the people with water at the Easter Vigil and at the dedication of a church will be treated in nos. 369 and 892-893 of this *Ceremonial*.

114   Objects being blessed are sprinkled with holy water in keeping with the provisions of the liturgical books.

---

[81] "When making the sign of the cross, he holds the palm of the right hand turned toward himself, with all the fingers joined and held straight, and makes the sign of the cross by moving this hand from head to chest and from left shoulder to right. If he blesses others or some object, he points the little finger at the person or thing to be blessed and in blessing extends the whole right hand with all the fingers joined and fully extended" (*Missale Romanum*, ed. 1962, *Ritus servandus in celebratione Missae*, III, 5).

VII. CARE OF LITURGICAL BOOKS AND WAYS OF PROCLAIMING VARIOUS LITURGICAL TEXTS

115   The liturgical books are to be treated with care and reverence, since it is from them that the word of God is proclaimed and the prayer of the Church offered. Care must therefore be taken, and especially in liturgical celebrations carried out by a bishop, to have on hand the official liturgical books in an edition that is current and is beautifully printed and bound.

116   In texts that are to be delivered in a clear, audible voice, whether by the bishop or by the ministers or by all, the tone of voice should correspond to the genre of the text, that is, accordingly as it is a reading, a prayer, an instruction, an acclamation, or a song; the tone should also be suited to the form of celebration and to the solemnity of the gathering.

117   Hence, in the rubrics and norms that follow in this *Ceremonial*, the words "say" (*dicere*), "recite" (*recitare*), "proclaim" (*proferre*) should be understood of both singing and speaking, in accordance with the principles set out in the respective liturgical books[82] and with the norms given in place in this *Ceremonial*.

118   The phrase "sing or say," which is used frequently in this *Ceremonial*, is to be understood as referring to singing, unless some other consideration rules out singing.

---

[82] See, for example, GIRM, nos. 18-19: DOL 208, nos. 1408-1409. See GILH, nos. 267-284: DOL 426, nos. 3697-3714. See MS, nos. 5-12: AAS 59 (1967), pp. 301-303; DOL 508, nos. 4126-4133. See Sacred Congregation for Divine Worship (hereafter, SC Worship), Circular Letter *Eucharistiae participationem*, on the eucharistic prayers, 27 April 1973, no. 17: AAS 65 (1973), pp. 346-347; DOL 248, no. 1991.

PART II
MASS

CHAPTER 1

STATIONAL MASS OF THE DIOCESAN BISHOP

INTRODUCTION

119   The preeminent manifestation of the local Church is present when the bishop, as high priest of his flock, celebrates the eucharist and particularly when he celebrates in the cathedral, surrounded by his college of presbyters and by his ministers, and with the full, active participation of all God's holy people.

This Mass, which is called the stational Mass, shows forth the unity of the local Church as well as the diversity of ministries exercised around the bishop and the holy eucharist.[1]

Hence, as many of the faithful as possible should come together for a stational Mass, priests should concelebrate with the bishop, deacons should assist in the celebration, and acolytes and readers should carry out their ministries.[2]

120   The form of the stational Mass should be retained especially on the greater solemnities of the liturgical year, on Holy Thursday for the blessing of the chrism and the Mass of the Lord's Supper,[3] at the celebration honoring the founder of the local Church or the patron of the diocese, on the anniversary of the bishop's episcopal ordination, at large gatherings of the Christian people, and during pastoral visitations.

121   The stational Mass should be a sung Mass, in accord with the provisions of the General Instruction of the Roman Missal.[4]

122   It is preferable that as a rule at least three deacons, properly so called, assist in a stational Mass: one to proclaim the gospel reading and minister at the altar, two to assist the bishop. If there are more than three deacons present, they should divide the ministries accordingly, and at least one of them should be charged with assisting the active participation of the faithful. If deacons properly so called are not available, their ministries should be carried out by presbyters, who, vested as priests,

---

[1] See SC, art. 41: DOL 1, no. 41.

[2] See SC, art. 26-28: DOL 1, nos. 26-28.

[3] See GIRM, nos. 157-158, a: DOL 208, nos. 1547-1548.

[4] See GIRM, nos. 12, 18, 19, 77, 313: DOL 208, nos. 1402, 1408, 1409, 1467, 1703. Where applicable, the *Ordo cantus Missae* should be followed. See Missale Romanum, *Ordo cantus Missae* (Vatican Polyglot Press, 1972), Introduction: DOL 535, nos. 4276-4302. See MS, nos. 7, 16, 29-31: AAS 59 (1967), pp. 302, 305, 308-309; DOL 508, nos. 4128, 4137, 4150, 4151.

concelebrate with the bishop, even if they must also celebrate another Mass for the pastoral benefit of the faithful.

123   If the cathedral has a chapter attached, all the canons should con-celebrate the stational Mass with the bishop,[5] but not to the exclusion of other presbyters.
     Bishops or canons who are not concelebrants assist wearing choir dress.

124   When an hour of the liturgy of the hours to which the chapter has a choral obligation cannot, in particular circumstances, be joined to the stational Mass, the chapter should celebrate the hour at some other suit-able time.[6]

125   Requisites for the stational Mass:
     a. *In the sanctuary (chancel) at the place belonging to each item:*
        — *The Roman Missal (Sacramentary);*
        — *Lectionary for Mass;*
        — texts for the concelebrants;
        — text for the general intercessions, both for the bishop and the deacon;
        — book for the singing;
        — large enough cup, covered by a veil;
        — [pall];
        — corporal;
        — purificators;
        — basin, pitcher of water, and towel;
        — vessel of water to be blessed, when holy water is used dur-ing the penitential rite;
        — communion plate for the communion of the faithful.
     b. *In a convenient place:*
        — bread, wine and water [and other gifts].
     c. *In the vesting room:*
        — Book of the Gospels;
        — censer and incense boat;
        — processional cross;
        — seven (or at least two) candlesticks with lighted candles.
     In addition:
        — for the bishop: basin, pitcher of water, and towel; amice, alb,

---

[5] See GIRM, no. 157: DOL 208, no. 1547.
[6] See GILH, nos. 31a and 93: DOL 426, nos. 3461 and 3523.

cincture, pectoral cross, stole, dalmatic, chasuble (pallium for a metropolitan), skullcap, miter, ring, pastoral staff;
— for concelebrants: amices, albs, cinctures, stoles, chasubles;
— for deacons: amices, albs, cinctures, stoles, dalmatics;
— for other ministers: amices, albs, and cinctures or cassocks and surplices, or other lawfully approved vesture.
Vestments should be of the color of the Mass or a festive color.[7]

Arrival and Preparation of the Bishop

126   After the reception of the bishop in the manner already indicated in no. 79, he is assisted by deacons and other ministers, who have vested beforehand. In the vesting room (sacristy) he takes off the cappa or the mozzetta and may also remove the rochet, if he is wearing one. He washes his hands and puts on the amice, alb, cincture, pectoral cross, stole, dalmatic, and chasuble.

The miter is then placed on his head by one of the deacons. An archbishop receives the pallium from the first deacon before the miter is put on.

During this time the concelebrating presbyters and any other deacons present put on their vestments.

127   When these preparations have been completed, the censerbearer comes forward, a deacon presents the incense boat, and the bishop puts incense into the censer and blesses it with the sign of the cross. The bishop then receives the pastoral staff from a minister. A deacon takes the Book of the Gospels and with reverence carries it unopened in the entrance procession.

Introductory Rites

128   As the entrance song is being sung, the procession moves from the vesting room (sacristy) to the sanctuary (chancel) in the following order:
— censerbearer carrying a censer with burning incense;
— an acolyte carrying the cross, with the image to the front, walks between seven other acolytes, or at least two, carrying candlesticks with lighted candles;
— clergy, two by two;

---

[7] See GIRM, no. 310: DOL 208, no. 1700.

– the deacon carrying the Book of the Gospels;
– deacons, if present, two by two;
– concelebrating presbyters, two by two;
– the bishop, walking alone, wearing the miter, carrying the pastoral staff in his left hand and blessing with his right;
– a little behind the bishop, the two deacons assisting him;
– finally, the ministers who assist with the book, the miter, and the pastoral staff.

There is neither a stop nor a genuflection if the procession passes in front of the blessed sacrament chapel.[8]

129   It is preferable that the processional cross be placed near the altar and serve as the altar cross; otherwise it is put away. The candlesticks are placed near the altar or on a side table or at some nearby place in the sanctuary (chancel). The Book of the Gospels is placed upon the altar.

130   On entering the sanctuary (chancel), all make a deep bow to the altar, two by two. Deacons and concelebrating presbyters go up to the altar, kiss it, then go to their places.

131   When he reaches the front of the altar, the bishop hands the staff to a minister and takes off the miter. Together with the deacons and other ministers accompanying him, the bishop makes a deep bow to the altar, then goes up to the altar and, together with the two deacons assisting him, kisses it.

If necessary, fresh incense is placed in the censer by an acolyte, and the bishop, accompanied by the two deacons assisting him, incenses the altar and the cross.[9]

When the altar has been incensed, the bishop, accompanied by the ministers, takes the most direct way to the chair. The two deacons stand on either side near the chair, ready to assist the bishop. If no deacons are present, two concelebrating presbyters serve in their place.

132   Then the bishop, the concelebrants, and the congregation, all standing, sign themselves with the sign of the cross as the bishop, facing the people, says, In the name of the Father.

With hands outstretched, the bishop greets the people, saying, Peace be with you, or one of the other greeting formularies given in The

---

[8] See no. 71 of this *Ceremonial*.

[9] On the manner of incensing the altar, as well as any images or relics exposed for veneration by the faithful, see nos. 93 and 95 of this *Ceremonial*.

Roman Missal (Sacramentary). The bishop himself, a deacon, or one of the concelebrants may very briefly introduce the faithful to the Mass of the day.[10] The bishop pronounces the invitation to the penitential rite, which he concludes with the words, May almighty God have mercy on us. If necessary, a minister may hold the book in front of the bishop.

When the third form of the penitential rite is used, the invocations are said by the bishop, by a deacon, or by another suitable minister.

133   On Sunday, it is commendable that the rite of blessing and sprinkling water replace the usual penitential rite.[11]

In this case, after the greeting, the bishop, standing at the chair, faces the congregation, and a minister holds a vessel of water in front of him. The bishop invites the people to pray and, after a brief pause for silent prayer, says the prayer of blessing. Where local custom recommends retaining the mixing of salt in the blessing, the bishop also blesses the salt, then adds it to the water.

Receiving the sprinkler from the deacon, the bishop sprinkles himself and the concelebrants, the ministers, the clergy, and the people; as the situation suggests, he may go through the church, accompanied by the deacons. During the sprinkling an accompanying song is sung.

When the bishop has returned to the chair and the singing has ended, he stands and, with hands outstretched, says the concluding prayer. Then, if called for by the rubrics, the *Gloria* is sung or recited.

134   After the penitential rite, the *Kyrie* is said, but not when the sprinkling of holy water has been carried out or the third form of the penitential rite has been used or the rubrics direct otherwise.

135   The *Gloria* is said when prescribed by the rubrics. It may be begun by the bishop, one of the concelebrants, or the cantors. During the *Gloria* all stand.

136   Next, with hands joined, the bishop invites the people to pray by singing or saying, Let us pray. After a brief pause for silent prayer, he says the opening prayer with hands outstretched, reading from the book held before him by a minister. For the conclusion of the prayer the bishop joins his hands, saying, We ask this through our Lord Jesus Christ or other relevant words. At the end the people reply with the acclamation Amen.

---

[10] See GIRM, no. 29: DOL 208, no. 1419.

[11] See *The Roman Missal (Sacramentary)*, 2nd English ed., (hereafter, RM), Appendix I, Rite of Blessing and Sprinkling of Holy Water.

The bishop then sits and, as a rule, receives the miter from one of the deacons. All sit. Deacons and the other ministers should be seated wherever the arrangement of the sanctuary (chancel) allows, but in such a way that they do not appear to be of the same rank as the presbyters.

LITURGY OF THE WORD

137   After the opening prayer, the reader goes to the ambo and proclaims the first reading, as all sit and listen. At the end of the reading the reader sings or says, This is the Word of the Lord, and all respond with the usual acclamation.

138   The reader retires and there is a brief pause for all to reflect on what they have heard. Then the psalmist or cantor or reader sings or recites the psalm in either of the ways described in the *Lectionary for Mass*.[12]

139   In the way just indicated, the second reading is proclaimed at the ambo by a second reader, as all sit and listen.

140   The *Alleluia* or some other song follows, depending on the liturgical season. When the *Alleluia* begins, everyone but the bishop stands.
     The censerbearer goes to the bishop and, as one of the deacons presents the incense boat, the bishop puts incense into the censer and blesses it, saying nothing.
     The deacon who is to proclaim the gospel reading makes a deep bow before the bishop and asks for a blessing, saying quietly, Father, give me your blessing. The bishop blesses him with the words The Lord be in your heart. The deacon signs himself with the sign of the cross and replies, Amen.
     Then the bishop takes off the miter and stands.
     The deacon goes to the altar, where he is joined by the censerbearer holding the censer with burning incense and by the acolytes with lighted candles. After bowing to the altar, the deacon reverently takes the Book of the Gospels and, without any further reverence to the altar, carries the book with solemnity to the ambo, preceded by the censerbearer and the acolytes with candles.

141   At the ambo the deacon, with hands joined, greets the people. At the words A reading from the holy gospel, he makes the sign of the

---

[12] See LM, Introduction, no. 20.

cross on the book and then on his forehead, lips, and breast, and all present do the same. At this point the bishop takes the pastoral staff. The deacon incenses the book and proclaims the gospel reading, as a rule with all present standing and facing him. After the gospel reading, the deacon takes the book to the bishop, who kisses it, saying inaudibly, May the words of the Gospel; alternatively, the deacon himself kisses the book and inaudibly says the same words. Finally the deacon and the other ministers return to their places. The Book of the Gospels is taken to a side table or some other suitable place.

142   Then, all sit and the bishop gives the homily. He may use the miter and pastoral staff. He gives the homily seated in the chair (cathedra), unless he prefers some other place in order to be easily seen and heard by all. As circumstances suggest, a period of silence may be observed after the homily.

143   Unless the celebration of a sacrament or a consecration or a blessing is to take place at this point in accordance with the provisions of The Roman Pontifical or The Roman Ritual, the bishop puts aside the miter and pastoral staff and stands. All present stand and, when the rubrics require, sing or recite the profession of faith.
    At the words By the power of the Holy Spirit, all bow; on Christmas and the Annunciation of the Lord all genuflect at these words.[13]

144   After the profession of faith, the bishop, standing at the chair with hands joined, introduces the general intercessions. Then one of the deacons, the cantor, a reader, or some other person announces the intentions, either from the ambo or from some other suitable place, and the people take part by responding. With hands outstretched, the bishop says the concluding prayer.

LITURGY OF THE EUCHARIST

145   At the end of the general intercessions, the bishop sits and puts on the miter. The concelebrants and the people also sit. The song for the presentation of the gifts (offertory song) is sung and continues at least until the gifts have been placed on the altar.
    The deacons and acolytes arrange the corporal, purificator, cup, and The Roman Missal (Sacramentary) on the altar.

---

[13] See GIRM, no. 98: DOL 208, no. 1488.

The gifts are then brought forward. As a sign of their participation, the faithful should present the bread and wine for the celebration of the eucharist, and even other gifts to meet the needs of the Church and of the poor. The deacons or the bishop receives the gifts of the faithful at a convenient place. The bread and wine are brought by the deacons to the altar; the other gifts are taken to a suitable place prepared beforehand.

146   The bishop goes to the altar, lays aside the miter, receives the paten with the bread from the deacon, and, holding the paten in both hands a little above the altar, says the appropriate formulary inaudibly. Then he places the paten with the bread on the corporal.

147   Meanwhile, the deacon pours wine and a little water into the cup, saying inaudibly, By the mystery.[14] He then hands the cup to the bishop, who holds it with both hands a little above the altar, saying the prescribed formulary inaudibly; the bishop then places the cup on the corporal and the deacon may cover it with the pall.

148   Bowing at the center of the altar, the bishop then says the prayer Lord God, we ask you inaudibly.

149   Next, the censerbearer goes to the bishop. As a deacon holds the incense boat, the bishop puts incense in the censer and blesses it. The bishop receives the censer from the deacon and, in the same way as at the beginning of Mass and accompanied by a deacon, incenses the gifts,[15] as well as the altar and the cross. After this, all rise, and a deacon, standing at the side of the altar, incenses the bishop, who stands without the miter, then the concelebrants, then the people. Care should be taken that the invitation Pray, brethren and the prayer over the gifts do not begin until the incensation has been completed.

150   After the bishop has been incensed, the ministers with a pitcher of water, basin, and towel go to him as he stands without the miter at the side of the altar. He washes and dries his hands. One of the deacons may remove the bishop's ring. As he washes his hands, the bishop says inaudibly, Lord, wash away my iniquity. Having dried his hands and put on his ring, the bishop returns to the middle of the altar.

---

[14] The deacon may carry out the preparation of the cup, that is, pour the wine and water, at a side table. See GIRM, no. 133: DOL 208, no. 1523.

[15] See nos. 91-93 of this Ceremonial on the way to incense.

151   The bishop, facing the people and extending, then joining his hands, invites the people to pray, saying, Pray, brethren.

152   After the response May the Lord accept, the bishop, with hands outstretched, sings or says the prayer over the gifts. The people respond with the acclamation Amen.

153   A deacon then removes the bishop's skullcap and hands it to a minister. The concelebrants come near the altar and stand around it in such a way that they do not interfere with the actions of the rite and the people have a clear view.

      The deacons stand behind the concelebrants, but in such a way that one of them may assist at the cup and the book as needed. But no one should stand between the bishop and the concelebrants or between the concelebrants and the altar.

154   The bishop begins the eucharistic prayer with the preface. With hands outstretched, he sings or says, The Lord be with you. As he continues with the words Lift up your hearts, he raises his hands, and then, with hands outstretched, continues with the words Let us give thanks to the Lord our God. When the people have responded with the words It is right to give him thanks and praise, the bishop continues with the preface. When it is finished, with hands joined, he sings the *Sanctus* along with the concelebrants, the ministers, and the people.

155   The bishop continues the eucharistic prayer in accordance with the provisions of nos. 171-191 of the General Instruction of the Roman Missal and the rubrics given in each eucharistic prayer. The parts that are said together by all the concelebrants with hands outstretched are to be recited by them in a quiet tone of voice, so that the voice of the bishop is heard clearly. In Eucharistic Prayer I, II, and III after the words N., our Pope, the bishop adds, and me, your unworthy servant. In Eucharistic Prayer IV, after the words especially N., our Pope, he adds, and me, your unworthy servant.

      If the cup and ciborium are covered, a deacon uncovers them before the epiclesis.

      One of the deacons puts incense into the censer and incenses the host and the cup at each elevation.

      The deacons remain kneeling from the epiclesis to the elevation of the cup.

      After the consecration, the deacon may cover the cup and the ciborium. When the bishop says, Let us proclaim the mystery of faith, the people respond with an acclamation.

156   The particular intercessions (interpolations), especially those connected with the celebration of a sacrament or a rite of consecration or blessing, should follow the structure of each eucharistic prayer and use the texts provided in *The Roman Missal (Sacramentary)* or the other liturgical books.[16]

157   In the Chrism Mass, the blessing of the oil of the sick, as provided in *The Roman Missal (Sacramentary)*, takes place before the bishop says, Through him you give us all these gifts, at the end of Eucharistic Prayer I or before the final doxology of the other eucharistic prayers, unless, for pastoral reasons, the blessing has taken place after the liturgy of the word.

158   At the final doxology of the eucharistic prayer the deacon, standing at the side of the bishop, holds up the cup while the bishop holds up the paten with the host until the people have made the acclamation Amen. The final doxology of the eucharistic prayer is proclaimed by the bishop alone or by all the concelebrants together with the bishop.

159   After the doxology of the eucharistic prayer, the bishop, with hands joined, introduces the Lord's Prayer, which all then sing or say; the bishop and the concelebrants hold their hands outstretched.

160   The embolism Deliver us, Lord is said by the bishop alone, with hands outstretched. The concelebrating presbyters, together with the people, conclude it with the acclamation For the kingdom.

---

[16] The following intercessions (interpolations) are given in RM.

    1. For Eucharistic Prayer I:

        a. Commemoration of the Living: for the godparents, in Ritual Masses, I. Christian Initiation, 2. The Scrutinies, and 3. Baptism.

        b. For the intercessions (interpolations), Father, accept this offering: for those to be baptized in Ritual Masses, I. Christian Initiation, 2. The Scrutinies; for the newly baptized, in Ritual Masses I. Christian Initiation, 3. Baptism; for those receiving confirmation, in Ritual Masses, I. Christian Initiation, 4. Confirmation; for those ordained as deacons, priests, or bishops, in Ritual Masses, II. Holy Orders; for husbands and wives, in Ritual Masses, IV. Wedding Mass; for those being consecrated to a life of virginity, in Ritual Masses, V. Consecration to a Life of Virginity; for those making religious profession, in Ritual Masses, VI. Religious Profession; for the dedication of a church, in Ritual Masses, Dedication of a Church.

    2. For the other eucharistic prayers:

        For the deceased, in Order of Mass, Eucharistic Prayers II and III; for the newly baptized in Eucharistic Prayers II, III, and IV, in Ritual Masses, I. Christian Initiation, 3. Baptism; for those being consecrated to a life of virginity in Eucharistic Prayers II, III, and IV, in Ritual Masses, V. Consecration to a Life of Virginity; for those making religious profession in Eucharistic Prayers II, III, and IV, in Ritual Masses, VI. Religious Profession; for the dedication of a church, in Ritual Masses, Dedication of a Church.

161   Then the bishop says the prayer Lord Jesus Christ, you said. After this, facing the people, he proclaims the greeting of peace, saying, The peace of the Lord. The people reply, And also with you. One of the deacons may give the invitation to an exchange of the sign of peace by facing the people and saying, Let us offer each other. The bishop gives the sign of peace at least to the two concelebrants nearest him, then to the first of the deacons. All exchange a sign of peace and charity that is in accord with local custom.[17]

162   The bishop begins the breaking of the bread and it is continued by some of the concelebrating priests. Meanwhile, the *Agnus Dei* is repeated as long as is necessary to accompany the breaking of the bread. The bishop puts a small piece of the host into the cup, saying inaudibly, May this mingling.

163   After saying inaudibly the prayer before communion, the bishop genuflects and takes the paten. One by one the concelebrants approach the bishop, genuflect, and reverently receive from him the body of Christ. They hold it in their right hand, under which they hold the left hand, and return to their places. The concelebrants, however, may remain in their places and there receive the body of Christ.
      Then the bishop takes the host, holding it a little bit above the paten, and, facing the people, says, This is the Lamb of God, then with the concelebrants and the people continues, Lord, I am not worthy.
      As the bishop receives the body of Christ the communion song is begun.

164   When the bishop has received the blood of the Lord, he hands the cup to one of the deacons and gives communion to the deacons and the faithful.
      The concelebrants go up to the altar and receive the blood of the Lord from a deacon, who presents the cup and wipes it with a purificator after the communion of each concelebrant.[18]

165   When the giving of communion is over, one of the deacons consumes the blood that remains, takes the cup to a side table, and there purifies and arranges it, or he may do so after Mass. Another deacon or one of the concelebrants takes any remaining consecrated particles to

---

[17] See nos. 99-103 of this *Ceremonial* on the kiss of peace.
[18] See GIRM, nos. 201-206, which describe other ways of distributing communion under both kinds: DOL 208, nos. 1591-1596.

the tabernacle, then at a side table cleanses the paten or ciborium over the cup before the cup is cleansed.

166   When the bishop returns to the chair after the communion, he puts on the skullcap and, if need be, washes his hands. All are seated and a period of prayerful silence may follow, or a song of praise or a psalm may be sung.

167   Standing at the chair as a minister holds the book or after returning to the altar with the deacons, the bishop sings or says, Let us pray. With hands outstretched, he continues with the prayer after communion, which is preceded by a brief period of silence, unless this has been observed immediately after communion. The people respond at the end of the prayer with the acclamation Amen.

Concluding Rite

168   When the prayer after communion has been said, any necessary, brief announcements are made.

169   Finally, the bishop receives the miter and, with hands outstretched, greets the people, saying, The Lord be with you, to which the people respond, And also with you. One of the deacons may give the invitation Bow your heads or use similar words. The bishop gives the solemn blessing, choosing an appropriate formulary from among those given in *The Roman Missal (Sacramentary)*, The Roman Pontifical, or The Roman Ritual. As he recites the invocations or prayer of the solemn blessing, the bishop holds his hands outstretched over the people. All reply, Amen. Then he takes the pastoral staff[19] and says, May almighty God bless you, and then, as he makes the sign of the cross three times over the people, continues, the Father, and the Son, and the Holy Spirit.
    The bishop may also give the blessing by using one of the formularies given in nos. 1120-1121.
    When, in keeping with the provisions of the law, the bishop imparts the apostolic blessing, this replaces the usual blessing. It is announced by the deacon and is pronounced by use of its proper formularies.[20]

---

[19] See PR, no. 36: AAS 60 (1968), p. 411; DOL 550, no. 4493.
[20] See in this *Ceremonial* nos. 1122-1126 on the rite and formularies for the apostolic blessing.

170   After the blessing, one of the deacons dismisses the people, saying, The Mass is ended, go in peace, or one of the other formulas. All reply, Thanks be to God. Then, as a rule, the bishop kisses the altar and makes the due reverence to it. The concelebrants also, and all in the sanctuary (chancel), reverence the altar, as at the beginning of Mass, and return to the vesting room (sacristy) in procession, following the order in which they entered.

When they reach the vesting room (sacristy), all make a reverence to the cross together with the bishop. Then the concelebrants bow to the bishop and carefully put away their vestments. All together the ministers also bow to the bishop, then lay aside the articles they have used in the celebration and their vestments. All are to be careful in observing silence, out of respect for a spirit of recollection and the holiness of the house of God.

CHAPTER 2

OTHER MASSES CELEBRATED BY THE BISHOP

171 Even when the bishop celebrates Mass with a smaller assembly of people and clergy, everything should be so arranged that he is seen as the high priest of his flock, engaged with the concerns of his entire Church. Hence, when he visits the parishes or communities of his diocese, it is fitting that the presbyters of the parish or community concelebrate with him.

172 At least one deacon should take part, wearing diaconal vestments. In the absence of a deacon, a presbyter should proclaim the gospel reading and minister at the altar; if he is not to concelebrate, he wears an alb and stole.

173 Everything described in the General Instruction of the Roman Missal for the celebration of Mass with a congregation should be observed.[21]

In addition, the bishop in vesting puts on the pectoral cross and, as a rule, the skullcap.

He may use the miter and pastoral staff, as the circumstances suggest.

At the beginning of Mass he greets the people, saying, Peace be with you or The grace of our Lord (or: The grace and peace of God our Father).

The person who proclaims the gospel reading, whether a deacon or a presbyter, even if he concelebrates, asks for and receives a blessing from the bishop. After the gospel reading, the book is either presented for the bishop to kiss, or the one who has proclaimed the gospel reading kisses it.

Before the preface, the deacon hands the bishop's skullcap to a minister.

In Eucharistic Prayers I, II, and III, the bishop, after the words N., our Pope, adds, and for me, your unworthy servant. In Eucharistic Prayer IV, after the words especially N., our Pope, he adds the words and me your unworthy servant.

At the end of Mass the bishop gives the blessing in the way described in nos. 1120-1121.

174 With the consent of the diocesan bishop (see nos. 47 and 59), a bishop who is not the local Ordinary may use the bishop's chair (cathedra) and the pastoral staff in the celebration of Mass.

---

[21] See GIRM, nos. 77-152: DOL 208, nos. 1467-1542.

CHAPTER 3

MASS AT WHICH THE BISHOP PRESIDES
BUT NOT AS CELEBRANT

175   In the teaching and tradition of the Church, it belongs to the bishop to oversee celebration of the eucharist in the communities of the diocese. It is most fitting, then, that when he is present at a Mass he should himself be the celebrant.

If he is present at a Mass but for good reason is not the celebrant, nor is another bishop the celebrant, he should preside at least by celebrating the liturgy of the word and by blessing the people at the end.[22] This is especially true of those eucharistic celebrations within which there is to be a sacramental rite or a rite of consecration or blessing.

When the bishop presides without celebrating, the provisions given in the present chapter are to be followed.

176   After being received in the way already described in no. 79, the bishop, in the vesting room (sacristy) or other convenient place, puts on an alb and over it the pectoral cross and a stole and cope of the color of the occasion. As a rule he uses the miter and pastoral staff. Two deacons assist the bishop, or at least one, wearing diaconal vestments. In the absence of deacons, the bishop should be assisted by presbyters wearing copes.

177   In the entrance procession the bishop walks behind the celebrant or concelebrants, escorted by the deacons and ministers.

178   Upon reaching the altar, the celebrant or concelebrants make a deep bow, but if the blessed sacrament is reserved in the sanctuary (chancel), they genuflect. Then they go up to the altar, kiss it, and go to their appointed places.

After handing the pastoral staff to a minister and taking off the miter, the bishop, together with the deacons and ministers, makes a deep bow to the altar (or genuflects, as the case may be). Then he goes up to the altar and kisses it.

If incense is used, the bishop, accompanied by the deacons, incenses the altar in the usual way, including the cross.

The bishop then goes in the most direct way to the chair (cathedra) along with his deacons, who stand close to the chair on either side, to be ready to assist him.

---

[22] See PR, no. 24: AAS 60 (1968), p. 410; DOL 550, no. 4481.

179   From the beginning of Mass until the end of the liturgy of the word, the directives already given for the stational Mass of the bishop should be observed (see nos. 128-144). But if there is to be a sacramental rite or a rite of consecration or blessing within the Mass, any special provisions for the profession of faith and the general intercessions should be followed.

180   After the general intercessions or after a sacramental rite or rite of consecration or blessing, the bishop sits and receives the miter. Then the deacon and ministers prepare the altar as usual. If the gifts are brought forward by the faithful, they are received by the celebrant of the Mass or by the bishop. After a deep bow to the bishop, the celebrant goes to the altar and begins the liturgy of the eucharist in accordance with the Order of Mass.

181   If there is an incensation, the bishop is incensed after the celebrant; he puts aside the miter and stands to receive the incensation. But if there is no incensation, he puts aside the miter and stands after the invitation Pray, brethren. He remains standing at the chair (cathedra) until the epiclesis in the eucharistic prayer.

182   From the epiclesis until after the elevation of the cup, the bishop kneels facing the altar on a kneeler provided for him either in front of the chair or in some other convenient place. After the elevation, he stands once again at the chair.

183   After the invitation Let us offer each other by the deacon, the bishop gives the sign of peace to his deacons.
    If the bishop receives communion, he takes the body and blood of the Lord at the altar, after the celebrant.

184   During the communion of the faithful, the bishop may remain seated until the beginning of the prayer after communion, which he says standing at the altar or at the chair (cathedra). After the prayer, the bishop blesses the people in the way indicated in nos. 1120-1121. One of the deacons assisting him dismisses the people (see no. 170).

185   Then the bishop and the celebrant reverence the altar with a kiss in the usual way. Finally, all make the prescribed bow and leave in the order in which they entered.

186   If the bishop does not preside in the manner just outlined, he should participate in the Mass wearing mozzetta and rochet, and at some suitable place other than the bishop's chair (cathedra).

PART III

LITURGY OF THE HOURS
AND
CELEBRATIONS OF THE WORD OF GOD

LITURGY OF THE HOURS

INTRODUCTION

187   The bishop represents Christ in an eminent and conspicuous way and is the high priest of his flock. He should, then, be the first of all the members of his Church in offering prayer.[1]
   For this reason it is most highly recommended that, whenever possible and especially in the cathedral church, the bishop celebrate the liturgy of the hours together with his presbyters and ministers and with the full and active participation of the people; this applies particularly to the celebration of morning and evening prayer.[2]

188   It is fitting that on major solemnities the bishop celebrate with his clergy and people in the cathedral either evening prayer I or morning prayer or evening prayer II, as local circumstances suggest, but always with respect for the correspondence between the canonical hour celebrated and the natural time of day.

189.   It is also fitting that the bishop celebrate in the cathedral the office of readings and morning prayer on Good Friday and Holy Saturday and the office of readings on Christmas Eve.

190   Finally, in keeping with the provisions of the General Instruction of the Liturgy of the Hours,[3] the bishop should, by word and example, instruct the people committed to his care on the importance of the liturgy of the hours, and he should encourage its communal celebration in parishes, in communities, and in various kinds of religious meetings.

---

[1] See GILH, no. 28: DOL 426, no. 3458.
[2] See GILH, no. 254: DOL 426, no. 3684.
[3] See GILH, nos. 1, 5-19, 20-27, 30-32: DOL 426, nos. 3431, 3435-3449, 3450-3457, 3460-3462.

CHAPTER 1

CELEBRATION OF EVENING PRAYER
ON MAJOR SOLEMNITIES

191   For the bishop's arrival at the church the provisions already given in no. 79 of the general norms are to be followed.

192   In the vesting room (sacristy) the bishop is assisted by the deacons and other ministers, who will have put on their vestments before his arrival. The bishop takes off the cappa or mozzetta and may also remove the rochet, and puts on the amice, alb, cincture, pectoral cross, stole, and cope. He then receives the miter and pastoral staff from one of the deacons.

During this time presbyters, and especially canons, may put on a cope over a surplice or alb; deacons may wear either a cope or a dalmatic.

193   When all is ready, the procession enters the church to the accompaniment of organ music or singing and in the following order:
    — an acolyte carrying the cross, between two acolytes holding candlesticks with lighted candles;
    — clergy, two by two;
    — deacons, if more than one are present, two by two;
    — presbyters, two by two;
    — the bishop walking alone, wearing the miter and carrying the pastoral staff in his left hand and blessing with his right;
    — a little behind the bishop, the two deacons assisting him, who may, if need be, hold up the cope on either side;
    — finally, the ministers who assist with the book, the miter, and the pastoral staff.

There is neither a stop nor a genuflection if the procession passes in front of the blessed sacrament chapel.[4]

194   It is preferable that the processional cross be placed near the altar and serve as the altar cross; otherwise it is put away. The candlesticks are placed near the altar or on a side table or at some nearby place in the sanctuary (chancel).

195   On entering the sanctuary (chancel), all make a deep bow to the altar two by two (or genuflect before the reserved blessed sacrament), then go to their places.

---

[4] See no. 71 of this *Ceremonial*.

196   When he reaches the front of the altar, the bishop hands the staff to a minister and takes off the miter. Together with the deacons and other ministers accompanying him, the bishop makes a deep bow to the altar, then goes up to the altar and, together with the two deacons assisting him, kisses it. Then he goes to the chair (cathedra), where he stands and, while making the sign of the cross, sings the verse God, come to my assistance. All reply, Lord, make haste to help me. The *Gloria Patri* is sung, followed by the *Alleluia*, depending on the rubrics.

197   The hymn is begun by the cantors and continued by the choir or the people, depending on the musical style of the hymn.

198   After the hymn, the bishop sits and, as a rule, takes the miter; everyone else also sits. The antiphons and psalms are begun by a cantor. Depending on local custom, all may stand during the singing of the psalms.
    When the psalm prayers are used, after the repetition of the antiphon, the bishop puts aside the miter, rises, and once everyone else has stood says, Let us pray. After a brief pause for silent prayer by all, he says the prayer corresponding to the psalm or canticle.

199   After the psalms, a reader, standing at the ambo, reads either the longer or the shorter reading as all sit and listen.

200   As circumstances suggest, the bishop, wearing the miter and with the pastoral staff if he wishes, may give a brief homily in explanation of the reading. He may do so either seated in the chair (cathedra) or in some other place where he can be better seen and heard by all.

201   As circumstances suggest, a brief period of silence may follow the reading or the homily.

202   In response to the word of God, a short responsory or responsorial song is sung.

203   During the antiphon for the Canticle of Mary, the bishop puts incense into the censer. When the choir begins the canticle, the bishop, wearing the miter, rises and all rise with him. Making the sign of the cross from forehead to breast, the bishop goes to the altar and, after making the appropriate reverence together with the ministers, goes up to the altar, but does not kiss it.

204   While the gospel canticle is being sung, the usual incensation of altar, cross, bishop, and others present is carried out in the manner already indicated for Mass in nos. 89, 93, 96, and 97.

205   After the canticle and the repetition of the antiphon, the intercessions follow. A minister holds the book and the bishop gives the introductory invitation. Then from the ambo or some other suitable place one of the deacons announces the intentions and the people respond.

The Lord's Prayer is sung or said by all, and, if the bishop so decides, without an introductory invitation.

With hands outstretched, the bishop sings or says the concluding prayer. All reply, Amen.

206   Then the bishop takes the miter and greets the people saying, The Lord be with you. One of the deacons may give the invitation Bow your heads or use similar words. With hands outstretched over the people, the bishop gives the solemn blessing, choosing an appropriate formulary from among those given in *The Roman Missal (Sacramentary)*.

He then takes the pastoral staff and says, May almighty God bless you, as he makes the sign of the cross three times over the people.

The bishop may also give the blessing by using one of the formularies given in nos. 1120-1121.

207   Then one of the deacons dismisses the people, saying, Go in the peace of Christ, and all reply, Thanks be to God.

208   The bishop leaves the chair (cathedra), wearing the miter and carrying the pastoral staff, and, as circumstances suggest, kisses the altar. The presbyters and all in the sanctuary (chancel) also reverence the altar. All return to the vesting room (sacristy) in procession, following the order in which they entered.

CHAPTER 2

SIMPLER FORM FOR THE CELEBRATION OF EVENING PRAYER

209   Even when the bishop presides at evening prayer apart from major solemnities or with a smaller group of people and clergy or in a parish church, it is desirable that a number of presbyters be present, preferably vested in cassock and surplice or in alb and cope, as well as two deacons or at least one, vested in alb and dalmatic. The bishop is vested either in the manner already described in no. 192 or in alb with stole and cope.

Everything is done as already indicated in nos. 191-208, with any necessary adaptations.

210   When the bishop takes part in a smaller gathering in a parish or in some other church, he may preside at evening prayer from the chair wearing choir dress[5] and with a few assisting ministers.

211   If the bishop takes part in a celebration of evening prayer at which a presbyter presides, the bishop gives the final blessing before the dismissal of the people.

---

[5] See no. 63 of this *Ceremonial*.

CHAPTER 3

MORNING PRAYER

212   Morning prayer may be celebrated in the same way as evening prayer, with the following changes.

213   If the invitatory is used, the bishop does not begin morning prayer with the verse God, come to my assistance, but with the verse Lord, open my lips, to which all reply, And my mouth will proclaim your praise. As they say this verse, all make the sign of the cross upon their lips. All remain standing and the invitatory psalm is sung, with the antiphon interspersed in the manner indicated in *The Liturgy of the Hours*.

After the invitatory psalm and the usual final repetition of the antiphon, the hymn is sung and the celebration of morning prayer continues in the manner already indicated for the celebration of evening prayer.

CHAPTER 4

OFFICE OF READINGS

214 The bishop, in choir dress, presides at the office of readings from the chair. In keeping with the rubrics, he begins the office with either Lord, open my lips or the words God, come to my assistance. Hymns, antiphons, and psalms are begun by the cantor; the readings are proclaimed by a reader. At the end the bishop sings or says the concluding prayer, and, if there is a dismissal, he blesses the people in the manner indicated in nos. 1120-1121 of this *Ceremonial*.

215 For the celebration of an extended vigil at the office of readings, a deacon solemnly proclaims the gospel reading, at a Sunday office from a gospel on the resurrection and at the office on other days from some other gospel. The deacon, vested in alb, stole, and dalmatic, first asks for the bishop's blessing and is then escorted by two acolytes with lighted candles and the censerbearer carrying a smoking censer in which incense has been placed and blessed by the bishop.
  As circumstances suggest, the bishop gives a homily.
  After the hymn *Te Deum*, if it is called for by the rubrics, the bishop sings or says the concluding prayer, and, if there is a dismissal, gives the blessing.

216 Whenever an extended vigil is celebrated in more solemn form and with a large attendance of the people, the bishop, presbyters, and deacons may be vested in the same manner as at evening prayer. During the singing of the psalms, the bishop, with miter, sits in the chair. For the gospel reading he lays aside the miter, rises, and takes the pastoral staff, which he holds even during the singing of the *Te Deum*. Everything else is done in the manner already indicated in no. 214.

217 On Christmas Eve, Good Friday, and Holy Saturday the office of readings as described in nos. 214-216 should be celebrated, if at all possible, with the bishop presiding, or at least present, and with the people taking part.

CHAPTER 5

DAYTIME PRAYER

(MIDMORNING, MIDDAY, MIDAFTERNOON)

218   The bishop may preside at the hours of daytime prayer, whether celebrated in the cathedral or elsewhere, in choir dress.[6] He begins the hour with the verse God, come to my assistance, and ends it with the concluding prayer.

   During the psalms all sit or stand, depending on local custom. After the psalms all sit and a reader, standing in a suitable place, proclaims the short reading. After the reading, as all stand, the cantors begin the verse, to which all make the response. There is no blessing. The hour ends with the acclamation Let us praise the Lord, to which all reply, And give him thanks.

---

[6] See no. 63 of this *Ceremonial*.

Chapter 6

NIGHT PRAYER

219   When the bishop presides at night prayer celebrated in a church, he wears choir dress,[7] and is assisted by a few ministers. The bishop begins the hour with the verse God, come to my assistance.

If there is an examination of conscience, it is made in silence or is made part of the penitential rite.

During the psalmody all sit or stand, depending on local custom. All sit as a reader, standing in a suitable place, proclaims the short reading. The reading is followed by the responsory Into your hands, Lord. The antiphon for the gospel canticle Lord, now you let is then said. As the canticle is begun all rise and sign themselves with the sign of the cross.

The bishop says the concluding prayer, then blesses those taking part with the words May the all-powerful Lord.

220   The hour is brought to a close with one of the antiphons in honor of the Blessed Virgin Mary, without any accompanying prayer.

---

[7] See no. 63 of this *Ceremonial*.

CHAPTER 7

CELEBRATIONS OF THE WORD OF GOD

INTRODUCTION

221 "The Church has always revered Sacred Scripture even as it has revered the body of the Lord, because, above all in the liturgy, it never ceases to receive the bread of life from the table both of God's word and of Christ's body and to offer it to the faithful."[8]

And every liturgical celebration is based on the word of God and sustained by that word.[9] The bishop should therefore strive to ensure that through a sound spiritual preparation all the faithful learn how to listen to the mystery of Christ and to reflect on it as that mystery is presented in the Old and the New Testament.

222 Therefore in the life of individuals and of communities celebrations of the word of God are an effective way to nurture their spirit and spiritual life, to foster a more intense love of God's word, and to ensure richer results from celebrations of the eucharist and the other sacraments.

223 Particularly in the cathedral, therefore, and with the bishop presiding, celebrations of the word of God should rightly take place especially on the vigils of major feasts, on some of the weekdays of Advent and Lent, and on Sundays and days of precept.

DESCRIPTION OF A CELEBRATION OF THE WORD

224 Celebrations of the word of God should be patterned on the structure of the liturgy of the word at Mass.

225 After being received in the manner already described in no. 79, the bishop, in the vesting room (sacristy) or other suitable place, puts on over the alb the pectoral cross, the stole, and a cope of the color of the occasion. As a rule he also takes the miter and pastoral staff. Two deacons, in diaconal vestments, assist the bishop. If no deacons are present, two priests, in alb or cassock and surplice, assist the bishop.

---

[8] Vatican Council II, Dogmatic Constitution on Divine Revelation *Dei verbum*, no. 21: DOL 14, no. 224.

[9] See LM, Introduction, no. 3.

226   After the introductory rites (consisting of a song, greeting, and prayer), one or more readings from Sacred Scripture are proclaimed, with songs or psalms or intervals of silence interspersed. The readings are explained in a homily that relates them to the lives of those present.

The homily may be followed by a period of silent reflection on the word of God. Then the whole congregation with one heart and voice should join in praying the intercessions, in litanic or other suitable form that encourages participation. Finally, the Lord's Prayer should be recited.

The bishop, as the one who presides over the assembly, concludes the celebration with a prayer and blesses the people in the manner indicated in nos. 1120-1121.

One of the deacons or ministers dismisses the people, saying, Go in the peace of Christ, and all reply, Thanks be to God.

PART IV

CELEBRATIONS
OF THE MYSTERIES OF THE LORD
THROUGH THE CYCLE
OF THE LITURGICAL YEAR

CELEBRATIONS OF THE MYSTERIES OF THE LORD THROUGH THE CYCLE OF THE LITURGICAL YEAR

INTRODUCTION

227   "The Church is conscious that it must celebrate the saving work of the divine Bridegroom by devoutly recalling it on certain days throughout the course of the year. Every week, on the day which the Church has called the Lord's Day, it keeps the memory of the Lord's resurrection, which it also celebrates once in the year, together with his blessed passion, in the most solemn festival of Easter.

"Within the cycle of a year, moreover, the Church unfolds the whole mystery of Christ, from his incarnation and birth until his ascension, the day of Pentecost, and the expectation of blessed hope and of the Lord's return.

"Recalling thus the mysteries of redemption, the Church opens to the faithful the riches of the Lord's powers and merits, so that these are in some way made present in every age in order that the faithful may lay hold of them and be filled with saving grace."[1]

Sunday, the Lord's Day

228   "The Church celebrates the paschal mystery on the first day of the week, known as the Lord's Day or Sunday. This follows a tradition handed down from the apostles and having its origin from the day of Christ's resurrection. Thus Sunday must be ranked as the first holy day of all."

Since Sunday is the nucleus and foundation of the yearly liturgical cycle by which the Church unfolds the entire mystery of Christ, the Sunday celebration gives way only to those solemnities or feasts of the Lord belonging to the General Roman Calendar. By its nature, then, Sunday excludes any other celebration's being permanently assigned to that day, with these exceptions: the feasts of the Holy Family and the Baptism of the Lord, the solemnities of the Holy Trinity and of Christ the King.

The Sundays of Advent, of Lent, and of the Easter season have precedence over all feasts of the Lord and over all solemnities.[2]

229   The bishop should therefore ensure that in his diocese the idea of the Lord's Day as the first holy day of all is proposed to the devotion

---

[1] SC, art. 102: DOL 1, no. 102.

[2] See SC Rites, General Norms for the Liturgical Year and the Calendar, 21 March 1969 (hereafter, GNLYC), nos. 4-6: DOL 442, nos. 3770-3772.

of the faithful and taught to them in such a way that it may become in fact a day of joy and of freedom from work.[3]

The bishop should be concerned that the directives of the Second Vatican Council and the reformed liturgical books concerning the proper character of the Sunday celebration are observed with fidelity and devotion. This has a particular application to the practice, frequently involving a Sunday, of assigning a special theme to a particular day, for example, dedicating a day to the promotion of peace and justice, vocations, or the missions. In such cases the liturgy to be celebrated is the Sunday liturgy, but the theme proposed may be brought out in the songs chosen or in the introductions, the homily, or the general intercessions.

On the Sundays in Ordinary Time one of the readings may be chosen from the *Lectionary for Mass* that serves to highlight the theme of the day.

Also on the Sundays in Ordinary Time when, by command or permission of the local Ordinary, there is a special celebration devoted to a particular theme, the Mass may be chosen from the Masses and Prayers for Various Needs and Occasions provided in *The Roman Missal* (*Sacramentary*).

230   Contemporary changes in the pattern of social life have influenced the changes in the composition of the liturgical calendar. Thus in certain regions some solemnities have been suppressed as days of precept and some of those that have been entered in the General Roman Calendar as solemnities of the mysteries of the Lord have been transferred to the following Sunday:

a. Epiphany to the Sunday falling between 2 January and 8 January;

b. Ascension to the Seventh Sunday of Easter;

c. the solemnity of the Body and Blood of Christ (Corpus Christi) to the Sunday after Trinity Sunday.

In regard to other celebrations of the Lord, of the Blessed Virgin Mary, and of the saints that occur during the week and are no longer to be observed as days of precept, the bishop should try to ensure that the Christian people continue to celebrate them with devotion, so that also on weekdays the faithful may have frequent opportunities to receive God's saving grace.

---

[3] See SC, art. 106: DOL 1, no. 106.

Liturgical Year

231　The celebration of the liturgical year possesses a distinct sacramental force and efficacy because Christ himself in his mysteries and in the memorials of his saints, especially of his Mother, continues his mission of infinite mercy. Therefore his faithful people not only recall and contemplate the mysteries of redemption but also lay hold of them, enter into communion with them, and live by them.[4]

232　The bishop should therefore strive to direct the faithful to observe with deep spirituality especially the feasts of the Lord and the privileged seasons of the liturgical year, so that what they celebrate and proclaim with their lips they may inwardly believe, and what they believe inwardly they may bring to bear on their personal and public lives.[5]

233　In addition to the liturgical celebrations that make up the liturgical year, many regions maintain their own popular customs and devout practices. The bishop as part of his pastoral charge should attach great importance to such customs and practices that build up piety, religious devotion, and an understanding of the mysteries of Christ. The bishop should also see to it that "they accord with the sacred liturgy, are in some way derived from it, and lead the people to it, since, in fact, the liturgy by its very nature far surpasses any of them."[6]

---

[4] See Paul VI, Motu Proprio *Mysterii paschalis*, 14 February 1969: AAS 61 (1969), pp. 223-224; DOL 440, no. 3755. See Pius XII, Encyclical *Mediator Dei*, 20 November 1947: AAS 39 (1947), p. 580.

[5] See SC, art. 108: DOL 1, no. 108. See Pius XII, Encyclical *Mediator Dei*, 20 November 1947: AAS 39 (1947), p. 577.

[6] SC, art. 13: DOL 1, no. 13.

Chapter 1

ADVENT AND THE CHRISTMAS SEASON

234   Next to the yearly celebration of the paschal mystery, the Church holds most sacred the commemoration of Christ's birth and first manifestations. This is the purpose of the Christmas season.[7]

235   The season of Advent, the preparation for this commemoration, has a twofold character: it is a time to prepare for Christmas, when Christ's First Coming is remembered; it is a time when that remembrance directs the mind and heart to await Christ's Second Coming in the last days. In this way Advent is a period of devout and joyful expectation.[8]

236   During Advent, the playing of the organ and other musical instruments as well as the floral decoration of the altar should be marked by a moderation that reflects the character of this season, but does not anticipate the full joy of Christmas itself.
         On the Third Sunday of Advent, called Gaudete Sunday, rose vestments may be worn.[9]

237   The bishop should see to the devout observance of Christmas, in a truly Christian spirit. This solemnity of the Lord's birth celebrates the mystery of the incarnation by which the Word of God humbled himself to share in our humanity, in order that he might enable us to become sharers in his divinity.

238   The custom of celebrating a vigil to begin the solemnity of Christmas is to be maintained and fostered, in keeping with the usage proper to each Church.[10]
         It is therefore most fitting that in the cathedral the bishop himself, as far as possible, preside at an extended vigil, in accord with the provisions already given in nos. 215-216.
         When the vigil is followed immediately by Mass, the bishop and presbyters may be vested as for Mass. After the gospel reading of the vigil or, if it is not an extended vigil, after the responsory, the *Gloria* is sung in place of the *Te Deum*, and the opening prayer of the Mass is said immediately, the introductory rites being omitted.

---

[7] See GNLYC, no. 32: DOL 442, no. 3798.

[8] See GNLYC, nos. 32, 39: DOL 442, nos. 3798, 3805.

[9] See GIRM, no. 308, f: DOL 208, no. 1698. See MS, no. 66: AAS 59 (1967), p. 319; DOL 508, no. 4187.

[10] See GILH, no. 71: DOL 426, no. 3501.

239   In keeping with a very ancient Roman practice, Mass may be celebrated three times on Christmas, provided each is celebrated at its proper
time, that is, at midnight, at dawn, and during the day.[11]

240   The ancient solemnity of the Epiphany of the Lord ranks among
the principal festivals of the whole liturgical year, since it celebrates in
the child born of Mary the manifestation of the one who is the Son of
God, the Messiah of the Jewish people, and a light to the nations.
       Whether the feast is observed as a day of precept or is transferred
to the following Sunday, the bishop will see to it that this solemnity is
celebrated in a proper manner. Hence:
       — there will be a suitable and increased display of lights;
       — after the singing of the gospel reading, depending on local cus-
       tom, one of the deacons or a canon or a beneficed cleric or some-
       one else, vested in cope, will go to the lectern and there announce
       to the people the movable feasts of the current year;
       — the custom of having a special presentation of gifts will be ob-
       served or renewed in accordance with local usage and tradition;
       — the invitations, comments, and homily will explain the full mean-
       ing of this day with its "three mysteries,"[12] that is, the adoration
       of the child by the Magi, the baptism of Christ, and the wedding
       at Cana.

---

[11] See RM, Proper of Seasons, the rubric printed at the end of the Mass of the vigil.

[12] See *The Liturgy of the Hours*, English ed., 1974 (hereafter, LH), Epiphany, Evening Prayer II, antiphon for the Canticle of Mary.

CHAPTER 2

FEAST OF THE PRESENTATION OF THE LORD

241   On this day Christ's faithful people, with candles in their hands, go out to meet the Lord and to acclaim him with Simeon, who recognized Christ as "a light to reveal God to the nations."

They should therefore be taught to walk as children of the light in their entire way of life, because they have a duty to show the light of Christ to all by acting in the works that they do as lighted lamps.

FIRST FORM: PROCESSION

242   At the appointed hour the people gather in a chapel or some other suitable place outside the church where the Mass will be celebrated. They carry unlighted candles.

243   In a convenient place the bishop puts on white Mass vestments. In place of the chasuble he may wear a cope for the procession. He puts on the miter and takes the pastoral staff, then with the ministers and, if there are any, concelebrants, who wear Mass vestments, he makes his way to the place where the candles are to be blessed.

While the candles are being lighted, the antiphon The Lord will come or another song is sung.[13]

244   When the bishop reaches the place where the candles are to be blessed and the singing has ended, he puts aside the miter and pastoral staff and, facing the people, says, In the name of the Father. Then he greets the people, saying, Peace be with you, and then gives the invitation to the service. But, as circumstances suggest, he may leave this invitation to a deacon or one of the concelebrants.

245   After the invitation, the bishop blesses the candles. With hands outstretched and as a minister holds the book, he says the prayer of blessing, then in silence sprinkles the candles with holy water. He puts on the miter again and in preparation for the procession places incense in the censer and blesses it. Finally, the bishop receives from a deacon the blessed candle that he is to carry in the procession.

246   When a deacon has announced, Let us go in peace to meet the Lord, the procession moves off to the church where Mass is to be cele-

---

[13] See RM, Proper of Saints, 2 February, Presentation of the Lord.

brated and in this order: censerbearer carrying a censer with burning incense; crossbearer, between two ministers carrying lighted candles in candlesticks; clergy; the deacon who carries the Book of the Gospels; other deacons present; concelebrants; minister with the bishop's pastoral staff; the bishop, wearing the miter and holding a candle; a little behind the bishop, the two deacons assisting him; after them the ministers who assist with the book and the miter; finally the faithful. All, ministers and faithful, carry candles.

As the procession moves forward, the antiphon Christ is the light of the nations, with the canticle Now, Lord, you have kept your word, is sung, or another suitable song is sung.

247   As the procession enters the church, the entrance antiphon of the Mass is sung. When the bishop comes to the altar, he reverences it and, as circumstances suggest, incenses it. Then he goes to the chair (where he replaces the cope with the chasuble, if he has worn the cope in the procession). After the singing of the *Gloria*, the bishop sings or says the opening prayer. The Mass continues as usual.

But if it seems more suitable, the following alternative may be used.

On reaching the altar, the bishop hands the candle to the deacon, lays aside the miter (replaces the cope with the chasuble), and reverences and incenses the altar. Then he goes to the chair (cathedra). The introductory rites of the Mass are omitted, and after the singing of the *Gloria* the bishop sings or says the opening prayer, and the Mass then continues as usual. [14]

Second Form: Solemn Entrance

248   When a procession is not feasible, the people, carrying unlighted candles, assemble in the church. The bishop, in white Mass vestments, is accompanied by his ministers and, if there are any, concelebrants, who wear Mass vestments, together with a representative group of the faithful. They go to a suitable place (either outside the door of the church or inside the church itself) where most of the congregation can easily take part.

When the bishop reaches the place appointed for the blessing of the candles, candles are lighted while the antiphon Christ the light or some other suitable song is sung.

Then the provisions already given in nos. 244-247 are followed.[15]

---

[14] See RM, Proper of Saints, 2 February, Presentation of the Lord.
[15] See RM, Proper of Saints, 2 February, Presentation of the Lord.

CHAPTER 3

LENT

249   The annual observance of Lent is the special season for the ascent to the holy mountain of Easter.

    Through its twofold theme of repentance and baptism, the season of Lent disposes both the catechumens and the faithful to celebrate the paschal mystery. Catechumens are led to the sacraments of initiation by means of the rite of election, the scrutinies, and catechesis. The faithful, listening more intently to the word of God and devoting themselves to prayer, are prepared through a spirit of repentance to renew their baptismal promises.[16]

250   As indicated in no. 406, the bishop should be deeply concerned to promote the formation of catechumens, as well as to preside at the rite of election or enrollment of names in the Lenten liturgy, as described in nos. 408-419, and, depending on the circumstances, at the presentation of the Creed and of the Lord's Prayer, described in nos. 420-424.

251   Catechesis should impress on the minds of the faithful not only the social consequences of sin but also the essence of the virtue of penance, namely, detestation of sin as an offense against God. The role of the Church in penitential practices is not to be neglected, and the people are to be exhorted to pray for sinners.

    During Lent penance should be not only inward and individual but also outward and social, and should be directed toward works of mercy on behalf of our brothers and sisters.[17]

    The faithful should be urged to take a greater and more fruitful share in the Lenten liturgy and penitential services. They should be advised particularly to approach the sacrament of penance during Lent, in accordance with the law and traditions of the Church, so that they may share in the joys of Easter Sunday with purity of heart. It is very appropriate for the sacrament of reconciliation to be celebrated during Lent in a more solemn form, as described in the *Rite of Penance*.[18]

---

[16] See SC, art. 109: DOL 1, no. 109. See GNLYC, no. 27: DOL 442, no. 3793.

[17] See SC, art. 105, 109-110: DOL 1, nos. 105, 109-110.

[18] See nos. 622-632 of this *Ceremonial*.

252   During Lent the altar is not to be decorated with flowers, and the use of musical instruments is allowed only to support the singing.

The Fourth Sunday of Lent, called Laetare Sunday, solemnities, and feasts are exceptions to this rule. On Laetare Sunday rose vestments may be used.[19]

---

[19] See GIRM, no. 308, f: DOL 208, no. 1698. See MS, no. 66: AAS 59 (1967), p. 319; DOL 508, no. 4187.

CHAPTER 4

ASH WEDNESDAY

253   On the Wednesday before the First Sunday of Lent the faithful, by receiving ashes, enter upon the season appointed for spiritual purification. This sign of penance, biblical in origin[20] and preserved among the customs of the Church until our own day, expresses the human condition as affected by sin. In this sign we outwardly profess our guilt before God and thereby, prompted by the hope that the Lord is kind and compassionate, patient and abounding in mercy, express our desire for inward conversion. This sign is also the beginning of the journey of conversion that will reach its goal in the celebration of the sacrament of reconciliation during the days leading to Easter.

254   In the Mass of Ash Wednesday the bishop blesses and imposes ashes in the cathedral church or in some other church that is more suitable pastorally.

255   Wearing the simple miter and carrying the pastoral staff, the bishop enters the church in the usual manner; with the presbyters, deacons, and other ministers, he reverences the altar, incenses it, then goes to the chair (cathedra), where he greets the people. The introductory rites of the Mass and, as circumstances suggest, also the *Kyrie* are omitted, and the bishop immediately says the opening prayer.

256   After the gospel reading and the homily the bishop, standing without the miter and with hands joined, invites the people to pray; after a brief pause for silent prayer, he blesses the ashes, held in front of him by an acolyte, by saying, with hands outstretched, the prayer provided in *The Roman Missal* (*Sacramentary*). In silence the bishop then sprinkles the ashes with holy water.

257   After the blessing, the appointed minister, a concelebrant or a deacon, places ashes on the bishop, as the bishop bows before him, and says, Turn away from sin and be faithful to the Gospel or Remember, man, you are dust and to dust you will return.

---

[20] See 2 Samuel 13:19; Esther 4:1; Job 42:6; 1 Maccabees 3:47, 4:39; Lamentations 2:10.

258   Then the bishop again puts on the miter and, seated at the chair or standing, places ashes on the concelebrants, the ministers, and the faithful. The bishop may be assisted if necessary by some of the concelebrants or deacons.

During this time Psalm 51 (50), with one of the antiphons, for example, Lord, take away our wickedness, or the responsory Direct our hearts to better things, or some other suitable song is sung.

259   After the imposition of ashes, the bishop washes his hands and proceeds to the general intercessions. The Mass continues in the usual way.

CHAPTER 5

LITURGICAL ASSEMBLIES DURING LENT

260   All the elements of Lenten observance should conspire to manifest more clearly and to promote the life of the local Church. For this
reason *The Roman Missal (Sacramentary)* strongly encourages the preser-
vation and development of the traditional form of gathering the local
Church after the fashion of the Roman "stations," at least in the larger
cities and in a way suited to the particular place. Especially with the chief
pastor of the diocese presiding, such assemblies of the faithful can gather
on Sunday or on more convenient weekdays, at the tombs of the saints,
in the principal churches or shrines of the city, or in other frequently
visited places of pilgrimage in the diocese. This may be done on Sundays or weekdays, in parish churches or places of pilgrimage. The manner of celebration will vary according to local needs.[21]

261   If, as local conditions permit, there is a procession preceding the
Mass that is celebrated for such assemblies, the people gather before-
hand in a chapel or other suitable place outside the church where the
Mass will be celebrated.

In a convenient place the bishop puts on purple Mass vestments.
In place of the chasuble he may wear a cope. He puts on a simple miter
and takes the pastoral staff, then with the ministers and, if there are any,
concelebrants, who wear Mass vestments, he goes to the gathering place,
to the accompaniment of a suitable song.

After the singing has ended, the bishop lays aside the pastoral staff
and miter and greets the people. The bishop, a concelebrant, or a deacon gives a brief introduction. Then, with hands outstretched, the bishop
says an opening prayer on the mystery of the holy cross or for the remis-
sion of sins or for the Church, especially the local Church, or he says
one of the prayers over the people given in *The Roman Missal (Sacramentary)*. He then takes the miter, and, as circumstances suggest, puts
incense in the censer. As the deacon announces, Let us go forth in peace,
the procession to the church is formed and during it the Litany of the
Saints is sung. The names of the holy patron or founder and the saints
of the local Church may be inserted at the proper places in
the litany. When the procession reaches the church, all go to their appointed places. When the bishop reaches the altar, he puts aside the pastoral staff and the miter, reverences the altar, and incenses it. He then

---

[21] See RM, Proper of Seasons, the rubric printed at the beginning of the Lenten season.

goes to the chair (cathedra) and takes off the cope, if he has worn it during the procession, and puts on the chasuble. The introductory rites of the Mass are omitted, and, as circumstances suggest, also the *Kyrie*. The bishop says the opening prayer of the Mass. The Mass continues in the usual way.

If this is preferable, the bishop may take off the cope and put on the chasuble as soon as he reaches the altar, before reverencing it.

262   At these assemblies, instead of Mass a celebration of the word of God may take place in the way already described in nos. 224-226, or in the form of the penitential services for the Lenten season provided in Appendix II of the *Rite of Penance* (see nos. 640-643 of this *Ceremonial*).

CHAPTER 6

PASSION SUNDAY (PALM SUNDAY)

263   On Passion Sunday (Palm Sunday) the Church enters upon the mystery of its crucified, buried, and risen Lord, who, by his entrance into Jerusalem, gave a glimpse of his own majesty. Christians carry branches as a sign of the royal triumph that Christ won by his acceptance of the cross. Since Saint Paul says: "Provided we suffer with him in order that we may also be glorified with him,"[22] the link between these two aspects of the paschal mystery should stand out clearly in the liturgical celebration and catechesis of Palm Sunday.

FIRST FORM: PROCESSION

264   At the scheduled time the congregation assembles in a secondary church or chapel or in some other suitable place distinct from the church to which the procession will move.
    The faithful carry branches.[23]

265   In a convenient place the bishop puts on red vestments for Mass. (The bishop may wear a cope instead of a chasuble. In this case he removes the cope at the end of the procession.) He puts on the miter and takes the pastoral staff and, together with the ministers and, if there are any, the concelebrants, who are vested for Mass, he goes to the place where the branches are to be blessed as the antiphon Hosanna or some other suitable song is being sung.

266   After the singing has ended, the bishop puts aside the miter and pastoral staff, and, facing the people, says, In the name of the Father, and of the Son, and of the Holy Spirit. Then he greets the people, saying, Peace be with you, and gives an introduction, inviting the people to take full part in the celebration. But, as circumstances suggest, he may leave this introduction to the deacon or one of the concelebrants.

267   After the introduction, the bishop, with hands outstretched, says the prayer of blessing over the branches, then sprinkles them with holy water in silence.

---

[22] Romans 8:17.
[23] See RM, Proper of Seasons, Passion Sunday (Palm Sunday), rubrics for the procession.

268   After the blessing of the branches, before the proclamation of the gospel reading, the bishop may distribute them to the concelebrants, the ministers, and some of the faithful. He himself first receives the branch set aside for him from a deacon or one of the concelebrants and hands it to a minister while he distributes the branches. During this time a suitable song is sung.

269   Next the bishop places incense in the censer, blesses the deacon who is to proclaim the gospel reading, and again takes the palm branch, which he holds during the gospel reading. If, as circumstances suggest, he gives a homily, the bishop lays aside the branch and, unless he decides not to, takes the miter and pastoral staff.

270   To begin the procession the bishop or a deacon may address the people in the words Let us go forth in peace, given in *The Roman Missal (Sacramentary)*, or in similar words. The procession to the church where Mass will be celebrated then begins. The censerbearer goes first, carrying a censer with burning incense, followed by the crossbearer (the cross may be suitably decorated with palm branches in accordance with local custom). The crossbearer is flanked by two other acolytes holding lighted candles. The rest of the procession follows in this order: clergy; a deacon who carries the Book of the Gospels; other deacons, if there are any, carrying books for the singing of the passion; concelebrants; a minister carrying the bishop's pastoral staff; then the bishop, wearing the miter and carrying a branch; next, a little behind the bishop, the two deacons assisting him; the ministers who assist with the book and the miter; finally the faithful. All, whether ministers or faithful, carry branches.

   During the procession the choir and people sing the songs provided in *The Roman Missal (Sacramentary)* or other suitable songs.

   As the procession enters the church, the responsory The children of Jerusalem or another song which refers to the Lord's entrance is sung.[24]

271   When the bishop comes to the altar, he hands the branch to the deacon, puts aside the miter, reverences the altar, and incenses it. He then goes to the chair (cathedra) and takes off the cope, if he has worn it, and puts on the chasuble. The introductory rites of the Mass and, as circumstances suggest, the *Kyrie* are omitted, and the bishop concludes the procession by saying the opening prayer of the Mass.

   If this is preferable, the bishop may take off the cope and put on the chasuble as soon as he reaches the altar, before reverencing it.

---

[24] See RM, Proper of Seasons, Passion Sunday (Palm Sunday), rubrics for the procession.

SECOND FORM: SOLEMN ENTRANCE

272   If the procession cannot be held outside the church, the blessing of branches may take the form of a solemn entrance.

The faithful, holding the branches, assemble either in front of the church door or inside the church. The bishop and ministers, with a representative group of the faithful, go to a place in the church where most of the people will be able to see the rite.

While the bishop makes his way to the appointed place, the antiphon Hosanna or some other suitable song is sung. Then everything is done as indicated in nos. 266-271.[25]

NARRATIVE OF THE PASSION

273   When the gospel acclamation has begun, everyone but the bishop rises. The Lord's passion is narrated without candles or incense. The deacons who are to proclaim the narrative of the passion ask for and receive a blessing (see no. 140 of this *Ceremonial*). Putting aside the miter, the bishop then rises. The greeting before the gospel reading and the signing of the book are omitted.

After the verse on the death of the Lord, all kneel and a brief pause is observed. At the end the words This is the Gospel of the Lord are said, but the book is not kissed.

After the narrative of the passion the bishop gives a short homily. After the homily, as circumstances suggest, there may be an interval of silence.

The Mass then continues in the usual way.

---

[25] See RM, Proper of Seasons, Passion Sunday (Palm Sunday), rubrics for the solemn entrance.

CHAPTER 7

CHRISM MASS

274   This Mass, which the bishop concelebrates with his college of presbyters and at which he consecrates the holy chrism and blesses the other oils, manifests the communion of the presbyters with their bishop.[26]

The holy chrism consecrated by the bishop is used to anoint the newly baptized, to seal the candidates for confirmation, and to anoint the hands of presbyters and the heads of bishops at their ordination, as well as in the rites of anointing pertaining to the dedication of churches and altars. The oil of catechumens is used in the preparation of the catechumens for their baptism. The oil of the sick is used to bring comfort and support to the sick in their infirmity.

Presbyters are brought together and concelebrate this Mass as witnesses and cooperators with their bishop in the consecration of the chrism because they share in the sacred office of the bishop in building up, sanctifying, and ruling the people of God.[27] This Mass is therefore a clear expression of the unity of the priesthood and sacrifice of Christ, which continue to be present in the Church.

To show the unity of the college of presbyters, the presbyters who concelebrate with the bishop should come from different parts of the diocese.[28]

Presbyters who take part but for some reason do not concelebrate may receive communion under both kinds.

275   The blessing of the oil of the sick and the oil of catechumens and the consecration of the chrism are ordinarily done by the bishop at the Chrism Mass celebrated on Holy Thursday morning.

If it is difficult for the clergy and the people to assemble with the bishop on Holy Thursday morning, the blessing may be held on an earlier day, near Easter, with the celebration of the proper Chrism Mass.[29]

276   Because of its meaning and pastoral importance in the life of the diocese, the Chrism Mass should be celebrated as a stational Mass in the cathedral church or, for pastoral reasons, in another church.

---

[26] See GIRM, no. 157: DOL 208, no. 1547. See RM, Proper of Seasons, Holy Thursday, rubrics preceding the text of the Chrism Mass.

[27] See Vatican Council II, Decree on the Ministry and Life of Priests *Presbyterorum Ordinis*, no. 2: DOL 18, no. 257.

[28] See RM, Proper of Seasons, Holy Thursday, rubrics preceding the text of the Chrism Mass.

[29] See The Roman Pontifical, *Rite of the Blessing of Oils and Consecrating the Chrism* (hereafter, BOCC), nos. 9-10: DOL 459, nos. 3869-3870; *The Roman Missal (Sacramentary)*.

277   According to the tradition of the Latin liturgy, the blessing of the oil of the sick takes place before the end of the eucharistic prayer; the blessing of the oil of catechumens and the consecration of the chrism, after communion.

For pastoral reasons, however, the entire rite of blessing may take place after the liturgy of the word.[30]

278   For the blessing of oils the following preparations are made in addition to what is needed for the celebration of a stational Mass:

a. *In the vesting room or some other convenient place:*
    — vessels of oil;
    — balsam or perfume for the preparation of the chrism, if the bishop wishes to mix the chrism during the liturgical service;
    — bread, wine and water for Mass, which are carried with the oils before the preparation of the gifts.

b. *In the sanctuary (chancel):*
    — *The Roman Missal (Sacramentary);*
    — table for the vessels of oil, placed so that the people may see the entire rite easily and take part in it;
    — chair for the bishop, if the blessing takes place in front of the altar.[31]

DESCRIPTION OF THE RITE

279   The preparation of the bishop, the concelebrants, and other ministers, their entrance into the church, and everything from the beginning of Mass until the end of the liturgy of the word follow the provisions already given in the rite for a stational Mass.[32]

280   For his homily the bishop, with miter and pastoral staff, is seated in the chair (cathedra), unless he decides otherwise. In the homily he should encourage the presbyters to fidelity in fulfilling their office in the Church and should invite them to renew publicly their priestly promises.

After the homily, the presbyters stand before the bishop, and he addresses them with the questions that call on them to renew their commitment to priestly service.[33]

---

[30] See BOCC, nos. 11-12: DOL 459, nos. 3871-3872.
[31] See BOCC, no. 13.
[32] See BOCC, no. 15.
[33] See RM, Proper of Seasons, Holy Thursday, rubrics for the Chrism Mass.

281   Then, putting aside the pastoral staff and miter, the bishop stands. The profession of faith is not said. In the intercessions, as given in *The Roman Missal* (*Sacramentary*), the faithful are invited to pray for their pastors.

282   Then the bishop sits in the chair, wearing the miter. The deacons and ministers appointed to carry the oils or, in their absence, some priests and ministers, together with the faithful who will carry the bread and the wine and water, go in procession to the vesting room (sacristy) or other place where the oils and other offerings have been prepared. Returning to the altar, they follow this order: first, the minister carrying the vessel of balsam, if the bishop wishes to mix the chrism; then the minister with the vessel for the oil of catechumens, if it is to be blessed; the minister with the vessel for the oil of the sick; lastly a deacon or presbyter carrying the oil for the chrism. The ministers or faithful who carry the bread and the wine and water for the celebration of the eucharist follow them.[34]

283   During the procession through the church, the choir leads the singing of the hymn *O Redemptor* or of some other suitable song in place of the song for the presentation of the gifts (offertory song).

284   The bishop receives the gifts at the chair or in a more convenient place. The deacon who carries the vessel of oil for the chrism shows it to the bishop, saying aloud, The oil for the holy chrism. The bishop takes the vessel and gives it to one of the deacons assisting him to place it on the table prepared for it. The same is done by those who carry the vessels for the oil of the sick and the oil of catechumens.[35]

The first says, The oil of the sick; the second says, The oil of catechumens. The bishop takes the vessels in the same way, and the ministers place them on the table.

The Mass continues in the usual way, unless the entire rite of blessing takes place immediately, in the way to be described in no. 291.

285   Before the bishop says the words Through Christ our Lord you give us all these gifts in Eucharistic Prayer I or the doxology Through him in the other eucharistic prayers, the one who carried the vessel for the oil of the sick brings it to the altar and holds it in front of the bishop, who blesses the oil by saying or singing the prayer God of all consolation.

---

[34] See BOCC, no. 16.
[35] See BOCC, nos. 17-18.

After the blessing, the vessel with the oil of the sick is returned to its place, and the Mass continues until the communion rite is completed.[36]

286   After the prayer after communion, the deacons place the oil of catechumens to be blessed and the chrism to be consecrated on a table that has been placed in the center of the sanctuary (chancel).

287   The bishop and the concelebrants go to the table with the deacons and ministers. The bishop stands facing the people, and the concelebrating presbyters stand around him on either side, in a semicircle, and the deacons and other ministers stand behind him.

288   When everything is ready, the bishop proceeds to the blessing of the oil of catechumens, if it is to be blessed. Without the miter, he stands facing the people and, with hands outstretched, says the prayer Lord God, protector of all who believe in you.[37]

289   Then the bishop sits, wearing the miter, and pours the balsam or perfume into the oil and in silence mixes the chrism, unless this has been done beforehand.

290   Without the miter, he stands and sings or says the invitation Let us pray that God.
    As circumstances suggest, he may then breathe over the vessel of chrism.
    Then, with hands outstretched, he says one of the consecratory prayers. At the words And so, Father, we ask you until the end of the consecratory prayer, all the concelebrants hold the right hand outstretched toward the chrism without saying anything.[38]

291   When for pastoral reasons the entire rite of blessing of oils is to be celebrated after the liturgy of the word, the procedure is as follows. The vessels with the oils to be blessed and of chrism to be consecrated are presented to the bishop, then placed by the deacons on a table that has been placed in the center of the sanctuary (chancel). Everything is done as already described in nos. 283-284 and 287-290. The Mass then proceeds in the usual way from the preparation of the gifts until the prayer after communion has been said.

---

[36] See BOCC, no. 20.

[37] See BOCC, nos. 21-22.

[38] See BOCC, nos. 23-25.

292   When the chrism has been consecrated after the communion rite, otherwise when the prayer after communion has been said, the bishop gives the blessing in the usual way; then he puts incense into the censer and blesses it. After the deacon has said, The Mass is ended, go in peace (or one of the other formulas), the procession to the vesting room (sacristy) is formed.

293   The censerbearer carrying a censer with burning incense leads the procession, and the blessed oils are carried, each by its own minister, immediately after the cross; the choir and people sing some verses of the hymn O Redemptor or some other suitable song.

294   In the vesting room (sacristy) the bishop may instruct the presbyters about the reverent use and safe custody of the holy oils.[39]

---

[39] See BOCC, nos 27-28.

CHAPTER 8

EASTER TRIDUUM

295   "Christ redeemed us all and gave perfect glory to God principally through his paschal mystery: dying he destroyed our death and rising he restored our life. Therefore the Easter Triduum of the Passion and Resurrection of the Lord is the culmination of the entire liturgical year. Thus the solemnity of Easter has the same kind of preeminence in the liturgical year that Sunday has in the week."[40]

Let the paschal fast be kept sacred. Let it be celebrated everywhere on Good Friday and, wherever possible, prolonged throughout Holy Saturday, as a way of coming to the joys of the Sunday of the resurrection with uplifted and welcoming heart.[41]

296   These days are therefore unique in the liturgical year and their celebration is of utmost importance in the spiritual and pastoral life of the Church. It is altogether fitting, then, that the bishop preside in his cathedral church at the Mass of the Lord's Supper, at the liturgical service of Good Friday, and at the Easter Vigil, particularly when this vigil is to include celebration of the sacraments of Christian initiation. It is also desirable that, if at all possible, the bishop take part with the clergy and people in the office of readings and morning prayer on Good Friday and Holy Saturday and in evening prayer of Easter Sunday, especially in places that have the custom of celebrating a "baptismal" evening prayer (see no. 371).

---

[40] GNLYC, no. 18: DOL 442, no. 3784.
[41] See SC, art. 110: DOL 1, no. 110.

CHAPTER 9

MASS OF THE LORD'S SUPPER

INTRODUCTION

297   With this Mass, celebrated in the evening of the Thursday in Holy Week, the Church begins the sacred Easter Triduum and devotes itself to the remembrance of the Last Supper. At this supper on the night he was betrayed, the Lord Jesus, loving those who were his own in the world even to the end, offered his body and blood to the Father under the appearances of bread and wine, gave them to the apostles to eat and drink, then enjoined the apostles and their successors in the priesthood to offer them in turn.[42]

This Mass is, first of all, the memorial of the institution of the eucharist, that is, of the memorial of the Lord's Passover, by which under sacramental signs he perpetuated among us the sacrifice of the New Law. The Mass of the Lord's Supper is also the memorial of the institution of the priesthood, by which Christ's mission and sacrifice are perpetuated in the world. In addition this Mass is the memorial of that love by which the Lord loved us even to death. The bishop should see to it that all these considerations are suitably presented to the faithful through the ministry of the word so that by their devotion they may be able to deepen their grasp of such great mysteries and reflect them more faithfully in the conduct of their lives.

298   Even if he has already celebrated the Chrism Mass in the morning, the bishop should be eager also to celebrate the Mass of the Lord's Supper with the full participation of presbyters, deacons, ministers, and faithful gathered around him.

Priests who have already concelebrated the Chrism Mass may also concelebrate the evening Mass.[43]

299   In addition to what is required for the celebration of a stational Mass, the following should be provided:

a. *In a convenient place in the sanctuary (chancel):*
   — ciborium with hosts that are to be consecrated for communion on Good Friday;
   — humeral veil;

---

[42] See Council of Trent, sess. 22, 17 Sept. 1562, Doctr. *De ss. Missae sacrificio*, ch. 1: *Concilium Tridentinum, Diariorum, Actorum, Epistolarum, Tractatuum nova collectio*, ed. Görres Gesellschaft, vol. 8, *Actorum*, part 5 (Freiburg, Br., 1919), p. 960.

[43] See GIRM, nos. 157 and 158, a: DOL 208, nos. 1547 and 1548.

    – second censer and incense boat;
    – torches and candles.

  b. *At the place for the footwashing:*
    – seats for the men chosen;
    – pitcher of water and basin;
    – towels for drying the feet;
    – linen apron (gremial) for the bishop;
    – requisites for washing the bishop's hands.

  c. *In the chapel where the blessed sacrament will be kept:*
    – tabernacle or repository for the blessed sacrament;
    – lights, flowers, and other suitable decorations.

DESCRIPTION OF THE RITE

300   The preparation, entrance into the church, and liturgy of the word follow the usual procedure for a stational Mass.

During the singing of the *Gloria,* the church bells are rung and then remain silent until the Easter Vigil, unless, according to circumstances, the conference of bishops or the bishop of the diocese decides otherwise.[44]

During the same period, the organ and other musical instruments may be used only to sustain the singing.

301   The homily should explain the chief mysteries that are commemorated in this Mass: the institution of the holy eucharist, the institution of the priesthood, and Christ's commandment to love one another. Depending on pastoral circumstances, the washing of feet follows the homily.

The men who have been chosen are led by the ministers to chairs provided in a suitable place. Then the bishop (laying aside the miter and chasuble but not the dalmatic, if he is wearing one) puts on a linen apron (gremial), as circumstances suggest. He then goes to each man and, with the help of the deacons, pours water on each one's feet and dries them. During the footwashing the antiphons provided in *The Roman Missal* (*Sacramentary*) or some other suitable songs are sung.[45]

302   After the footwashing, the bishop returns to the chair, washes his hands, and puts on the chasuble. Since the profession of faith is not said in this Mass, the general intercessions follow immediately.[46]

---

[44] See RM, Proper of Seasons, Holy Thursday, Mass of the Lord's Supper (hereafter, HT), rubric for the *Gloria.*

[45] See RM, HT, rubrics for the washing of feet.

[46] See RM, HT, the rubric for the general intercessions.

303   At the beginning of the liturgy of the eucharist there may be a procession of the faithful with gifts for the poor. During the procession the song Where charity and love are found or some other suitable song may be sung.[47]

304   From the preparation of the gifts up to and including the communion rite everything is done as in a stational Mass. The proper texts provided in *The Roman Missal (Sacramentary)* for the eucharistic prayer are used.[48]

305   After the communion of the faithful, the ciborium with hosts for Good Friday is left on the altar and the prayer after communion is said.[49]

306   After the prayer after communion, the concluding rites of the Mass are omitted. Standing before the altar, the bishop puts incense into the censer and blesses it, then, kneeling, incenses the blessed sacrament. Then he receives the humeral veil, goes up to the altar, genuflects, and, with the help of the deacon, takes the ciborium and covers it with the ends of the veil.[50]

307   The blessed sacrament is carried through the church in procession to the place of reposition, prepared in a chapel suitably decorated for the occasion. The procession is led by a crossbearer, accompanied by acolytes holding lighted candles; after them come clergy; deacons; concelebrants; a minister holding the bishop's pastoral staff; two censerbearers carrying censers with burning incense; then the bishop, carrying the blessed sacrament; a little behind the bishop, the two deacons assisting him; and finally the ministers who assist with the book and the miter. All in the procession carry lighted candles, and around the blessed sacrament torches are carried.

During the procession the hymn *Pange, lingua* (exclusive of the last two stanzas) or some other eucharistic song is sung, in keeping with local custom.[51]

308   When the procession reaches the place of reposition, the bishop hands the ciborium to the deacon, who places it on the altar or in the tabernacle, the door of which is left open. While *Tantum ergo Sacramen-*

---

[47] See RM, HT, rubric for the beginning of the liturgy of the eucharist.
[48] See RM, Preface no. 47 and Eucharistic Prayer I.
[49] See RM, HT, the rubric printed after the communion rite.
[50] See RM, HT, rubrics for the transfer of the eucharist.
[51] See RM, HT, rubrics for the transfer of the eucharist.

tum or some other suitable song is being sung, the bishop, kneeling, incenses the blessed sacrament. Then the deacon places the blessed sacrament in the tabernacle (if this has not been done already) and/or closes its door.[52]

309   After a period of silent adoration, all rise, genuflect, and return to the vesting room (sacristy). The bishop wears the miter and carries the pastoral staff.[53]

310   At a suitable time the altar is stripped and, if possible, the crosses are removed from the church. It is desirable to cover any crosses that remain in the church, unless they have already been covered by directive of the conference of bishops.[54]

311   The faithful should be encouraged to continue adoration before the blessed sacrament for a suitable period of time during the night, according to local circumstances, but there should be no solemn adoration after midnight.[55]

---

[52] See RM, HT, rubrics for the transfer of the eucharist.
[53] See RM, HT, rubrics for the transfer of the eucharist.
[54] See RM, HT, rubrics for the transfer of the eucharist.
[55] See RM, HT, rubrics for the transfer of the eucharist.

CHAPTER 10

CELEBRATION OF THE LORD'S PASSION

INTRODUCTION

312 On this day, when "Christ our paschal lamb was sacrificed,"[56] what had long been promised in signs and figures was at last revealed and brought to fulfillment. The true lamb replaced the symbolic lamb, and the many offerings of the past gave way to the single sacrifice of Christ.[57]

"The wonderful works of God among the people of the Old Testament were a prelude to the work of Christ the Lord. He achieved his task of redeeming humanity and giving perfect glory to God, principally by the paschal mystery of his blessed passion, resurrection from the dead, and glorious ascension, whereby 'dying he destroyed our death and rising he restored our life' (Preface of Easter). For it was from the side of Christ as he slept the sleep of death upon the cross that there came forth the sublime sacrament of the whole Church."[58]

In contemplating the cross of its Lord and Bridegroom, the Church commemorates its own origin and its mission to extend to all peoples the blessed effects of Christ's passion that it celebrates on this day in a spirit of thanksgiving for his marvelous gift.

313 The celebration of the Lord's passion takes place in the afternoon, about three o'clock, unless pastoral reasons suggest a later hour. The celebration consists of three parts: liturgy of the word, veneration of the cross, and holy communion.[59]

314 The altar should be completely bare, without cross, candles, or altar cloths.[60]

315 For the celebration of the Lord's passion, the following should be prepared:

    a. *In the vesting room (sacristy):*
        — for the bishop and the deacons, red Mass vestments; the bishop uses a simple miter, but not the ring or pastoral staff;
        — for the other ministers, albs or other lawfully approved vesture.

---

[56] 1 Corinthians 5:7.

[57] See Leo the Great, Sermo 58, *De Passione Domini* 1: PL 54, 332.

[58] SC, art. 5: DOL 1, no. 5.

[59] See RM, Proper of Seasons, Good Friday, Celebration of the Lord's Passion (hereafter, GF), no. 3.

[60] See RM, GF, no. 2.

b. *In a convenient place:*
 — cross [veiled if the first form of veneration is to be used];
 — two candlesticks;
c. *In the sanctuary (chancel):*
 — *The Roman Missal (Sacramentary);*
 — copies of the *Lectionary for Mass* and/or books for the reading of the Lord's passion;
 — altar cloth;
 — corporal;
 — red stoles for the presbyters and deacons receiving communion;
d. *In the chapel of reposition of the blessed sacrament:*
 — red or white humeral veil for the deacon;
 — two candlesticks for the acolytes.

INTRODUCTORY RITES

316 The bishop and the deacons, wearing red Mass vestments, go to the altar in silence. At the altar the bishop lays aside the miter and, after reverencing the altar, prostrates himself or, as circumstances suggest, kneels on a bare priedieu. All pray for a while in silence.[61]

317 Then the bishop goes to the chair (cathedra) with the deacons. He faces the people and, with hands outstretched, says the prayer Lord, by shedding his blood or Lord, by the suffering of Christ your Son. After the prayer, he sits and again puts on the miter.[62]

LITURGY OF THE WORD

318 All sit and the first reading, from the book of the prophet Isaiah (52:13–53:12), is proclaimed, with its responsorial psalm. The second reading, from the letter to the Hebrews (4:14-16; 5:7-9) follows.[63]

319 As the gospel acclamation begins, all but the bishop rise. Neither incense nor candles are used for the narrative of the passion. The deacons who are to proclaim it ask for and receive a blessing from the bishop

---

[61] See RM, GF, no. 4.
[62] See RM, GF, no. 5.
[63] See RM, GF, no. 6.

in the usual way. The bishop lays aside the miter and rises. Then the passion according to John (18:1–19:42) is read. The greeting of the people and the signing of the book are omitted.

After the verse on the death of the Lord, all kneel and a brief pause is observed. At the end the words This is the Gospel of the Lord are said, but the book is not kissed.

After the reading of the passion, the bishop gives a short homily. After the homily, the bishop or a deacon may invite the faithful to spend a short time in silent prayer.[64]

320   After the homily, the bishop, without miter, stands at the chair or, as circumstances suggest, at the altar. With hands outstretched, he says or sings the prayers of the general intercessions provided in *The Roman Missal* (*Sacramentary*), but he may, if necessary, select those that are the most relevant.

As circumstances suggest, a deacon or deacons may proclaim at the ambo the introductions that state the intentions of each prayer.

The people may either kneel or stand throughout the entire period of the general intercessions.[65]

VENERATION OF THE CROSS

321   Then the showing and veneration of the cross takes place, by use of one of the two forms provided in *The Roman Missal* (*Sacramentary*).

a. *First form of showing the cross*

As a deacon, accompanied by two acolytes with lighted candles, carries the veiled cross to the altar, the bishop goes to the altar with the two deacons assisting him. There, standing without the miter, he receives the cross, and in three successive stages he uncovers it and shows it to the faithful for their veneration. At the beginning of each unveiling he begins the invitation This is the wood of the cross (if necessary a deacon or the schola may continue the singing of the invitation). All respond, Come, let us worship. After the singing, all kneel and venerate the cross briefly in silence; the bishop remains standing and holds the cross high. Accompanied by two acolytes with lighted candles, a deacon carries the cross to the entrance of the sanctuary (chancel) or to another suitable

---

[64] See RM, GF, nos. 8-9.

[65] See RM, GF, no. 10-13.

place. There he lays the cross down or hands it to the ministers to hold. Candles are placed on either side of the cross.[66]

b. *Second form of showing the cross*

The bishop, without miter, stands at the chair. A deacon, accompanied by acolytes, goes to the church door. There he takes the uncovered cross, and the acolytes take lighted candles. They go in procession through the church to the sanctuary (chancel). Near the entrance of the church, in the middle of the church, and at the entrance to the sanctuary (chancel), the deacon stops, lifts up the cross, and sings the invitation This is the wood of the cross. All respond, Come, let us worship. After each response, the bishop remains standing and everyone else kneels and venerates the cross briefly in silence. The deacon then places the cross at the entrance to the sanctuary (chancel) or at another place, in the way already indicated.[67]

322 For the veneration of the cross, the bishop lays aside miter, chasuble, and, as circumstances suggest, his shoes, and, with head uncovered, goes first to the cross. He kneels before it and kisses it. He then returns to the chair (cathedra), where he puts on his shoes and the chasuble, then sits without the miter. After the bishop, the deacons who assist him, then the clergy and faithful approach to venerate the cross in a kind of procession. They make a simple genuflection or perform some other appropriate sign of reverence according to local custom, for example, kissing the cross.

During the veneration the antiphon We worship you, Lord, the reproaches, or some other suitable songs are sung. All who venerate the cross then return to their places and sit.[68]

323 Only one cross should be used for the veneration. If the number of people makes it impossible for everyone to venerate the cross individually, the bishop, after some of the clergy and faithful have venerated it, goes to the altar, receives the cross from a deacon, and stands in the center in front of the altar. In a few words he invites the people to venerate the cross and then holds it up briefly for them to venerate in silence.[69]

---

[66] See RM, GF, nos. 15-16.
[67] See RM, GF, no. 17.
[68] See RM, GF, no. 18.
[69] See RM, GF, no. 19.

HOLY COMMUNION

324   After the veneration, the cross is carried by a deacon to its place at the altar and the bishop returns to the chair. The lighted candles are placed around the altar or near the cross. The altar is covered with a cloth, and the corporal and book are placed on it.[70]

325   Then without any procession a deacon, wearing the humeral veil, brings the ciborium with the blessed sacrament to the altar. Two acolytes with lighted candles accompany the deacon, and they place their candles near or on the altar.
       During this time the bishop and all present rise and remain standing in silence.[71]

326   The deacon places the ciborium on the altar and uncovers it. Then the bishop, with the deacons assisting him, comes from his chair (cathedra), genuflects, and goes up to the altar. Then in the manner indicated in *The Roman Missal (Sacramentary)*, the Lord's Prayer with its embolism is said and holy communion takes place.[72]

327   If the bishop has been present at the celebration but not as celebrant, it is fitting that after the veneration of the cross he put on a red stole and cope over the rochet and at least preside at the communion rite. Otherwise he should put on a stole for communion and, after the celebrant, give himself communion.

328   When the giving of communion has been completed, a deacon may take the ciborium to a place prepared outside the church or, if circumstances require, may place it in the tabernacle.[73]

329   A period of silence may now be observed. The bishop then says the prayer after communion.[74]

---

[70] See RM, GF, nos. 20-21.
[71] See RM, GF, no. 21.
[72] See RM, GF, nos. 22-25.
[73] See RM, GF, no. 26.
[74] See RM, GF, no. 27.

CONCLUDING RITE

330   When the prayer after communion has been said, the bishop stands facing the people for the dismissal; with hands outstretched over them, he says the prayer Lord, send down your abundant blessing.[75]

331   After a genuflection before the cross, the bishop again takes the miter and all depart in silence.
     The altar is stripped at a convenient time.[76]

---

[75] See RM, GF, no. 28.
[76] See RM, GF, no. 28.

CHAPTER 11

EASTER VIGIL

INTRODUCTION

332 In accord with ancient tradition, this night is a night of vigil for the Lord,[77] and, as the memorial of the holy night of Christ's resurrection, the Vigil celebrated is "the mother of all holy vigils."[78] The Church this night awaits the Lord's resurrection and celebrates it with the sacraments of Christian initiation.

333 The entire celebration of the Easter Vigil takes place at night; it should not begin before nightfall; it should end before daybreak of Sunday.[79]

334 Since the Easter Vigil is the supreme, most exalted of all solemnities in the liturgical year, the bishop should not fail to celebrate it in person.

335 The Mass of the Vigil is a paschal Mass of Easter Sunday. Those who celebrate or concelebrate the Mass at night may celebrate or concelebrate the second Mass of Easter.[80]

336 In addition to what is required for the celebration of a stational Mass, the following should be prepared:
   a. *For the blessing of the fire:*
      — large fire (at the gathering place of the people outside the church);
      — Easter candle;
      — [five grains of incense, stylus];
      — some means of lighting the Easter candle from the new fire;
      — lamp (torch) to illuminate the texts to be read by the bishop;
      — candles for those taking part in the Vigil;
      — tongs so that the censerbearer can put charcoal lighted from the new fire into the censer;
   b. *For the Easter proclamation (Exsultet):*
      — stand for the Easter candle beside the ambo;

---

[77] See Exodus 12:42.
[78] See Augustine, *Sermo* 219: PL 38, 1088.
[79] See RM, Proper of Seasons, Easter Vigil (hereafter, EV), no. 3.
[80] See RM, EV, no. 5.

      – if the stand cannot be placed beside the ambo, a lectern near the candle for the deacon (or if necessary for the cantor)[81] who is to sing the Easter proclamation;

  c. *For the baptismal liturgy:*
      – vessel of water;
      – when the sacraments of Christian initiation are to be celebrated, oil of catechumens, holy chrism, baptismal candle, *Rite of Christian Initiation of Adults* and/or *Rite of Baptism for Children*.

All the lights in the church are put out.

Blessing of the Fire and Lighting of the Candle

337   In the vesting room (sacristy) or some other suitable place, the bishop, concelebrants, and deacons put on white Mass vestments, which are worn from the very beginning of the Vigil.[82]

338   The bishop, with miter and pastoral staff, goes with the concelebrants, clergy, and ministers to the place where the people are gathered for the blessing of the fire. One of the acolytes carries the Easter candle ahead of the ministers. The processional cross and candles are not carried. The censerbearer carries the censer but with charcoal unlighted.

339   The bishop lays aside the pastoral staff and miter and, facing the people, says, In the name of the Father, and of the Son, and of the Holy Spirit, then greets the people saying, Peace be with you. Then he or a deacon or one of the concelebrants briefly instructs the people about the Vigil in the words Dear friends in Christ, given in *The Roman Missal* (*Sacramentary*), or in similar words.[83]

340   Then as he blesses the fire, the bishop, with hands outstretched, says the prayer Father, we share in the light of your glory. After the prayer, he puts on the miter and, assisted by the deacon, lights the Easter candle from the new fire in silence. The censerbearer lights the charcoal in the censer from the new fire.[84]

---

[81] See RM, EV, no. 17.
[82] See RM, EV, no. 6.
[83] See RM, EV, no. 8.
[84] See RM, EV, no. 9.

341   Depending on the character of the congregation, it may seem appropriate to stress the dignity of the Easter candle by means of other symbolic rites. After the blessing of the new fire, an acolyte or one of the ministers brings the Easter candle to the bishop, who, standing and wearing the miter, cuts a cross in the wax with a stylus. Then he traces the Greek letter *alpha* above the cross, the letter *omega* below, and the numerals of the current year between the arms of the cross. As he does so, he says, Christ yesterday and today. When the cross and the other marks have been made, the bishop may insert five grains of incense into the candle. He does so in the form of a cross, saying, By his holy and glorious wounds. Then he lights the Easter candle from the new fire, saying, May the light of Christ.

Any or all of the preceding rites may be used, depending on local pastoral circumstances. The conference of bishops may also decide on other rites that are better adapted to the culture of the people.[85]

PROCESSION

342   After lighting the Easter candle, the bishop puts incense into the censer. The deacon receives the Easter candle from an acolyte.

343   The entrance procession into the church is then formed in this way: the censerbearer carrying censer with burning incense precedes the deacon carrying the Easter candle, then a minister carrying the pastoral staff, the bishop with the deacons assisting him, concelebrants, clergy, and faithful. All hold unlighted candles.

At the door of the church the deacon stops and, lifting high the Easter candle, sings, Christ our light, and all respond, Thanks be to God. The bishop lights his candle from the Easter candle.

Then the deacon goes to the middle of the church, stops, and, lifting high the Easter candle, sings a second time, Christ our light, and all respond, Thanks be to God. All light their candles from the Easter candle, passing the light from one to the other.

When the deacon arrives before the altar, he stops, faces the people, and sings for the third time, Christ our light, and all respond, Thanks be to God. The deacon then places the Easter candle on a stand prepared in the middle of the sanctuary (chancel) or near the ambo. Then the lights in the church are lit.[86]

---

[85] See RM, EV, nos. 10-12.
[86] See RM, EV, nos. 14-16.

EASTER PROCLAMATION

344   When he reaches the sanctuary (chancel), the bishop goes to the chair (cathedra), hands his candle to the deacon, and sits, wearing the miter. He puts incense into the censer and blesses it, as at the gospel reading of the Mass. The deacon goes to the chair (cathedra) and asks for a blessing from the bishop, who says in a low voice, The Lord be in your heart and on your lips, that you may worthily proclaim his Easter praise. In the name of the Father, and of the Son, ✠ and of the Holy Spirit. The deacon replies, Amen.[87]

345   As the deacon goes to the ambo, the bishop lays aside the miter and rises to hear the Easter proclamation, while holding a lighted candle.

In the same way, all in the assembly stand and hold lighted candles.

At the ambo or the stand near the Easter candle, the deacon, after incensing the book and the candle, sings the Easter proclamation.[88]

LITURGY OF THE WORD

346   After the Easter proclamation, the candles are put aside and all sit. Before the readings begin, the bishop, seated and wearing the miter, speaks to the people in the words provided in *The Roman Missal* (*Sacramentary*), Dear friends in Christ, or in similar words. But he may also assign this task to a deacon or to one of the concelebrants.[89]

347   In this Vigil nine readings are provided, seven from the Old Testament and two from the New Testament (the epistle and the gospel reading). The number of readings from the Old Testament may be reduced for pastoral reasons, but it must always be kept in mind that the reading of the word of God is a fundamental part of the Easter Vigil. At least three readings from the Old Testament should be read, although for more serious reasons the number may be reduced to two. The reading of Exodus chapter fourteen, however, is never to be omitted.[90]

---

[87] See RM, EV, no. 17. When a presbyter rather than a deacon is to sing the Easter proclamation, he also, like a deacon, goes to receive the blessing from the bishop. But when it is necessary to have a cantor sing the Easter proclamation, the cantor does not go to the bishop for the blessing, does not incense the book, nor say the bracketed words My dearest friends in the proclamation or the greeting The Lord be with you.

[88] See RM, EV, nos. 17-19.

[89] See RM, EV, no. 22.

[90] See RM, EV, nos. 20-21.

348   As all sit and listen, a reader goes to the ambo and proclaims the first reading, after which the cantor leads the psalm, and the people respond. Then, laying aside the miter, the bishop rises, and all rise with him. He sings or says, Let us pray. When all have prayed silently for a while, he sings or says the prayer belonging to the reading. The same is done after each reading from the Old Testament.[91]

349   After the final reading from the Old Testament with its responsorial psalm and prayer, the candles on the altar are lit, and the bishop solemnly intones the *Gloria*, which is taken up by all present. The church bells are rung, according to local custom.[92]

350   At the end of the hymn, the bishop, in the usual way, sings or says the opening prayer, Lord God, you have brightened this night.[93]

351   The bishop then sits and puts on the miter. All in the assembly sit, and a reader proclaims the reading from the Apostle Paul.[94]

352   After this reading, as occasion suggests and if it is in keeping with local custom, one of the deacons or the reader goes to the bishop and says to him, Most Reverend Father, I bring you a message of great joy, the message of Alleluia.
       After this greeting or, if it does not take place, immediately after the reading, all rise. Standing and without miter, the bishop solemnly intones the *Alleluia*, assisted if necessary by one of the deacons or concelebrants. He sings it three times, a little higher each time. In the same key as the bishop, all present repeat the *Alleluia* each time.
       The psalmist or cantor sings the verses of the responsorial psalm, and the people answer, Alleluia.[95]

353   Then the bishop sits and in the usual way puts incense into the censer and blesses the deacon assigned to proclaim the gospel reading. Candles are not carried for the gospel reading.[96]

354   The homily follows the gospel reading, and then the liturgy of baptism begins.[97]

---

[91] See RM, EV, no. 23.
[92] See RM, EV, no. 31.
[93] See RM, EV, no. 32.
[94] See RM, EV, no. 33.
[95] See RM, EV, no. 34.
[96] See RM, EV, no. 35.
[97] See RM, EV, no. 36.

LITURGY OF BAPTISM

355   It is eminently fitting for the bishop himself to be the celebrant for the sacraments of baptism and confirmation at the Easter Vigil.[98]

356   The liturgy of baptism is carried out either at the font or in the sanctuary (chancel). In places where there is a baptistery outside the main body of the church, it is a long-standing practice to go there for the celebration of the baptismal liturgy.[99]

357   First the catechumens are called forward and introduced by their godparents. If there are children, they are brought forward by their parents and godparents.[100]

358   Then, if the procession to the baptistery or font is to take place, it should be formed immediately. An acolyte with the Easter candle leads, followed by the candidates with their godparents, then the deacons, the concelebrants, and the bishop with miter and pastoral staff. During the procession the Litany of the Saints is sung. After the litany, the bishop lays aside the pastoral staff and miter and gives the introduction Dear friends in Christ.[101]

359   But if the baptismal liturgy takes place in the sanctuary (chancel), the bishop lays aside the pastoral staff and miter and gives the introduction Dear friends in Christ. The Litany of the Saints is then sung by two cantors. All stand (as is customary during the Easter season) and sing the responses.[102]

360   After the litany and his introduction mentioned in no. 358, the bishop stands at the baptismal font, without the miter and with hands outstretched, and says the prayer Father, you give us grace. As he says, We ask you, Father, he may lower the Easter candle into the water either once or three times, as indicated in The Roman Missal (Sacramentary).[103]

---

[98] See The Roman Ritual, *Rite of Christian Initiation of Adults*, Eng. ed., 1985 (hereafter, RCIA), Introduction, no. 12. (No. 12 of the Introduction of RCIA adds the qualifier "at least for the initiation of those who are fourteen years old or older.")

[99] See RM, EV, no. 37.

[100] See RM, EV, no. 37.

[101] See RM, EV, nos. 39, 41, 38.

[102] See RM, EV, nos. 38-39.

[103] See RM, EV, nos. 42-43.

361   After the blessing of the water and the people's acclamation at the end, the bishop sits and takes the miter and pastoral staff. He then asks the candidates the questions on the renunciation of sin, addressing the adult elect in the manner indicated in the *Rite of Christian Initiation of Adults*,[104] and addressing the parents and godparents of children to be baptized in the manner indicated in the *Rite of Baptism for Children*.[105]

362   If the anointing of the adult elect with the oil of catechumens has not been anticipated as a preparatory rite, it takes place at this point, in the manner indicated in the *Rite of Christian Initiation of Adults*; if necessary presbyters may assist with the anointing.[106]

363   Informed again by the godparents of the name of each of the adult elect, the bishop asks the elect individually the questions pertaining to the profession of faith, in the manner indicated in the *Rite of Christian Initiation of Adults*.[107] In the case of children, he asks for the profession of faith in the Father, Son, and Holy Spirit from all the parents and godparents as a group, in the manner indicated in the *Rite of Baptism for Children*.[108]

364   After the questioning, the bishop puts aside the pastoral staff, stands, and baptizes the elect and the children, with the help, if necessary, of presbyters and also deacons, in the manner indicated in the *Rite of Christian Initiation of Adults*[109] and the *Rite of Baptism for Children*.[110]

365   Then the bishop sits. After their baptism, infants are anointed with chrism by presbyters or by deacons, particularly when a large number have been baptized; and over all the infants as a group, the bishop says the formulary of anointing, The God of power. All those baptized, both adults and children, receive the baptismal garment, as the bishop says, N. and N., you have become a new creation.[111] Next the bishop or a deacon receives the Easter candle from an acolyte and says the invitation Godparents, please come forward, and the candles of the newly bap-

---

[104] See RCIA, no. 217 (U.S. ed., no. 224).
[105] See *Rite of Baptism for Children* (hereafter, RBC), nos. 56-57.
[106] See RCIA, no. 218.
[107] See RCIA, no. 219 (U.S. ed., no. 225).
[108] See RBC, no. 58.
[109] See RCIA, no. 220 (U.S. ed., no. 226).
[110] See RBC, nos. 60-61.
[111] See RCIA, no. 223 (U.S. ed., no. 229); RBC, no. 63.

tized are lighted as the bishop says, You have been enlightened by Christ.[112] In the case of infants the presentation of a lighted candle and the ephphetha rite are omitted at the Easter Vigil, as indicated in the *Rite of Baptism for Children*.[113]

366   After the baptism and the explanatory rites, unless the whole service has taken place before the altar, all return to the sanctuary (chancel) in procession as before, the newly baptized or the godparents and parents carrying lighted candles. During the procession a baptismal song is sung, for example, You have put on Christ.

367   If adults have been baptized, the bishop should confer the sacrament of confirmation in the sanctuary (chancel), in keeping with the provisions of the *Rite of Christian Initiation of Adults*.[114]

Renewal of Baptismal Promises

368   After the baptism and confirmation or, if the sacraments have not been celebrated, after the blessing of water, the bishop, taking the miter and pastoral staff, stands before the people and receives the renewal of their baptismal profession of faith, for which they stand and hold lighted candles.[115]

369   After the renewal of baptismal promises, the bishop, still wearing the miter, sprinkles the people with the blessed water. He is assisted, if necessary, by presbyters and, as circumstances suggest, he may pass through the body of the church. During this time all sing the antiphon I saw water or some other song that is baptismal in character.[116]

Meanwhile the newly baptized are led to their place among the faithful.

If the blessing of the baptismal water does not take place in the baptistery, a deacon and acolytes reverently carry the vessel of water to the font.

After the people have been sprinkled, the bishop returns to the chair. The profession of faith is omitted, and the bishop, standing with-

---

[112] See RCIA, no. 224 (U.S. ed., no. 230); RBC, no. 64.

[113] See RBC, no. 28, 3.

[114] See RCIA, nos. 225-229 (U.S. ed., nos. 231-235).

[115] See RM, EV, no. 46.

[116] See RM, EV, no. 47.

out miter, presides over the general intercessions, in which the newly baptized take part for the first time.[117]

LITURGY OF THE EUCHARIST

370   Next the liturgy of the eucharist begins, celebrated in the form of a stational Mass.

It is fitting that the bread and wine be brought forward by the newly baptized,[118] or, if the newly baptized are infants, by their parents or godparents.

The eucharistic prayer should include the intercessions (interpolations) for the baptized and their godparents, as provided in *The Roman Missal* (*Sacramentary*) for each of the eucharistic prayers.[119]

Before the words This is the Lamb of God of the communion rite, the bishop may briefly address the newly baptized on the excellence of this great mystery, which is the high point of Christian initiation and the center of the whole Christian life.

It is most desirable that the neophytes, together with their godparents, parents, spouses, and catechists, receive communion under both kinds.

At the dismissal of the faithful the deacon adds a double *Alleluia* to the usual dismissal formulary The Mass is ended, go in peace (or one of the other formularies), and the faithful do the same in their response.[120]

For the blessing at the end of Mass the bishop may use the formulary provided in *The Roman Missal* (*Sacramentary*) for the solemn blessing at the Easter Vigil[121] or, depending on the circumstances, he may use the formulary for the final blessing provided in the *Rite of Baptism for Children*.[122]

---

[117] See RM, EV, nos. 48-49.

[118] See RM, EV, no. 51.

[119] See RM, Ritual Masses, I. Christian Initiation, 3. Baptism.

[120] See RM, EV, no. 56.

[121] See RM, Solemn Blessings, no. 6, Easter Vigil and Easter Sunday.

[122] See RBC, no. 70 and nos. 247-249.

CHAPTER 12

EASTER SEASON

371 The fifty days from Easter Sunday to Pentecost are celebrated in joyful exultation as one feast day, or better as one "great Sunday."[123]

These above all others are the days for the singing of the *Alleluia*.

On Easter Sunday, wherever it is in force, the custom should be continued of celebrating a "baptismal" evening prayer, that is, a celebration in which the psalms are sung during a procession to the baptismal font.

372 The Easter candle is lighted for Mass and morning prayer and evening prayer of all the more solemn liturgical celebrations of this season. After the feast of Pentecost, the Easter candle should be kept in the baptistery with due honor; during the celebration of baptism, the candles given to the newly baptized are lighted from it.[124]

The water blessed at the Easter Vigil is used throughout the Easter season in the celebration of baptism.[125]

373 The first eight days of the Easter season make up the octave of Easter and are celebrated as solemnities of the Lord. At the end of Mass a double *Alleluia* is added to the usual dismissal formulary, to which all reply, Thanks be to God, alleluia, alleluia.[126]

374 Wherever there are neophytes, the Easter season, and particularly the first week, is the period of postbaptismal catechesis or mystagogy. The community shares with them a deepening understanding of the paschal mystery and an ever greater assimilation of it in daily life through meditation, participation in the eucharist, and the practice of charity. The main setting of this period is the Sunday Masses of Easter, because these celebrations include particularly suitable readings from the *Lectionary for Mass*, especially the readings for Year A, which are to be explained in the homily.[127]

375 On the fortieth day after Easter or, where it is not a holy day of obligation, on the Seventh Sunday of Easter, the Ascension of the Lord

---

[123] Athanasius, *Epist. festal.*, 1: PG 26, 1366. See GNLYC, no. 22: DOL 442, no. 3788.

[124] See RM, Proper of Seasons, Pentecost, rubric printed at the end of the Mass during the day.

[125] See RBC, *Christian Initiation*, General Introduction, no. 21: DOL 294, no. 2270. See RCIA, p. xiii (U.S. ed., p. xvii).

[126] See RM, Proper of Seasons, Easter Sunday, rubric for the dismissal.

[127] See RCIA, no. 237 (U.S. ed., no. 247).

is celebrated. This solemnity directs our attention to Christ, who ascended into heaven before the eyes of his disciples, who now is seated at the right hand of the Father, invested with royal power, who is there to prepare a place for us in the kingdom of heaven, and who is destined to come again at the end of time.

376   The weekdays from Ascension to the Saturday before Pentecost inclusive are days of preparation for the coming of the Holy Spirit, the Paraclete.

This sacred season of fifty days comes to an end on Pentecost Sunday, which commemorates the giving of the Holy Spirit to the apostles, the beginnings of the Church and its mission to every tongue and people and nation. On Pentecost the bishop as a rule celebrates a stational Mass and presides over the liturgy of the hours, particularly morning and evening prayer.

CHAPTER 13

ORDINARY TIME

377 Apart from those seasons having their own distinctive character, thirty-three or thirty-four weeks remain in the yearly cycle that do not celebrate a particular element of the mystery of Christ. Rather, especially on the Sundays, these weeks are devoted to the mystery of Christ in its entirety. This period is known as Ordinary Time.[128]

378 Ordinary Time begins on Monday after the Sunday following 6 January and continues until Tuesday before Ash Wednesday inclusive. It begins again on Monday after Pentecost and ends before Evening Prayer I of the First Sunday of Advent.[129]

379 Since Sunday is the first holy day of all, the nucleus and foundation of the liturgical year,[130] the bishop should ensure that, in view of nos. 228-230 of this *Ceremonial*, on the Sundays in Ordinary Time the proper Sunday liturgy is celebrated, even when such Sundays are days to which special themes are assigned.

380 For the pastoral advantage of the people, it is permissible to observe on the Sundays in Ordinary Time those celebrations that fall during the week and have special appeal to the devotion of the faithful, provided these celebrations take precedence over the Sundays in the table of liturgical days. The Mass for such celebrations may be used at all the Masses at which a congregation is present.[131]

---

[128] See GNLYC, no. 43: DOL 442, no. 3809.

[129] See GNLYC, no. 44: DOL 442, no. 3810.

[130] See SC, art. 106: DOL 1, no. 106. See GNLYC, no. 4: DOL 442, no. 3770.

[131] See GNLYC, no. 58: DOL 442, no. 3809. See the Table of Liturgical Days in Appendix II of this *Ceremonial* (also in DOL 442, no. 3825).

CHAPTER 14

ROGATION AND EMBER DAYS

381   On the rogation and ember days the practice of the Church is to offer prayers to the Lord for the needs of all people, especially for the productivity of the earth and for human labor, and to give the Lord public thanks.[132]

382   In order to adapt the rogation and ember days to various regions and the different needs of the people, the conference of bishops should arrange the time and plan of their celebration.

Consequently, the competent authority should lay down norms, in view of local conditions, determining whether such celebrations should involve one or several days and whether they should be repeated during the year.[133]

383   It is important that in each diocese, after taking into account local circumstances and customs, the bishop take great care that suitable means are found to preserve the liturgy of the rogation and ember days and to devote the liturgy of these days to the ministry of charity. In this way the devotion of the people of God will be fostered and their perception of the mystery of Christ deepened.

384   On each day of these celebrations the Mass should be one of the votive Masses for various needs and occasions that is best suited to the intentions of the petitioners.[134]

---

[132] See GNLYC, no. 45: DOL 442, no. 3811.
[133] See GNLYC, no. 46: DOL 442, no. 3812.
[134] See GNLYC, no. 47: DOL 442, no. 3813.

CHAPTER 15

SOLEMNITY OF THE BODY AND BLOOD OF CHRIST

INTRODUCTION

385   The institution of the eucharist has as a special memorial the Mass of the Lord's Supper, when Christ the Lord shared a meal with his disciples and gave them the sacrament of his body and blood to be celebrated in the Church. The solemnity of the Body and Blood of Christ (Corpus Christi) further proposes the cultus of the blessed sacrament to the faithful so that they may celebrate the wonderful works of God, signified by the sacrament and accomplished by the paschal mystery of Christ. This solemnity is also intended to teach the faithful how to share in the eucharistic sacrifice and to have it more profoundly influence their life, to revere the presence of Christ the Lord in this sacrament, and to offer the thanks due for God's gifts.[135]

386   In its devotion the Church has handed down as a distinctive feature of the celebration of this solemnity a procession in which the eucharist is carried solemnly and with singing through the streets, and the Christian people give public witness to their belief in the sacrament of the eucharist and to their devotion.

It is therefore desirable to continue this procession where circumstances permit and when it can truly be a sign of common faith and adoration. In the principal districts of large cities there may be additional processions for pastoral reasons at the discretion of the diocesan bishop.

It is for the diocesan bishop to decide on both the advisability of such processions in today's conditions and on the time, place, and plan for them that will ensure their being carried out with decorum and without any loss of reverence toward the blessed sacrament.

If the procession cannot be held on the solemnity of the Body and Blood of Christ, it is fitting to hold some kind of public celebration for the entire city or its principal districts in the cathedral church or in other convenient places.[136]

---

[135] See GIRM, no. 3: DOL 208, no. 1378.

[136] See The Roman Ritual, *Holy Communion and Worship of the Eucharist outside Mass* (hereafter, HCWE), nos. 101-102: DOL 279, nos. 2219-2220. See SC Rites, Instruction *Eucharisticum mysterium*, 25 May 1967, no. 59: AAS 59 (1967), p. 570; DOL 179, no. 1288.

126

EUCHARISTIC PROCESSION

387 It is fitting that a eucharistic procession begin after the Mass at which the host to be carried in the procession is consecrated. A procession may take place, however, at the end of a lengthy period of public adoration that has been held after Mass.[137]

388 The following preparations are made in addition to what is needed for the celebration of a stational Mass:
  a. *In the sanctuary (chancel):*
     — on the paten a host to be consecrated for the procession;
     — monstrance;
     — humeral veil;
     — second censer and incense boat;
  b. *In a convenient place:*
     — copes, white or of some other festive color (see no. 390 of this *Ceremonial*);
     — torches and candles;
     — [baldachin (canopy)].

389 After the communion of the faithful, the deacon places the monstrance on the altar, then reverently places the consecrated host in it. The bishop and the deacons assisting him genuflect and return to the chair (cathedra), where the bishop says the prayer after communion.

390 After the prayer after communion, the concluding rites are omitted, and the procession takes place. The bishop presides, wearing a chasuble as at Mass or a white cope. When the procession does not begin immediately after Mass, the bishop wears a cope.[138]
  It is fitting that canons and presbyters who were not concelebrants of the Mass wear a cope over the cassock and surplice.

391 When incense has been placed in the censer and blessed, the bishop, kneeling before the altar, incenses the blessed sacrament.
  He then receives the humeral veil and goes up to the altar, genuflects, and, assisted by a deacon, takes the monstrance and holds it with hands covered by the two ends of the veil.
  The procession is then formed in this order: first the crossbearer, accompanied by acolytes carrying candlesticks with lighted candles;

---

[137] See HCWE, nos. 101-102: DOL 279, no. 2221.
[138] See HCWE, no. 105.

next, the clergy; deacons of the Mass; canons and presbyters, wearing copes; concelebrants; visiting bishops, wearing copes; the minister carrying the bishop's pastoral staff; two censerbearers carrying censers with burning incense; the bishop carrying the blessed sacrament; a little behind him the two deacons assisting him; the ministers who assist with the book and the miter. All carry candles, and torchbearers escort the blessed sacrament.

Whether or not a baldachin (canopy) is held over the bishop as he carries the blessed sacrament depends on local custom.

If the bishop is unable to carry the blessed sacrament, he should walk in the procession immediately before the priest carrying the blessed sacrament. The bishop is vested and walks with head uncovered, carrying the pastoral staff, but not blessing as he walks.

Other bishops present for the procession vest in choir dress and take their places in the procession after the one carrying the blessed sacrament, in the order indicated in no. 1100 of this *Ceremonial*.

392   The procession should be arranged in accordance with local custom in regard to the decoration of the streets and the order to be followed by the faithful who take part.

In the course of the procession there may be stations where eucharistic benediction is given, if there is such a custom and some pastoral advantage recommends it. Songs and prayers should be planned with the purpose of expressing the faith of the participants and keeping their attention centered on the Lord alone.[139]

393   It is fitting that the procession go from one church to another. But, when local circumstances require, the procession may return to the church where it began.[140]

394   At the end of the procession, eucharistic benediction is given in the church where the procession ends or in some other suitable place.

The ministers, deacons, and presbyters on entering the sanctuary (chancel) go directly to their places. When the bishop has gone up to the altar, he remains standing, and the deacon on his right takes the monstrance from the bishop and places it on the altar. Then the bishop, together with the deacon, genuflects and, laying aside the humeral veil, kneels before the altar.

After incense has been placed in the censer and blessed, the bishop takes the censer from a deacon, bows with the deacons assisting him,

---

[139] See HCWE, no. 104.
[140] See HCWE, no. 107.

and incenses the blessed sacrament, swinging the censer back and forth three times. After bowing once more to the blessed sacrament, the bishop returns the censer to the deacon. During the incensation the hymn *Tantum ergo Sacramentum* or some other eucharistic hymn is sung.

Then the bishop rises and says, Let us pray. A short pause for silent prayer follows. If necessary, a minister holds the book open before the bishop, who then continues with the prayer Lord Jesus Christ, you gave us the eucharist or some other prayer from *Holy Communion and Worship of the Eucharist outside Mass.*

After the prayer, the bishop receives the humeral veil, goes up to the altar and genuflects. Then, assisted by the deacon, he takes the monstrance, holds it elevated in both hands, which are covered with the humeral veil, and, facing the people, makes the sign of the cross in silence.

After the blessing, the deacon takes the monstrance from the bishop and places it on the altar. The bishop and deacon genuflect. Then, while the bishop remains kneeling in front of the altar, the deacon reverently takes the blessed sacrament to the chapel of reservation.

As circumstances suggest, after the blessing, the people may sing an acclamation.

The procession returns to the vesting room (sacristy) in the usual way.

CHAPTER 16

ALL SOULS

395   The Church offers the eucharistic sacrifice and its own intercession for the dead not only at their funerals and anniversaries but also in the yearly remembrance of all the sons and daughters of the Church who sleep in Christ. The Church seeks to help the faithful departed by earnest prayer to God for their entry into the communion of the saints in heaven. In this way, because of the communion of all Christ's members with one another, the Church obtains spiritual help for the dead and brings the consolation of hope to the living.[141]

396   In celebrating this commemoration the bishop should be intent on affirming Christian hope for eternal life, but in such a way that he does not give the impression of a disregard or contempt for attitudes or practices of the people of his diocese in regard to the dead. In such matters as family traditions, local customs, burial societies, he should willingly acknowledge whatever he perceives to be good and try to transform whatever seems alien to the Gospel. Then the funeral ceremonies for Christians will both manifest paschal faith and be true examples of the spirit of the Gospel.[142]

397   On All Souls there are no flowers on the altar, and the use of the organ and other instruments is permitted only to sustain the singing.[143]

398   On All Souls, wherever it is the custom of the faithful to gather in church or at a cemetery, the bishop should celebrate Mass with the people and take part with his Church in the custom of offering prayers for the dead.

399   At the cemetery, in churches where the dead are buried, at the entrance to burial vaults, or at the tombs of the bishops of the diocese, Mass may be followed by the sprinkling and incensing of burial sites, as described in the following paragraphs.

400   After the prayer after communion, the bishop puts on the simple miter, and either he or a deacon or a concelebrant or other suitable min-

---

[141] See The Roman Ritual, *Rite of Funerals* (hereafter, RF), no. 1: DOL 416, no. 3373. In the English edition of 1985, The Roman Ritual, *Order of Christian Funerals* (hereafter, OCF), nos. 1-13.

[142] See RF, no. 2: DOL 416, no. 3374. See OCF, nos. 9-10.

[143] See MS, no. 66: AAS 59 (1967), p. 319; DOL 508, no. 4187.

ister gives a brief introduction to the rite of sprinkling carried out for the dead.

401   While a suitable song from the *Order of Christian Funerals*[144] is sung, the bishop, with miter and pastoral staff, goes to the burial sites and, after laying aside the pastoral staff, sprinkles them with holy water and incenses them. Then, after laying aside the miter, he says one of the prayers chosen from those given in the *Order of Christian Funerals*.[145] The dismissal follows in the usual way.

402   The bishop may use this rite even outside Mass. In this case he wears a purple cope and the simple miter; the blessing of the graves follows a liturgy of the word, celebrated by use of elements from the Funeral Liturgy outside Mass, as described in the *Order of Christian Funerals*.[146]

403   The rite of sprinkling and incensing of burial sites just described is for use only in a place where the bodies of the deceased actually lie buried.

[144] See RF, nos. 145-166 and 187-191; see OCF, Part III, 16, no. 347 and Part V, 20, no. 403.
[145] See RF, nos. 170-176; see OCF, Part V, 20, no. 398.
[146] See RF, no. 45; see OCF, nos. 301-306.

Part V

SACRAMENTS

CHAPTER 1

CHRISTIAN INITIATION

Introduction

404   The bishop is the chief steward of the mysteries of God and the overseer of all liturgical life in the Church entrusted to his care.[1] He therefore regulates the conferral of baptism, which brings with it a share in Christ's royal priesthood, and he is the primary minister of confirmation.[2] The bishop also has responsibility for the entire process of Christian initiation, a responsibility he carries out either personally or through the presbyters, deacons, and catechists of his diocese.

Ecclesiastical tradition has viewed pastoral responsibility in this regard to be so peculiarly the bishop's own as to declare without qualification, in the words of Ignatius of Antioch: "It is not permitted to baptize without the authorization of the bishop."[3]

There is special reason for the bishop to be involved in the Christian initiation of adults and to celebrate its principal steps. And he should exercise his ministry in the sacraments of initiation for both adults and children at the solemn celebration of the Easter Vigil and, as far as possible, during pastoral visitations.[4]

405   Apart from cases of necessity, the bishop is not to celebrate the sacraments of Christian initiation in chapels or private homes; rather, as a rule, he is to celebrate these sacraments in the cathedral church or in parish churches so that the Christian community can take part in the celebration.

I. Christian Initiation of Adults

406   In person or through his delegate, the bishop sets up, regulates, and promotes the program of pastoral formation for catechumens and admits the candidates to their election and to the sacraments. It is hoped that, presiding if possible at the Lenten liturgy, he will himself celebrate the rite of election and, at the Easter Vigil, the sacraments of initiation, at least for the initiation of those who are fourteen years old or older.

---

[1] See CD, no. 15: DOL 7, no. 194.

[2] See LG, no. 26: DOL 4, no. 146.

[3] Ignatius of Antioch, *Ad Smyrnaeos*, 8, 2; F. X. Funk, ed., *Opera Patrum apostolicorum* (2 v., Tübingen, 1878-81), I, p. 283.

[4] See RBC, *Christian Initiation*: General Introduction, no. 12: DOL 294, no. 2261. See also RCIA, p. xii (U.S. ed., p. xvi).

Finally, when pastoral care requires, the bishop should depute catechists, truly worthy and properly prepared, to celebrate the minor exorcisms and the blessings of the catechumenate.[5]

407   The bishop may therefore rightly reserve to himself the rite of election or enrollment of names and also, in keeping with circumstances, the presentation of the Creed and of the Lord's Prayer, as well as the actual celebration of the sacraments of initiation from the Litany of the Saints to the end, but with the assistance of presbyters and deacons, as will be indicated in this chapter. When the bishop chooses to preside at any of the other rites belonging to Christian initiation, he does so in the manner indicated in the *Rite of Christian Initiation of Adults*.

Rite of election or enrollment of names [6]

408   Through celebration of the rite of election or enrollment of names at the beginning of Lent, the Church hears the testimony of the godparents and the catechists, as well as the catechumens' reaffirmation of intent, and then judges whether the catechumens are sufficiently prepared to receive the Easter sacraments.[7]

409   However much or little involved in the deliberation prior to the rite, the bishop has the responsibility of showing in the homily or elsewhere during the celebration the religious and ecclesial significance of the election.

He also declares before all present the Church's decision and, if appropriate in the circumstances, asks the community to express its approval of the candidates. He then asks the candidates to give a personal expression of their intention and, in the name of the Church, he carries out the act of admitting them as elect.[8]

410   Unless some other time is regarded as more suitable, the rite of election should normally be celebrated by the bishop within Mass, with the Mass texts of the First Sunday of Lent,[9] in the cathedral or some other church, in accord with pastoral considerations.

---

[5] See RCIA, Introduction, no. 12.
[6] See RCIA, nos. 105-124 (U.S. ed., nos. 118-137).
[7] See RCIA, nos. 106-107 (U.S. ed., nos. 119-120).
[8] See RCIA, no. 112 (U.S. ed., no. 125).
[9] See RCIA, no. 113 (U.S. ed., no. 126).

When celebrated at a time other than the First Sunday of Lent, the rite begins with the liturgy of the word, and the readings may be those of the First Sunday of Lent[10] or others that are thought suitable.

Mass for the election or enrollment of names may be celebrated on any day except those listed in nos. 1-4 of the table of liturgical days. The vestments for Mass are purple.[11]

411 The preparation of the bishop, concelebrants, and other ministers, their entry into the church, the introductory rites and liturgy of the word up to and including the gospel reading take place in the usual way.

412 The homily should be suited to the actual situation and should address not just the catechumens but the entire community of the faithful, so that all will be encouraged to give good example and to accompany the elect along the path of the paschal mystery.[12]

413 After the homily, the profession of faith is omitted. The priest in charge of the catechumens' initiation, or a deacon, a catechist, or a representative of the community presents the candidates to the bishop, who is seated at the chair, wearing the miter. The presenter may use the words indicated in the *Rite of Christian Initiation of Adults* or similar words.

414 After the presentation, the bishop directs that the candidates be called. One by one, the candidates and their godparents are called by name. Each candidate, accompanied by a godparent (or godparents), comes forward and stands before the bishop.[13]

415 When all have come before him, the bishop, seated at the chair and wearing the miter, asks the godparents for their testimony and the candidates for a declaration of their intention to proceed to the reception of the sacraments of Christian initiation. When the candidates have done so, he invites them to give their names.

416 During the actual inscription of their names a suitable song is sung, for example, Psalm 16 (15).[14]

---

[10] See LM, nos. 22-24 (Proper of Seasons, First Sunday of Lent) and 744 (Ritual Masses, I. Christian Initiation, 1. Order of Catechumens and Christian Initiation, On the day of election or enrollment of names).

[11] See GIRM, no. 330: DOL 208, no. 1720. See Appendix II of this *Ceremonial*.

[12] See RCIA, no. 116 (U.S. ed., no. 129).

[13] See RCIA, no. 117 (U.S. ed., no. 130).

[14] See RCIA, nos. 118-119 (U.S. ed., nos. 131-132).

417 When the enrollment of names has ended, the bishop takes the pastoral staff and, turning to the catechumens, declares that they have been elected to receive the sacraments at Easter. He then invites the godparents to place a hand on the shoulder of the candidate whom they are receiving into their care, or to make some other gesture to indicate the same intent.[15]

Putting aside the pastoral staff and miter, the bishop stands and introduces the intercessions for the elect. The deacon announces the intentions; the bishop, with hands outstretched over the elect, says the concluding prayer.

418 After the intercessions, the bishop dismisses the elect and with the faithful proceeds to the liturgy of the eucharist. If for serious reasons the elect cannot leave but must remain with the baptized, they are to be instructed that though they are present at the eucharist, they cannot take part in it as the baptized do.

419 When the rite of election or enrollment of names is celebrated outside Mass, the bishop wears alb, pectoral cross, stole, and, as circumstances suggest, purple cope. He wears the simple miter and carries the pastoral staff.

The bishop is assisted by a deacon in the vestments of his order and by other ministers in albs or other lawfully approved vesture.

After the entrance into the church or other suitable place chosen for the rite, there is a celebration of the word of God, with readings chosen from the *Lectionary for Mass* or with other suitable readings.

All then continues as described in nos. 412-418. The rite is concluded with a suitable song and the dismissal of both the elect and the faithful.[16]

Presentations of the Creed and of the Lord's Prayer

420 When the formation of the catechumens has been completed or is sufficiently far advanced, the presentations of the Creed and of the Lord's Prayer are celebrated. In these rites the Church lovingly entrusts to the elect the ancient texts that have always been regarded as expressing the heart of the Church's faith and prayer.

---

[15] See RCIA, no. 120 (U.S. ed., no. 133).

[16] See RCIA, nos. 115 and 123 (U.S. ed., nos. 128, 136); see LM, nos. 22-24 (Proper of Seasons, First Sunday of Lent).

421   The presentations should preferably be celebrated during the week in the presence of a community of the faithful within Mass after the liturgy of the word. The readings are those provided in the *Lectionary for Mass* for each presentation.[17]

If circumstances permit, the bishop should preside at the presentations because of their significance, provided that the presentations are not anticipated but take place after the rite of election.[18]

422   The vestments for Mass are purple. Mass is celebrated in the usual way up to and including the verse before the gospel reading.

In the rite of presentation of the Lord's Prayer the deacon invites the elect before the gospel reading to come forward and stand in front of the bishop. When they have taken their place, the bishop, laying aside the miter, rises and, after addressing the elect with the words Listen to the gospel or some similar invitation, proclaims the Lord's Prayer from the gospel according to Matthew.[19]

But in the rite of presentation of the Creed the gospel reading takes place in the usual way.

423   In the homily the bishop, basing his words on the readings, explains the meaning and importance of the Creed and of the Lord's Prayer in relation to the teaching that the elect have already received and to the Christian life they are to live.

In the rite of presentation of the Creed after the homily, the deacon invites the elect to come forward and stand before the bishop. When they have taken their place, the bishop, laying aside the miter, rises and, after addressing the elect with the words My dear friends, listen or a similar invitation, recites the Creed, joined by the entire community, as the elect listen.[20]

424   Next in these rites the bishop, standing and without miter, invites the faithful to pray. All pray in silence. Then the bishop, with hands outstretched over the elect, says the prayer for them. After the intercessions, the bishop dismisses the elect and proceeds with the faithful to the liturgy of the eucharist. If for serious reasons the elect cannot leave but must remain with the baptized, they are to be instructed that though they are present at the eucharist, they cannot take part in it as the baptized do.

---

[17] See LM, nos. 748-749 (Ritual Masses, I. Christian Initiation, 1. Order of Catechumens and Christian Initiation, Presentation of the Creed and Presentation of the Lord's Prayer).

[18] See RCIA, nos. 134, 144 (U.S. ed., nos. 147, 157).

[19] See RCIA, nos. 167-168 (U.S. ed., nos. 180-181).

[20] See RCIA, nos. 136, 147-150, 165-171 (U.S. ed., nos. 149, 160-163, 178-184).

Mass continues in the usual way. In Eucharistic Prayer I there is a remembrance of the elect and their godparents (RM, Ritual Masses, I. Christian Initiation, 2. The Scrutinies).

Celebration of the sacraments of initiation

425   Besides the requisites for celebration of a stational Mass, the following should be prepared: vessel of water, oil of catechumens, holy chrism, baptismal candle, Easter candle, the *Rite of Christian Initiation of Adults*, a cup large enough for communion under both kinds, pitcher of water, basin and towel for the washing of hands.

426   Since the initiation of adults is normally celebrated at the Easter Vigil, the provisions already set out in nos. 356-367 for the celebration of the sacraments of initiation at the Vigil are followed.

But even when the celebration of Christian initiation takes place apart from the Easter Vigil, care should be taken to ensure that the celebration has a markedly paschal character.

When the celebration takes place on a day when ritual Masses are permitted,[21] the ritual Mass for baptism (RM, Ritual Masses, I. Christian Initiation, 3. Baptism), with its proper readings, may be celebrated. The vestments for the Mass are white.

If the ritual Mass is not said, one of its readings, as provided in the *Lectionary for Mass*, may be used.[22]

But on the days listed in nos. 1-4 of the table of liturgical days,[23] the Mass of the day, with its proper readings, is celebrated.

427   For the conferral of the sacraments themselves, the provisions in nos. 356-367 for the Easter Vigil are to be followed, but the explanatory rites are carried out by a priest.

428   The profession of faith is omitted and Mass continues in the usual way. It is fitting that during the song for the presentation of the gifts (offertory song) the bread and the wine and water for the celebration of the eucharist be brought forward by some of the newly baptized.

The eucharistic prayer should include the intercessions (interpolations) provided in *The Roman Missal* (*Sacramentary*) for the newly baptized and their godparents.

---

[21] See Appendix III of this *Ceremonial*.

[22] See LM, nos. 751-755 (Ritual Masses, I. Christian Initiation, 1. Order of Catechumens and Christian Initiation of Adults, Christian Initiation apart from the Easter Vigil).

[23] See Appendix II of this *Ceremonial*.

It is most desirable that the newly baptized receive the eucharist under both kinds; their parents, godparents, catechists, and friends may do so also.

Period of postbaptismal catechesis or mystagogy

429 In order to establish a pastoral relationship with the new members of his Church, the bishop, particularly if he could not preside at the sacraments of initiation himself, should arrange to meet the recently baptized at least once in the year, preferably on a Sunday of the Easter season or on the anniversary of their baptism, and to preside at a celebration of the eucharist with them. At this Mass they may receive the eucharist under both kinds.[24]

Christian initiation of adults in exceptional circumstances

430 If in extraordinary circumstances the bishop must preside at the Christian initiation of an adult in a simpler form, that is, an initiation in one step, all the rites preceding the blessing of water are carried out by a priest. The bishop himself, following the provisions of nos. 356-367 given for the Easter Vigil, blesses the baptismal water, leads the renunciation of sin and the profession of faith, and confers baptism and confirmation. The explanatory rites are carried out by a priest.[25]

II. BAPTISM OF CHILDREN

431 For the celebration of baptism the following should be prepared:
a. vessel of water;
b. oil of catechumens;
c. holy chrism;
d. baptismal candle;
e. *Rite of Baptism for Children;*
in addition, for the bishop, miter, pastoral staff, pitcher of water, basin and towel for the washing of hands.

432 It is preferable that at least one presbyter, normally the parish priest (pastor), as well as a deacon and several ministers, assist the bishop.

[24] See RCIA, nos. 234-241 (U.S. ed., nos. 244-251).
[25] See RCIA, nos. 307-345 (U.S. ed., nos. 331-369).

The presbyter welcomes the children and carries out those rites that precede the liturgy of the word; he also says the prayer of exorcism and does the prebaptismal anointing. After the baptism, the presbyter does the anointing with chrism, the clothing with the baptismal garment, the giving of the lighted candle, and the ephphetha rite.

Celebration of baptism within Mass

433   The bishop, the presbyters who, as is fitting, are to concelebrate with him, and the deacons put on the vestments for Mass, which are white or of another festive color. If there is to be communion under both kinds, a large enough cup should be provided.

434   On days when ritual Masses are permitted,[26] the ritual Mass for baptism (RM, Ritual Masses, I. Christian Initiation, 3. Baptism), with its proper readings, may be celebrated.
       If a Mass other than the ritual Mass for baptism is used, one of the readings may be chosen from those provided in the *Lectionary for Mass* for this ritual Mass.[27]
       On days listed in nos. 1-4 of the table of liturgical days[28] the Mass of the day, with its proper readings, is celebrated.
       One of the formularies for the final blessing given in the *Rite of Baptism for Children* (nos. 70, 247-249) may always be used.

435   After the usual entrance into the church, the bishop first puts aside the miter and pastoral staff, then with the presbyters, deacons, and ministers, reverences the altar and, as circumstances suggest, may incense it. Then he goes to the chair (cathedra) and greets the people, then puts on the miter and sits.

436   The parish priest (pastor) or another presbyter goes with the ministers to the door of the church and carries out the rite of reception of the children as set out in the *Rite of Baptism for Children*.

437   After all have taken their place in the church, the bishop puts aside the miter and stands. The penitential rite and *Kyrie* are omitted, and the bishop begins the *Gloria*, when called for by the rubrics, and says the opening prayer.

---

[26] See Appendix III of this *Ceremonial*.
[27] See LM, nos. 756-760 (Ritual Masses, I. Christian Initiation, 2. Christian Initiation of Children).
[28] See Appendix II of this *Ceremonial*.

438   The liturgy of the word follows, with the homily being given by the bishop. The profession of faith is omitted, since the parents and god-parents will make a profession of faith later, to which the bishop and the community will join their assent.

439   The bishop introduces the general intercessions. When these are over, the bishop remains standing at the chair as a presbyter says the prayer of exorcism and carries out the prebaptismal anointing.

440   After the anointing, the bishop takes the miter and pastoral staff, and a procession to the baptistery is formed if the baptistery is outside the church or out of sight of the congregation. Those to be baptized, the parents, and the godparents follow the bishop in the procession to the baptistery.

But if, instead, a vessel of baptismal water has been prepared in a place visible to the congregation, the bishop and the parents and god-parents with the children go there. The others remain in their place.

If the baptistery is not large enough to accommodate all present, the baptism may be celebrated in a more suitable place in the church, to which the parents and godparents go at the appointed time.

During these arrangements, if this can be done in a proper manner, a suitable song is sung, for example, Psalm 23 (22).

441   At the font or the place where the rite of baptism is to be carried out, the bishop introduces this part of the celebration by reminding the assembly of the wonderful plan of God, who chose to make both body and soul holy by means of water.

Then, laying aside the pastoral staff and miter, the bishop faces the font and says the blessing of water that corresponds to the liturgical season.[29]

442   The bishop then sits and, after taking the miter and pastoral staff, addresses the parents and godparents with the questions pertaining to the renunciation of sin and the profession of faith.[30]

443   After the renunciation of sin and the profession of faith, the bishop lays aside the pastoral staff, rises, and baptizes the children. If a large number are to be baptized, priests and deacons are to join in baptizing the children.[31]

---

[29] See RBC, nos. 53-55, 223-224.
[30] See RBC, nos. 18b, 56-59.
[31] See RBC, nos. 60-61.

444   After the baptisms, the bishop sits, wearing the miter, and recites the prescribed formularies from the *Rite of Baptism for Children* as the parish priest (pastor) or another presbyter carries out the anointing with chrism, the clothing with a baptismal garment, the presentation of a lighted candle, and, if this is used, the ephphetha rite.[32]

445   Unless the baptism has taken place in the sanctuary, a procession to the altar follows, in which the bishop precedes the newly baptized and the parents and godparents, and the lighted candles are carried for the baptized.[33]

446   The profession of faith is omitted, and Mass continues in the usual way. It is fitting that during the song for the presentation of the gifts (offertory song) the bread and the wine and water for the celebration of the eucharist be brought forward by some of the parents and godparents of the newly baptized.

The eucharistic prayer should include the intercessions (interpolations) provided in *The Roman Missal* (*Sacramentary*) for the newly baptized and their godparents (Ritual Masses, I. Christian Initiation, 3. Baptism).

The parents, godparents, and relatives of the newly baptized may receive communion under both kinds.

447   For the blessing at the end of Mass the bishop may appropriately use one of the formularies provided in the *Rite of Baptism for Children*.[34]

The mothers, holding their children, and the fathers stand before the bishop. The bishop stands facing them, wearing the miter, and says, The Lord be with you.[35] A deacon may then say the invitation before the blessing; with hands outstretched over the people, the bishop says the invocations of the blessing. He then takes the pastoral staff and says, May almighty God bless you, and makes the sign of the cross three times over the people.

For the blessing the bishop may also use one of the formularies provided in this *Ceremonial*, nos. 1120-1121.

448   Then the deacon dismisses the people, saying, The Mass is ended, go in peace (or one of the other formulas), and all reply, Thanks be to God.

---

[32] See RBC, nos. 62-66.

[33] See RBC, no. 67.

[34] See RBC, nos. 29, 5; 70, or nos. 247-249.

[35] See RBC, no. 70.

Celebration of baptism outside Mass

449   The bishop vests in alb, pectoral cross, stole, and a cope of festive color; presbyters wear a stole over either a surplice and cassock or over an alb; a deacon may appropriately wear a dalmatic.

450   After the usual entrance into the church, the bishop reverences the altar, goes to the chair (cathedra), greets the people, then sits.

451   The rite of reception of the children is carried out by a presbyter at the door of the church, in the manner set out in the *Rite of Baptism for Children*.

452   When all have taken their proper place, a celebration of the word of God follows, with the homily given by the bishop. All else is done as already set out in nos. 435-445.

453   After the celebration of baptism, when all have gathered around the altar, the bishop lays aside the miter and introduces the Lord's Prayer, which he then says with all present.

454   Again putting on the the miter, the bishop gives the blessing in the manner already indicated in no. 447. The celebration ends with the singing of the Canticle of Mary or some other suitable song.

III. CONFIRMATION

455   The ordinary minister of confirmation is the bishop. Normally a bishop confers the sacrament so that there will be a clearer reference to the first pouring forth of the Holy Spirit on Pentecost: after the apostles were filled with the Holy Spirit, they themselves gave the Spirit to the faithful through the laying on of hands. Thus the reception of the Spirit through the ministry of the bishop shows the close bond that joins the confirmed to the Church and the mandate received from Christ to bear witness to him before all.[36]

456   For a serious reason, as sometimes is present because of the large number of those to be confirmed, the bishop may associate presbyters

---

[36] See *The Roman Pontifical*, English ed., 1978, Part I, Christian Initiation, ch. 3, Confirmation (hereafter, RC), Introduction, no. 7: DOL 305, no. 2516.

with himself as ministers of the sacrament. It is preferable that the presbyters who are so invited:

a. either have a particular function or office in the diocese, being, namely, either vicars general, episcopal vicars, or district or regional vicars;

b. or be the parish priests (pastors) of the places where confirmation is conferred, parish priests (pastors) of the places where the candidates belong, or presbyters who have had a special part in the catechetical preparation of the candidates.[37]

457 Requisites for the celebration of confirmation:

a. the vestments for the celebration, accordingly as it is within or outside Mass, as indicated in nos. 458 and 473;

b. chairs for the presbyters assisting the bishop;

c. vessel (or vessels) containing the holy chrism;

d. *The Roman Pontifical*;

e. requisites for the washing of hands after the anointing of those confirmed;

f. when confirmation is to be given within Mass and communion received under both kinds, a large enough cup.[38]

The celebration normally takes place at the bishop's chair (cathedra). But when necessary for the participation of the faithful, a chair for the bishop should be placed in front of the altar or in some other convenient place.

Confirmation within Mass

458 It is eminently fitting that the bishop celebrate this Mass. The presbyters who are to assist him in conferring confirmation should concelebrate with him. Hence the bishop and the presbyters wear the required Mass vestments.

But if the Mass is celebrated by someone other than the bishop, it is proper that he preside over the liturgy of the word and that he give the blessing at the end of Mass, in the manner described earlier in nos. 175-185. In this case the bishop is vested in alb, pectoral cross, stole, and cope of the color appropriate to the Mass; he wears a miter and carries the pastoral staff. If the presbyters who are to assist the bishop in con

[37] See RC, no. 8, a and b (as emended in accord with CIC).
[38] See RC, no. 19: DOL 305, no. 2526.

ferring confirmation do not concelebrate, they wear a stole over a surplice and cassock or over an alb and, if circumstances suggest, a cope.

459   On days when ritual Masses are permitted,[39] the ritual Mass for
confirmation (RM, Ritual Masses, I. Christian Initiation, 4. Confirmation),
with its proper readings,[40] may be celebrated. The vestments for the Mass
are red or white or of some other festive color.
    If the ritual Mass is not celebrated, one of the readings may be
taken from those provided in the *Lectionary for Mass* for the ritual Mass
for confirmation.
    On the days listed in nos. 1-4 of the table of liturgical days,[41] the
Mass of the day, with its readings, is celebrated.
    The final blessing proper to the ritual Mass may always be used.

460   The entrance into the church, introductory rites, and liturgy of the
word, including the gospel reading, take place in the usual way.

461   After the gospel reading, the bishop, wearing the miter, sits in his
usual chair or in the special chair prepared for the occasion. The presbyters assisting him in the confirmation take seats near him.
    The parish priest (pastor) or another presbyter, deacon, or cate-
chist presents the candidates for confirmation, according to the custom
of the region. If possible, each candidate is called by name and comes
individually to the sanctuary. If the candidates are children, they are accompanied by one of their sponsors or parents and stand before the
bishop. If there are very many candidates, they are not called by name,
but simply take a suitable place in front of the bishop.[42]

462   The bishop then gives a brief homily. He should explain the readings and so lead the candidates, their sponsors and parents, and the whole
assembly to a deeper understanding of the mystery of confirmation.[43] He
may, if he chooses, use the words of address given in *The Roman Pontifical*.

463   After the homily, the bishop, seated and with the miter and pastoral staff, addresses the candidates standing before him with the questions pertaining to the renewal of their baptismal promises.[44] He accepts

[39] See Appendix III of this *Ceremonial*.
[40] See LM, nos. 764-768 (Ritual Masses, I. Christian Initiation, 4. Confirmation).
[41] See Appendix II of this *Ceremonial*.
[42] See RC, no. 21.
[43] See RC, no. 22.
[44] See RC, no. 23.

their profession of faith by proclaiming the faith of the Church, to which all in the assembly respond with some acclamation or song expressing their assent.

464   Then, putting aside the miter and pastoral staff, the bishop stands (and the presbyters he has associated with himself to confer confirmation stand near him). He faces the people and, with hands joined, gives the invitation My dear friends. All pray in silence for a brief period.[45]

The bishop (and the presbyters who will minister confirmation with him) lays (lay) hands upon all the candidates. But the bishop alone says the prayer All-powerful God, Father of our Lord Jesus Christ.[46]

465   Then the bishop sits and takes the miter. The deacon brings the vessel or vessels of chrism to the bishop. When there are presbyters to assist the bishop in giving the anointing, the deacon brings all the vessels of holy chrism to the bishop, and each of the presbyters assisting him in turn receives the vessel of chrism from the bishop.

466   Each candidate goes to the bishop (or to a presbyter), or, if circumstances suggest, the bishop, with miter and staff, (and the presbyters) may go to the individual candidates.

The one who presented the candidate places his or her right hand on the candidate's shoulder and gives the candidate's name to the bishop; or the candidate may give his or her own name.[47]

467   The bishop (or presbyter) dips his right thumb into the chrism and makes the sign of the cross on the forehead of the one to be confirmed, as he says the sacramental formulary. When the candidate has responded, Amen, the bishop (or presbyter) adds, Peace be with you, and the newly confirmed responds, And also with you. During the anointing a suitable song may be sung.[48]

468   After the anointing, the bishop (and the presbyters) washes his hands (wash their hands).

469   Then the bishop, standing and without the miter, introduces the general intercessions and says the concluding prayer.

---

[45] See RC, no. 24.
[46] See RC, no. 25.
[47] See RC, nos. 26 and 28.
[48] See RC, no. 27.

470   The Creed is not said, since there has already been a profession of faith. Mass continues in the usual way.

It is appropriate that during the song for the presentation of the gifts (offertory song) some of those confirmed bring up the bread and the wine and water for the celebration of the eucharist.

The eucharistic prayer includes the intercessions (interpolations) provided in *The Roman Missal* (*Sacramentary*) for those confirmed (Ritual Masses, I. Christian Initiation, 4. Confirmation).

The newly confirmed, their sponsors, parents, wives and husbands, catechists, and relatives may receive communion under both kinds.[49]

471   For the final blessing of the Mass the bishop should use the solemn blessing or the prayer over the people provided in *The Roman Pontifical.*[50]

The newly confirmed stand in front of the bishop. The bishop, standing and wearing the miter, says, The Lord be with you. Then one of the deacons may give the invitation before the blessing. With hands outstretched over the people, the bishop says the invocations belonging to the blessing. Then he takes the pastoral staff and says, May almighty God bless you, and makes the sign of the cross three times over the people.

The bishop may also use one of the formularies provided in nos. 1120-1121 to bestow the blessing.

472   Then the deacon dismisses the people, saying, The Mass is ended, go in peace (or one of the other formulas), and all reply, Thanks be to God.

Confirmation outside Mass

473   The bishop vests in alb, pectoral cross, and stole and cope of festive color; he wears the miter and carries the pastoral staff. Presbyters associated with the bishop as ministers of confirmation wear a stole of festive color over surplice and cassock or over an alb, and, as circumstances suggest, also a cope of festive color. Deacons wear alb and stole, and other ministers wear an alb or other lawfully approved vesture.

474   When the candidates, their sponsors and parents, and the whole assembly have gathered, the bishop with the presbyters, deacons, and

---

[49] See RC, nos. 31-32.
[50] See RC, no. 33.

other ministers proceed to the sanctuary (chancel) as a suitable song is sung. After reverencing the altar, the bishop goes to the chair, where he lays aside the pastoral staff and miter, then greets the people. Then he says the opening prayer, God of power and mercy (or one of the other prayers provided in *The Roman Pontifical*).

475   The celebration of the word of God, the presentation of the candidates, the homily, and the rest follow, as provided in nos. 461-469.

476   After the general intercessions, which the bishop may introduce with a suitable invitation, the Lord's Prayer is said by all. Then the bishop adds the prayer God, our Father.

477   The bishop imparts the blessing in the manner described in no. 471. Then the deacon dismisses the people, saying, Go in peace, and all reply, Thanks be to God.

Chapter 2

SACRAMENT OF HOLY ORDERS

Introduction

478   "For the shepherding and continual increase of the people of God, Christ the Lord instituted in his Church various ministries that work together for the good of the whole Body."[51]

"Christ, whom the Father has sanctified and sent into the world, through his apostles has made their successors, the bishops, sharers in his consecration and mission. They in turn have lawfully handed on to different individuals in the Church in varying degrees a participation in this ministry. Thus the divinely established ecclesiastical ministry is exercised at different levels by those who from antiquity have been called bishops, presbyters, and deacons."[52]

Marked with the fullness of the sacrament of orders, bishops are stewards of the grace of the high priesthood, and, in union with their college of presbyters, they govern the particular Churches entrusted to them as vicars and legates of Christ.[53]

"Even though they do not possess the fullness of the priesthood and in the exercise of their power are subordinate to the bishops, presbyters are nevertheless linked to the bishops in priestly dignity. By virtue of the sacrament of orders, in the image of Christ the eternal High Priest, they are consecrated to preach the Gospel, to shepherd the faithful, and to celebrate divine worship as true priests of the New Testament."[54]

"At a lower level of the hierarchy are deacons, who receive the laying on of hands, not unto priesthood, but for a ministry of service. Strengthened by sacramental grace, they have as their service for the people of God, in communion with the bishop and his college of presbyters, the *diakonia* of liturgy, word, and charity."[55]

I. Admission to Candidacy for Ordination as Deacons and Priests

479   The rite of admission is a rite by which one who aspires to ordination as deacon or presbyter publicly manifests his will to offer himself to God and the Church so that he may exercise a sacred order. The Church

---

[51] LG, no. 18.

[52] LG, no. 28: DOL 4, no. 148.

[53] See LG, nos. 26, 27: DOL 4, nos. 146 and 147. See CD, no. 1.

[54] LG, no. 28: DOL 4, no. 148.

[55] LG, no. 29: DOL 4, no. 149.

in accepting this offering chooses and calls him to prepare himself to receive a sacred order. In this way he is properly admitted into the ranks of candidates for the diaconate or presbyterate.[56]

Professed members of a clerical religious institute who aspire to the priesthood are not bound to the celebration of this rite.

480   The rite of admission is celebrated when the candidates have reached a maturity of purpose and are shown to have the necessary qualifications.

Depending on the status of the candidate, the rite is celebrated either by the bishop or by the major superior of a clerical religious institute.[57]

481   The rite of admission may be celebrated on any day, but preferably on feast days, in a church or other suitable place, within Mass or within a celebration of the word. Because of its nature, the rite is never to be joined to an ordination or to the institution of readers or acolytes.[58]

482   The bishop should be assisted by a deacon or presbyter appointed to call the candidates, as well as by other requisite ministers.

If the rite is celebrated within Mass, the bishop vests for Mass and uses the miter and pastoral staff. If it is celebrated outside Mass, the bishop wears over the alb a pectoral cross, stole, and cope of appropriate color. But he may also simply wear the pectoral cross and stole over rochet and mozzetta, and in this case he does not use the miter or pastoral staff.

483   If the rite is celebrated within Mass, the Mass for vocations to holy orders (RM, Masses and Prayers for Various Needs and Occasions, I. For the Church, 9. For Priestly Vocations) may be said, with readings chosen from those in the *Lectionary for Mass* for the ritual Mass of admission to candidacy for ordination.[59] The vestments for the Mass are white.

On the days listed in nos. 1-4 of the table of liturgical days,[60] the Mass of the day is celebrated.

When the Mass for vocations to holy orders is not said, one of the readings may be chosen from those given in the *Lectionary for Mass* for

---

[56] See Paul VI, Motu Proprio *Ad pascendum*, laying down norms regarding the order of diaconate, 15 August 1972: AAS 64 (1972), p. 538; DOL 319, no. 2576.

[57] See *The Roman Pontifical*, Part III, Ordination of Deacons, Priests, and Bishops, ch. 7, Admission to Candidacy for Ordination as Deacons and Priests (hereafter, AC), Introduction, nos. 1-2.

[58] See AC, no. 3.

[59] See LM, nos. 775-779 (Ritual Masses, III. Admission to Candidacy for Ordination as Deacons and Priests).

[60] See Appendix II of this *Ceremonial*.

the rite of admission to candidacy for ordination, except on the days listed in nos. 1-4 of the table of liturgical days.[61]

484   If the rite of admission is celebrated simply within a celebration of the word, the celebration may begin with an appropriate antiphon and, after the greeting by the bishop, the opening prayer of the Mass for vocations to holy orders. The readings are chosen from those given in the *Lectionary for Mass* for the rite of admission to candidacy for ordination.

485   After the gospel reading, the bishop gives the homily; he may, according to circumstances, do so seated in the bishop's chair (cathedra) and with miter and pastoral staff. He concludes the homily with the words provided in *The Roman Pontifical* or other similar words.[62]

486   Then the appointed deacon or presbyter calls the candidates by name. Each one answers, Present, and goes to the bishop, before whom he makes a sign of reverence.[63]

487   The bishop speaks to the candidates in the words provided in the *The Roman Pontifical* or in others that the conference of bishops may determine. If it wishes, the conference of bishops may also determine the manner in which the bishop is to accept the candidates. The bishop concludes by saying, The Church receives your declaration with joy, and all reply, Amen.[64]

488   Putting aside the pastoral staff and miter, the bishop stands and all stand with him. If called for by the rubrics, the profession of faith is said. Then the bishop invites the faithful to pray, saying, Brothers and sisters, let us ask our God and Lord. The deacon or other suitable minister proclaims the intentions, and all respond with an appropriate acclamation. Then the bishop says the concluding prayer, Lord, hear our prayers or Lord, help your servants.[65]

489   If the rite of admission is celebrated within Mass, the Mass continues in the usual way.

---

[61] See Appendix II of this *Ceremonial*.
[62] See AC, no. 5.
[63] See AC, no. 6.
[64] See AC, no. 7.
[65] See AC, nos. 8-10.

But if the rite takes place within a celebration of the word, the bishop greets and blesses the faithful, and the deacon dismisses them, saying, Go in peace, and all reply, Thanks be to God.[66]

490 "Candidates for the permanent diaconate and for the transitional diaconate, as well as candidates for the presbyterate itself, are to receive the ministries of reader and acolyte, unless they have already done so, and are to exercise them for a suitable period, in order to be better disposed for the future service of the word and of the altar."[67]

The rite of institution of readers and acolytes is described in nos. 790-820 of this Ceremonial.

II. SOME GENERAL NORMS FOR THE RITE OF ORDINATION

491 The ordination of deacons and presbyters and especially the ordination of a bishop should take place in the presence of as large a gathering of the faithful as possible, on a Sunday or feast day, unless pastoral reasons suggest another day. Thus, for example, the ordination of a bishop might be celebrated on the feast of an apostle.[68]

492 Ordinations are to be celebrated within a Mass celebrated in the form of a stational Mass and, as a rule, in the cathedral. For pastoral reasons, however, ordinations may be celebrated in another church or oratory.

493 Ordinations should normally take place at the chair (cathedra) of the bishop, but if necessary for the participation of the faithful, ordinations may take place before the altar or in some other suitable place.

The chairs for those to be ordained should be so placed as to allow the faithful a clear view of the liturgy.

494 When ordinations are celebrated on any day except those listed in nos. 1-4 of the table of liturgical days[69] or the feast of an apostle, the Mass may be arranged in the following manner:

[66] See AC, no. 11.

[67] Paul VI, Motu Proprio Ad pascendum, laying down norms regarding the order of diaconate, 15 August 1972: AAS 64 (1972), p. 539; DOL 319, no. 2582.

[68] See The Roman Pontifical, Part III, Ordination of Deacons, Priests, and Bishops, ch. 8, Ordination of Deacons (hereafter, OD), Introduction, no. 1; ch. 10, Ordination of Priests (hereafter, OP), Introduction, no. 1; ch. 12, Ordination of a Bishop (hereafter, OB), Introduction, no. 1.

[69] See Appendix II of this Ceremonial.

a. the entrance antiphon and communion antiphon from the ritual Mass for holy orders are sung;

b. the pertinent orations are chosen from those for the bishop, for priests, for the ministers of the Church that are provided in *The Roman Missal* (*Sacramentary*) among the Masses and Prayers for Various Needs and Occasions;

c. the readings are chosen from those provided in the *Lectionary for Mass*, for the ritual Mass for holy orders;[70]

d. at the ordination of priests, unless the rubrics call for a more proper preface, the preface of the priesthood (Chrism Mass) may be used;[71]

e. Eucharistic Prayer I includes the intercessions (interpolations) for the newly ordained, as provided in *The Roman Missal* (*Sacramentary*) among the Ritual Masses (II. Holy Orders).

But when the ritual Mass is not said, one of the readings may be chosen from those provided in the *Lectionary for Mass* for the ritual Mass for holy orders.

When ordinations are celebrated on the days listed in nos. 1-4 of the table of liturgical days or on the feast of an apostle, the Mass of the day is celebrated, with its proper readings.

III. Ordination of Deacons

495   Those to be ordained wear an alb (with amice and cincture unless other provisions are made). A stole and dalmatic for each should also be laid out.

The vestments for the Mass are of the color proper to the Mass being celebrated, but they may also be white or of another festive color.[72]

496   Besides the vestments just mentioned and the requisites for celebration of a stational Mass, there should be ready:

a. *The Roman Pontifical*;

b. chair for the bishop, if the ordination is not to take place at the usual chair (cathedra);

c. cup large enough for communion under both kinds.

---

[70] See LM, nos. 770-774 (Ritual Masses, II. Holy Orders).

[71] See RM, Ritual Masses, II. Holy Orders.

[72] See GIRM, no. 310: DOL 208, no. 1700.

497   When everything is ready, the procession moves through the church to the altar in the usual way. The candidates walk in front of the deacon who carries the Book of the Gospels.

498   The introductory rites and the liturgy of the word up to and including the gospel reading take place in the usual way.
    After the gospel reading, the deacon places the Book of the Gospels back on the altar, where it remains until its presentation to each newly ordained deacon.

499   The ordination begins after the gospel reading. The bishop, wearing the miter, sits in the chair (cathedra) or in a chair provided for the occasion.

500   The candidates are called by the deacon: Those to be ordained deacons, please come forward. Then their names are called by the deacon. Each one answers, Present, and goes to the bishop, before whom he makes a sign of reverence.[73]

501   When all the candidates are in their places before the bishop, the presbyter designated by the bishop presents them, using the words provided in *The Roman Pontifical*. The bishop concludes the presentation by saying, We rely on the help of the Lord God, and all reply, Thanks be to God, or give their assent to the choice in some other way determined by the conference of bishops.[74]

502   Then all sit and the bishop, with miter and pastoral staff (unless he decides otherwise), gives the homily. Taking his theme from the text of the Mass readings just proclaimed, he addresses the people and the candidates on the duties of a deacon. He may do this in the words provided in *The Roman Pontifical* or in his own words. If there are candidates who are to make the commitment to celibacy, the bishop speaks also on the importance and meaning of celibacy in the Church.[75]

503   After the homily, the public acceptance of celibacy is made by candidates for priesthood in the order of presbyterate and by unmarried candidates for the diaconate. As the deacon calls them, these candidates stand before the bishop. He speaks to them in the words provided in *The Roman Pontifical* or in similar words.

---

[73] See OD, nos. 10-11.
[74] See OD, nos. 12-13.
[75] See OD, no. 14.

504   Then the candidates manifest their intention of a commitment to celibacy by answering, I am, to the question put by the bishop, or by some external sign determined by the conference of bishops.

The bishop ends by saying, May the Lord help you to persevere in this commitment. The candidates answer, Amen.[76]

505   Then the candidates for the diaconate who are not obliged to make the commitment to celibacy come forward. As the candidates stand before him, the bishop questions them all together in the words provided in *The Roman Pontifical* (no. 15), including the question on the celebration of the liturgy of the hours.[77]

506   The bishop then puts aside the pastoral staff. Each of the candidates goes to the bishop and, kneeling before him, places his joined hands between those of the bishop.

The bishop asks from each a promise of obedience by using one of the formularies given in *The Roman Pontifical.*

If the gesture mentioned seems less suitable in some places, the conference of bishops may choose another gesture or sign.[78]

507   Putting aside the miter, the bishop stands, and all stand with him. He faces the people and, with hands joined, invites them to pray: My dear people, let us pray. The deacon says, Let us kneel. The bishop kneels before his chair, the candidates prostrate themselves, the others in the assembly kneel at their places.

But during the Easter season and on Sundays the deacon does not say, Let us kneel, and all in the assembly remain standing, except the candidates, who prostrate themselves.

The cantors then begin the Litany of the Saints; they may add, at the proper places, names of other saints (for example, the patron saint, the titular of the church, the founder of the church, the patron saints of those to be ordained); they may also add petitions suitable to the occasion, since the litany takes the place of the general intercessions.[79]

508   After the litany, the bishop alone stands and, with hands outstretched, says the prayer Lord God, hear our petitions. At the end of

[76] See OD, no. 14.
[77] See OD, no. 15.
[78] See OD, no. 16.
[79] See OD, nos. 17-18.

this prayer the deacon (if he had given the invitation to kneel before the litany) says, Let us stand, and all stand.[80]

509   One by one, the candidates go to the bishop and kneel before him. The bishop, wearing the miter, lays his hands on the head of each, in silence.[81]

510   The bishop then puts aside the miter. The candidates kneel before the bishop, who, with hands outstretched, sings or says the prayer of consecration.[82]

511   After the prayer of consecration, the bishop, wearing his miter, sits, and the newly ordained stand. Some of the deacons assisting him or presbyters put a deacon's stole and then a dalmatic on each of the newly ordained. Meanwhile, Psalm 84 (83) with its antiphon or some other suitable song may be sung. The singing continues until dalmatics have been put on all the newly ordained.[83]

512   Vested as deacons, the newly ordained go to the bishop and kneel before him. He places the Book of the Gospels in the hands of each one and says, Receive the Gospel of Christ.[84]

513   Lastly, the bishop stands and gives the kiss of peace to each of the new deacons, saying, Peace be with you. The deacon responds, And also with you.
        If circumstances permit, other deacons present also give the kiss of peace to the newly ordained as a sign of their being joined in the order of the diaconate.
        Meanwhile, Psalm 146 (145) with its antiphon or some other suitable song may be sung.[85]

514   When called for by the rubrics, the profession of faith is said; the general intercessions are omitted.

515   In the liturgy of the eucharist the Order of Mass is followed. Some of the new deacons bring the gifts for the celebration to the bishop, and at least one of them assists him at the altar.

---

[80] See OD, no. 19.

[81] See OD, no. 20.

[82] See OD, no. 21.

[83] See OD, nos. 22-23.

[84] See OD, no. 24.

[85] See OD, nos. 25-26.

516 In Eucharistic Prayer I there is a commemoration of the newly ordained, by means of the formulary provided in *The Roman Missal* (*Sacramentary*) among the Ritual Masses (II. Holy Orders).

517 The new deacons receive communion under both kinds. The deacon who assists the bishop ministers the cup. Some of the new deacons assist the bishop in giving communion to the people.[86]

The parents and relatives of the new deacons may also receive communion under both kinds.

The concluding rite of the Mass takes place in the usual way.

IV. ORDINATION OF PRESBYTERS

518 All the presbyters concelebrate with the bishop in their ordination Mass. It is most fitting that the bishop admit other presbyters to the concelebration; in this case and on this day the newly ordained presbyters take the first place ahead of the others who concelebrate.[87]

519 Those to be ordained wear an alb (with amice and cincture unless other provisions are made) and deacon's stole. A chasuble should be provided for each candidate.

The vestments for the Mass should be of the color proper to the Mass being celebrated, but they may be white or of another festive color.

520 In addition to what is listed above and whatever is needed for the celebration of a stational Mass, the following should be provided:

a. *The Roman Pontifical*;

b. stoles for nonconcelebrating presbyters who lay hands on the candidates;

c. linen apron (gremial);

d. holy chrism;

e. whatever is needed for the bishop and candidates to wash their hands;

f. chair for the bishop, if the ordination does not take place at the usual chair (cathedra);

g. cup large enough for the concelebrants and others who are to receive communion under both kinds.[88]

---

[86] See OD, no. 28.

[87] See OP, no. 3.

[88] See OP, no. 4.

521   In the entrance procession the candidates follow other deacons and precede the concelebrating presbyters.[89]

522   The introductory rites and the liturgy of the word up to and including the gospel reading take place in the usual way.

523   The ordination begins after the gospel reading. The bishop, wearing the miter, sits in the chair (cathedra) or in a chair provided for the occasion.

524   The candidates are called by the deacon: Those to be ordained priests, please come forward. Then their names are called by the deacon. Each one answers, Present, and goes to the bishop, before whom he makes a sign of reverence.[90]

525   When the candidates are in their places before the bishop, the presbyter designated by the bishop presents them, in the words provided in *The Roman Pontifical*.[91] The bishop concludes the presentation of candidates by saying, We rely on the help of the Lord God, and all say, Thanks be to God, or give their assent to the choice in some other way determined by the conference of bishops.

526   Then all sit and the bishop, with miter and pastoral staff (unless he decides otherwise), gives the homily. Taking his theme from the text of the Mass readings just proclaimed, he addresses the people and the candidates on the duties of a priest. He may do this in the words provided in *The Roman Pontifical* or in his own words.[92]

527   After the homily, the candidates stand before the bishop, who questions all of them together, as prescribed in *The Roman Pontifical*.[93]

528   The bishop then puts aside the pastoral staff. Each of the candidates goes to the bishop and, kneeling before him, places his joined hands between those of the bishop.
    The bishop asks from each a promise of obedience by using one of the formularies given in *The Roman Pontifical*.
    If the gesture mentioned seems less suitable in some places, the conference of bishops may choose another gesture or sign.[94]

---

[89] See OP, no. 5.
[90] See OP, nos. 10-11.
[91] See OP, nos. 12-13.
[92] See OP, no. 14.
[93] See OP, no. 15.
[94] See OP, no. 16.

529   Putting aside the miter, the bishop stands, and all stand with him. He faces the people and, with hands joined, invites them to pray: My dear people, let us pray. The deacon says, Let us kneel. The bishop kneels before his chair, the candidates prostrate themselves, the others in the assembly kneel at their places.

But during the Easter season and on Sundays the deacon does not say, Let us kneel, and all in the assembly remain standing, except the candidates, who prostrate themselves.

The cantors then begin the Litany of the Saints; they may add, at the proper places, names of other saints (for example, the patron saint, the titular of the church, the founder of the church, the patron saints of those to be ordained); they may also add petitions suitable to the occasion, since the litany takes the place of the general intercessions.[95]

530   After the litany, the bishop alone stands and, with hands outstretched, says the prayer Hear us, Lord our God. At the end of this prayer the deacon (if he had given the invitation to kneel before the litany) says, Let us stand, and all stand.[96]

531   One by one, the candidates go to the bishop and kneel before him. The bishop, wearing the miter, lays his hands on the head of each, in silence.[97]

532   Next all the concelebrating presbyters and all other presbyters present, provided they are vested with a stole worn over an alb or over a cassock and surplice, lay their hands on each of the candidates, in silence. After the laying on of hands, the presbyters remain on either side of the bishop until the prayer of consecration is completed.[98]

533   The candidates kneel before the bishop. Putting aside the miter and with hands outstretched, he sings or says the prayer of consecration.[99]

534   After the prayer of consecration, the bishop, wearing the miter, sits, and the newly ordained stand. The presbyters assisting the bishop re-

---

[95] See OP, nos. 17-18.

[96] See OP, no. 19.

[97] See OP, no. 20.

[98] See OP, no. 21; SC Worship, Third Instruction Liturgicae instaurationes, on the orderly carrying out of the Constitution on the Liturgy, 5 September 1970, no. 8c: AAS 62 (1970), p. 701; DOL 52, no. 526.

[99] See OP, no. 22.

turn to their places, but some help the newly ordained to arrange the stole in the manner proper to presbyters and to put on the chasuble.[100]

535   Next the bishop receives a linen apron (gremial) and anoints with chrism the palms of each new presbyter as he kneels before him. The bishop says, The Father anointed. Then the bishop and the newly ordained wash their hands.[101]

536   While the newly ordained are being vested in stoles and chasubles, and the bishop is anointing their hands, the hymn *Veni, Creator Spiritus* or Psalm 110 (109), with the antiphon provided in *The Roman Pontifical,* or some other suitable song is sung.[102]
    The singing continues until all the newly ordained have returned to their places.

537   Next some of the faithful bring up a paten holding the bread and a cup containing the wine mixed with water for the celebration of Mass. The deacon receives the paten and chalice and brings them to the bishop, who hands them to each of the newly ordained as he kneels before him. The bishop says, Accept from the holy people of God.[103]

538   Lastly, the bishop stands and gives each of the newly ordained the kiss of peace, saying, Peace be with you. The presbyter responds, And also with you.
    If circumstances permit, the other presbyters present may also give the newly ordained the kiss of peace as a sign of their being joined in the order of the presbyterate.
    Meanwhile, Psalm 100 (99), with the antiphon You are my friends, or the responsory No longer do I call you servants, or some other suitable song may be sung.[104] The singing continues until all have received the kiss of peace.

539   When called for by the rubrics, the profession of faith is said; the general intercessions are omitted.

540   In the liturgy of the eucharist the order for the concelebration of Mass is followed, but the preparation of the cup is omitted.[105]

---

[100] See OP, no. 23.
[101] See OP, no. 24.
[102] See OP, no. 25.
[103] See OP, no. 26.
[104] See OP, no. 27.
[105] See OP, no. 29.

541   In Eucharistic Prayer I there is a commemoration of the newly ordained, by means of the formulary provided in *The Roman Missal*
(*Sacramentary*) among the Ritual Masses (II. Holy Orders).

542   The parents and relatives of the newly ordained may also receive
communion under both kinds.[106]
The concluding rite of the Mass takes place in the usual way.

V. Ordination of Deacons and Presbyters in the Same Celebration[107]

543   For the preparation of the candidates and of the celebration, the
provisions of nos. 495-496 and 518-520 are to be followed.

544   In the entrance procession those to be ordained deacons precede
the deacon carrying the Book of the Gospels; those to be ordained presbyters follow the other deacons assisting the bishop and precede the concelebrating presbyters.

545   The introductory rites and the liturgy of the word up to and including the gospel reading take place in the usual way.

546   The ordination begins after the gospel reading. The bishop, wearing the miter, sits in the chair (cathedra) or in a chair provided for the
occasion.

547   The candidates, first for the diaconate, then for the priesthood in
the presbyteral order are called by the deacon and presented, as prescribed
in nos. 500-501 and nos. 524-525.

548   Afterward, all sit, and the bishop, seated and with miter and pastoral staff (unless he decides otherwise), gives the homily. Taking his
theme from the texts just proclaimed, he addresses the people and the
candidates on the office of deacon and presbyter, and, if there are candidates for the diaconate who are to commit themselves to celibacy, he
speaks also on the importance and meaning of celibacy in the Church.
He may do so in the words provided in *The Roman Pontifical* (no. 10) or
in his own words.[108]

---

[106] See GIRM, no. 242, 13: DOL 208, no. 1632.

[107] See *The Roman Pontifical*, Appendix III, Ordination of Deacons and Priests in the Same Celebration (hereafter, ODP).

[108] See ODP, no. 10.

549   After the homily, the candidates who are to manifest their intention of a commitment to celibacy rise and stand before the bishop. He speaks to them in the words of the invitation provided in *The Roman Pontifical* or in other similar words.[109]

550   The candidates manifest their intention of a commitment to celibacy by answering, I am, to the question put by the bishop, or by some external sign determined by the conference of bishops.
        The bishop ends by saying, May the Lord help you to persevere in this commitment. The candidates answer, Amen.

551   Then the candidates for the diaconate who are not obliged to make the commitment to celibacy come forward. As the candidates stand before him, the bishop questions them all together in the words provided in *The Roman Pontifical* (no. 11), including the question on the celebration of the liturgy of the hours.[110]

552   The bishop then puts aside the pastoral staff. Each of the candidates for the diaconate goes to the bishop and, kneeling before him, places his joined hands between those of the bishop.
        The bishop asks from each a promise of obedience by using one of the formularies given in *The Roman Pontifical* (no. 12).
        If the gesture mentioned seems less suitable in some places, the conference of bishops may choose another gesture or sign.[111]

553   After this, those to be ordained deacons move aside, and those to be ordained presbyters stand before the bishop, who questions all of them together. Then each of the candidates for ordination goes to the bishop and kneels before him. With the same gesture and the same formularies indicated in no. 506, the bishop asks from each a promise of obedience.[112]

554   Putting aside the miter, the bishop stands, and all stand with him. The Litany of the Saints is said with its introduction and concluding prayer, as already indicated in nos. 507-508.
        After the litany, the candidates for priesthood in the presbyteral order return to their places, and the ordination of deacons begins.[113]

---

[109] See ODP, no. 10.
[110] See ODP, no. 11.
[111] See ODP, no. 12.
[112] See ODP, nos. 12-13.
[113] See ODP, no. 16.

555   The ordination of deacons proceeds in the manner already indicated in nos. 509-512, but the kiss of peace is deferred until after the ordination of presbyters.

556   The newly ordained deacons return to their places, and the candidates for priesthood in the presbyteral order come forward.
    Putting aside the miter, the bishop stands and all stand with him. He faces the people and, with hands joined, invites them to pray: My dear people, let us pray. The deacon says, Let us kneel. The bishop kneels before his chair, the candidates prostrate themselves, the others in the assembly kneel at their places.
    But during the Easter season and on Sundays the deacon does not say, Let us kneel, and all in the assembly remain standing.[114]

557   The ordination of presbyters follows, in the manner indicated in nos. 531-538.

558   Lastly, the bishop stands and gives the newly ordained, first the presbyters, then the deacons, the kiss of peace. If circumstances permit, the other presbyters present may also give the new presbyters the kiss of peace as a sign of their being joined in the order of the presbyterate; similarly other deacons present may give the new deacons the kiss of peace.
    Meanwhile, Psalm 100 (99), with the antiphon You are my friends, or the responsory No longer do I call you servants, or some other suitable song is sung.[115]

559   When called for by the rubrics, the profession of faith is said; the general intercessions are omitted.

560   In the liturgy of the eucharist the order for the concelebration of Mass is followed, but the preparation of the chalice is omitted. One of the newly ordained deacons assists the bishop at the altar.

561   In Eucharistic Prayer I there is a commemoration of the newly ordained, by means of the formulary provided in *The Roman Missal* (*Sacramentary*) among the Ritual Masses (II. Holy Orders).[116]

---

[114] See ODP, nos. 22-24.
[115] See ODP, nos. 31-32.
[116] See ODP, no. 33.

562   The new deacons receive communion under both kinds. The deacon who assists the bishop ministers the cup. Some of the new deacons assist the bishop in giving communion to the people.

The parents and relatives of the newly ordained may also receive communion under both kinds.[117]

The concluding rite of the Mass takes place in the usual way.

VI. Ordination of a Bishop

563   The ordination of a bishop most appropriately takes place in his cathedral church. In this case the rite will include the presentation and reading of the apostolic letter and the seating of the newly ordained bishop in the chair of the bishop (cathedra), as indicated in nos. 573 and 589.

564   The principal consecrator must be assisted by at least two other consecrating bishops, who will also concelebrate the Mass with him and the bishop-elect. But it is fitting that all the bishops present ordain the bishop-elect with the principal consecrator.[118]

565   It is most appropriate for all the consecrating bishops and the presbyters assisting the bishop-elect to concelebrate the Mass with the principal consecrator and the bishop-elect. If the ordination takes place in the bishop-elect's own church, some presbyters of his diocese should also concelebrate.[119]

But the distinction between bishops and presbyters should be made abundantly clear, even by means of the places they are assigned.

566   Two presbyters assist the bishop-elect.[120]

567   The principal consecrator and the concelebrating bishops and presbyters wear the vestments required for Mass. The bishop-elect wears all the priestly vestments, the pectoral cross, and the dalmatic.

If the consecrating bishops are not to concelebrate, they wear the alb, pectoral cross, stole, and, as circumstances suggest, cope and miter. If the presbyters assisting the bishop-elect are not to concelebrate, they wear a cope over an alb or over surplice and cassock.[121]

---

[117] See ODP, no. 34.
[118] See OB, no. 2.
[119] See OB, no. 4.
[120] See OB, no. 3.
[121] See OB, no. 6.

The vestments for the Mass should be of the color proper to the Mass being celebrated, but they may be white or of another festive color.

568   Besides the requisites for concelebration of a stational Mass, there should be ready:

a. *The Roman Pontifical;*

b. copies of the consecratory prayer for the consecrating bishops;

c. linen apron (gremial);

d. holy chrism;

e. ring, pastoral staff, and miter for the bishop-elect;

f. cup large enough for the concelebrants and others who will receive communion under both kinds.[122]

569   As indicated in *The Roman Pontifical,*[123] the blessing of the ring, pastoral staff, and miter ordinarily takes place at a convenient time prior to the ordination service.

570   Seats for the principal consecrator, consecrating bishops, the bishop-elect, and concelebrating presbyters are arranged as follows:

a. for the liturgy of the word, the principal consecrator sits at the chair (cathedra), with the consecrating bishops near the chair, on either side; the bishop-elect sits between the presbyters assisting him, in an appropriate place within the sanctuary (chancel);

b. the ordination should usually take place at the chair (cathedra) or, to enable the faithful to participate more fully, seats for the principal consecrator and consecrating bishops may be placed before the altar or elsewhere; seats for the bishop-elect and the presbyters assisting him should be placed so that the faithful may have a complete view of the liturgical rites.[124]

571   When everything is ready, the procession moves through the church to the altar in the usual way.

The bishop-elect, between the presbyters assisting him, follows the concelebrating presbyters and precedes the consecrating bishops.[125]

572   The introductory rites and the liturgy of the word up to and including the gospel reading take place in the usual way.

---

[122] See OB, no. 8.

[123] See *The Roman Pontifical,* Appendix V, Blessing of Pontifical Insignia, p. 383.

[124] See OB, no. 9b.

[125] See OB, no. 10.

573　If the bishop is ordained in his cathedral church, after the greeting of the people, one of the deacons or concelebrating presbyters presents the apostolic letter to the college of diocesan consultors, in the presence of the chancellor, who records the proceedings. Then the deacon or presbyter reads the letter at the ambo, as all sit and listen, and at the end express their assent by saying, Thanks be to God, or by some other suitable means.

In newly erected dioceses, the apostolic letter is presented to the clergy and people assembled in the cathedral, and the senior presbyter present records the proceedings.

574　After the gospel reading, the deacon reverently replaces the Book of the Gospels on the altar, where it remains until it is held above the head of the new bishop.

575　The ordination begins after the gospel reading. While all stand, the hymn Veni, Creator Spiritus or another hymn similar to it, depending on local custom, is sung.[126]

576　The principal consecrator and the consecrating bishops, wearing their miters, go to the seats prepared for the ordination and sit.[127]

577　The bishop-elect is led by the presbyters assisting him to the chair of the principal consecrator, to whom he makes a sign of reverence. One of the presbyters assisting him asks the principal consecrator to proceed with the ordination of the bishop-elect. The principal consecrator orders the reading of the apostolic mandate; all sit and listen and at the end give their assent to the choice by saying, Thanks be to God, or by some other suitable means, in accord with local custom.[128]

578　Then the principal consecrator gives the homily; taking his theme from the biblical readings just proclaimed, he addresses the clergy, the people, and the bishop-elect on the duties of a bishop. He may do so in the words provided in The Roman Pontifical or in similar words of his own.[129]

579　After the homily, the bishop-elect rises and stands in front of the principal consecrator, who addresses to him the questions indicated in

---

[126] See OB, no. 13.
[127] See OB, no. 14.
[128] See OB, nos. 15-17.
[129] See OB, no. 18.

The Roman Pontifical, on his resolve to hold fast to the faith and to carry out his responsibilities.[130]

580   Putting aside their miters, the consecrating bishops stand and all stand with them. The principal consecrator, with hands joined, faces the people and invites them to pray, saying, My dear people, let us pray that.

Then the deacon says, Let us kneel. The principal consecrator and the consecrating bishops kneel before their chairs, the bishop-elect prostrates himself, and the others in the assembly kneel.

But during the Easter season and on Sundays the deacon does not say, Let us kneel, and all in the assembly remain standing, except the bishop-elect, who prostrates himself.

The cantors then begin the Litany of the Saints; they may add, at the proper places, names of other saints (for example, the patron saint, the titular of the church, the founder of the church, the patron saint of the one to be ordained); they may also add petitions suitable to the occasion, since the litany takes the place of the general intercessions.[131]

581   After the litany, the principal consecrator stands and, with hands outstretched, says, Lord, be moved. At the end of this prayer, the deacon (if he had given the invitation to kneel before the litany) says, Let us stand, and all stand.[132]

582   The bishop-elect rises, goes to the principal consecrator, and kneels before him.

The principal consecrator, wearing the miter, lays his hands upon the head of the bishop-elect, in silence.

Then one after another all the bishops go to the bishop-elect and lay hands on him, in silence, then remain alongside the principal consecrator until the prayer of consecration has been said.[133]

583   Then the principal consecrator receives the Book of the Gospels from a deacon and places it, open, upon the head of the bishop-elect; two deacons, standing on either side of the bishop-elect, hold the Book of the Gospels above his head until the prayer of consecration is completed.[134]

---

[130] See OB, no. 19.

[131] See OB, nos. 20-21.

[132] See OB, no. 22.

[133] See OB, nos. 23-24.

[134] See OB, no. 25.

584   Next the principal consecrator puts aside the miter, and the consecrating bishops, also without miter, remain by his side. With hands outstretched he sings or says the prayer of consecration, God the Father of our Lord.

The part of the prayer from the words So now pour out through the words glory and praise of your name is said by all the consecrating bishops, with hands joined.

The rest of the prayer of consecration is said by the principal consecrator alone. At the conclusion of the prayer all say, Amen.[135]

585   After the prayer of consecration the deacons remove the Book of the Gospels, which they have been holding above the head of the new bishop. One of them holds the book until it is presented to the new bishop. The principal consecrator and the other bishops, wearing their miters, sit, as do all in the assembly.[136]

586   After putting on a linen apron (gremial) and taking the holy chrism from one of the deacons, the principal consecrator anoints the head of the new bishop, who kneels before him, and says, God has brought you to share. After the anointing, the principal consecrator washes his hands.[137]

587   Taking the Book of the Gospels from the deacon, he presents it to the newly ordained bishop, saying, Receive the Gospel. Afterward the deacon takes the Book of the Gospels and returns it to its place.[138]

588   Finally the principal consecrator invests the new bishop with the pontifical insignia. First, he places the ring on the ring finger of the new bishop's right hand, saying, Take this ring. Then the principal consecrator places the miter on the head of the new bishop, in silence. Lastly, he gives the pastoral staff to the new bishop, saying, Take this staff.[139]

If the new bishop is entitled to use the pallium, the principal consecrator, following the rite described in no. 1154, presents it to him before the presentation of the miter.

589   All then stand. If the ordination takes place in the new bishop's own church, the principal consecrator invites him to occupy the chair

---

[135] See OB, no. 26.

[136] See OB, no. 27.

[137] See OB, no. 28.

[138] See OB, no. 29.

[139] See OB, nos. 30-32.

(cathedra), and leads him to it. If the ordination takes place in front of the altar, he leads him to the chair provided for the occasion.

If the ordination does not take place in the new bishop's own church, he is invited by the principal consecrator to take the first place among the concelebrating bishops.[140]

590   The newly ordained sets aside his pastoral staff, rises, and receives the kiss of peace from the principal consecrator and all the other bishops.

After the presentation of the staff and until the end of the ordination rite, Psalm 96 (95) with its antiphon or some other suitable song may be sung.[141]

The singing continues until all have exchanged the kiss of peace.

591   If the ordination has taken place in the new bishop's own church, the principal consecrator may ask the newly ordained bishop to preside over the concelebration of the eucharistic liturgy. If the ordination does not take place in the new bishop's own church, the principal consecrator presides at the concelebration; in this case the new bishop takes the first place among the other concelebrants.[142]

592   When called for by the rubrics, the profession of faith is said; the general intercessions are omitted.

593   In the liturgy of the eucharist the order for the concelebration of a stational Mass is followed.

In Eucharistic Prayer I there is a commemoration of the new bishop, said by one of the concelebrating bishops, who uses the formulary provided in *The Roman Missal* (*Sacramentary*) among the Ritual Masses (II. Holy Orders).[143]

The parents and relatives of the new bishop may receive communion under both kinds.

594   At the conclusion of the prayer after communion, the hymn *Te Deum* is sung, or another hymn similar to it, depending on local custom. Meanwhile the newly ordained bishop, after taking the miter and pastoral staff, is led by two of the consecrating bishops through the church, and he blesses the congregation.[144]

---

[140] See OB, no. 33.

[141] See OB, no. 35.

[142] See OB, no. 5.

[143] See OB, no. 37.

[144] See OB, no. 38.

595   After the hymn, the new bishop may stand at the altar or, if he is in his own church, at the chair (cathedra), and address the people briefly.[145]

596   Afterward the bishop who presided at the eucharistic liturgy gives the blessing. Facing the people and wearing the miter, he says, The Lord be with you. Then one of the deacons may give the invitation before the blessing. With hands outstretched over the people, the bishop says the invocations belonging to the blessing. Taking the pastoral staff, he then says, May almighty God bless you, as he makes the sign of the cross three times over the people.
      The text for the blessing invocations varies depending on who presides, the newly ordained bishop or the principal consecrator.

597   After the blessing and the dismissal of the people by the deacon, the procession returns to the vesting room (sacristy) in the usual way.[146]

---

[145] See OB, no. 38.
[146] See OB, no. 40.

Chapter 3

SACRAMENT OF MARRIAGE

Introduction

598 Mindful of Christ the Lord's attendance at the wedding feast of Cana, the bishop should make it his concern to bless occasionally the marriages of his people, and particularly those of the poor.

To prevent his participation from bearing the mark of favoritism[147] or from being a mere sign of outward show, it should be the bishop's normal practice not to assist at marriages in a private chapel or home but in the cathedral or parish church. In this way the ecclesial character of the celebration of the sacrament will more surely stand out and the local community will have the opportunity to participate in the celebration.

599 For the celebration of marriage, in addition to the usual requisites for the nuptial blessing imparted by a presbyter, the miter and pastoral staff should be made ready.

600 The bishop should be assisted by at least one presbyter, who as a rule will be the parish priest (pastor), and at least one deacon, along with several ministers.

I. Celebration of Marriage Within Mass

601 If the bishop himself celebrates the Mass, he wears Mass vestments and uses the miter and pastoral staff. If a presbyter concelebrates, he also wears Mass vestments.

If the bishop presides at the Mass but does not celebrate, he wears an alb, pectoral cross, stole, and white cope, and uses the miter and pastoral staff.

A deacon wears the vestments of his order. The other ministers wear an alb or other lawfully approved vesture.

In addition to the requisites for the celebration of Mass, the following should be provided:

a. *Rite of Marriage;*
b. vessel of holy water with sprinkler;
c. rings for the bridegroom and bride;
d. cup large enough for communion under both kinds.

---

[147] See SC, art. 32: DOL 1, no. 32.

602   At the appointed time the parish priest (pastor) or other presbyter, vested with a stole over a cassock and surplice or over an alb, or if he is to celebrate, vested for Mass, goes with the ministers to receive the bride and bridegroom at the door of the church or, if more suitable, at the altar. He greets them, then leads them to their places.[148]

Then the bishop goes to the altar and reverences it. The bride and bridegroom are presented to him by the parish priest (pastor) or another presbyter. Meanwhile, the entrance song is sung.

603   On days when ritual Masses are permitted[149] one of the wedding Masses (RM, Ritual Masses, IV. Wedding Mass, 1. For the Celebration of Marriage) may be celebrated, with its proper readings. The vestments for the Mass are white or of some other festive color.

On the days listed in nos. 1-4 of the table of liturgical days, the Mass of the day is celebrated, with the nuptial blessing included and, as circumstances suggest, the proper solemn blessing.

But if the Mass in which the sacrament of marriage is celebrated is a regular parish Mass, the Mass of the day is celebrated, even on the Sundays of the Christmas season and of Ordinary Time.

When the ritual Mass is not celebrated, one of the readings may be chosen from those provided for this ritual Mass in the *Lectionary for Mass*, except on those days listed in nos. 1-4 of the table of liturgical days.[150]

604   When a marriage is celebrated during Advent or Lent or on other days of penance, the parish priest (pastor) should advise the couple to take into consideration the special nature of these liturgical seasons.[151]

605   The introductory rites and the liturgy of the word take place in the usual way.

606   After the gospel reading, the bishop, seated and with miter and pastoral staff (unless he decides otherwise), gives the homily, drawn from the sacred text. He speaks about the mystery of Christian marriage, the dignity of wedded love, the grace of the sacrament, and the responsibilities of married people.[152]

---

[148] See The Roman Ritual, *Rite of Marriage*, English ed., 1969 (hereafter, RMar), no. 19.

[149] See Appendix III of this *Ceremonial*.

[150] See Appendix II of this *Ceremonial*; LM, nos. 801-805 (Ritual Masses, IV. Wedding Mass).

[151] See RMar, Introduction, no. 11: DOL 349, no. 2979.

[152] See RMar, no. 22.

607   After the homily, the bishop, with miter and pastoral staff, stands before the bride and bridegroom and questions them about their freedom, faithfulness to each other, and the acceptance and upbringing of children. He then invites the couple to declare their consent.[153]

608   Putting aside the pastoral staff (and also the miter if he uses the alternative, deprecatory formulary of blessing), the bishop blesses the rings and, as circumstances suggest, sprinkles them with holy water and hands them to the bridegroom and bride, who place them on each other's ring finger.[154]

609   When called for by the rubrics, the profession of faith is said; the general intercessions take place in the usual way.

610   In Eucharistic Prayer I there is a commemoration of the bride and bridegroom, in the formulary provided in *The Roman Missal* (*Sacramentary*) among the Ritual Masses (IV. Wedding Mass).

611   After the Lord's Prayer, the embolism Deliver us, Lord is omitted. The bishop, if he is celebrant of the eucharist, otherwise the presbyter who is the celebrant, faces the bride and bridegroom and, with hands joined, invites the assembly to pray: My dear friends, let us turn to the Lord. All pray silently for a short while. Then, with hands outstretched, the bishop pronounces the prayer of blessing, Father, by your power (or one of the other prayers of blessing provided in the *Rite of Marriage*).[155]

612   The married couple, their parents, witnesses, and relatives may receive communion under both kinds.[156]

613   In place of the usual blessing of the people at the end of Mass, the bishop uses one of the blessing formularies provided in the *Rite of Marriage* for this Mass.[157]
      With miter and with hands outstretched, the bishop greets the people, saying, The Lord be with you. One of the deacons may then give the invitation before the blessing. With hands outstretched over the people, the bishop says the blessing invocations. Taking the pastoral staff,

---

[153] See RMar, nos. 24-26.
[154] See RMar, nos. 27-28.
[155] See RMar, no. 33.
[156] See RMar, no. 36.
[157] See RMar, nos. 125-127.

he then pronounces the blessing, as he makes the sign of the cross three times over the people.

The bishop may also impart the blessing by using one of the formularies given in nos. 1120-1121 of this *Ceremonial*.

II. CELEBRATION OF MARRIAGE OUTSIDE MASS

614   The bishop is vested in the way indicated in no. 176 for a Mass at which he presides but does not celebrate. The presbyter assisting him wears a stole over a cassock and surplice or over an alb; the deacon wears the vestments of his order.

615   The bride and bridegroom and the bishop enter the church in the way already indicated in no. 602, while the entrance song is being sung.

616   After the singing, the bishop greets all present and says the opening prayer from *The Roman Missal* (*Sacramentary*) among the Ritual Masses (IV. Wedding Mass) or the *Rite of Marriage*. The liturgy of the word follows in the same way as at Mass.

617   The questions about freedom of choice, the expression of consent, and the exchange of rings take place in the manner already indicated in nos. 607-608.

618   The intercessions follow. Then, omitting the prayer that concludes the intercessions, the bishop, with hands outstretched, blesses the bride and bridegroom. He uses the text provided in the *Rite of Marriage* for this blessing within Mass.[158]

The Lord's Prayer is then recited.

619   If communion is to be given within this rite, the deacon takes the ciborium or pyx with the body of the Lord, places it on the altar, and, with the bishop, genuflects. Then the bishop introduces the Lord's Prayer, which all recite together.

Then the bishop genuflects. Taking the host, he raises it slightly over the ciborium or pyx and, facing those who will receive communion, says, This is the Lamb of God.

Communion is distributed as at Mass.

After communion, a period of silence may be observed, or a psalm or song of praise may be sung. Then the prayer Lord, we who have shared

---

[158] See RMar, nos. 33, 120-121.

the food of your table, provided in the *Rite of Marriage,* or some other suitable prayer is said.[159]

620   The bishop then gives the final blessing in the manner already indicated in no. 613. The deacon says the dismissal formula, Go in peace, and all reply, Thanks be to God, and leave.

---

[159] See RMar, no. 123; HCWE, nos. 50 and 210-222.

CHAPTER 4

SACRAMENT OF PENANCE

INTRODUCTION

621   The Church is minister of the mystery of reconciliation that Christ brought to fulfillment through his death and resurrection; it shares in the sufferings of Christ by patience in its own trials and continually seeks the conversion proposed by the Gospel through the practice of charity and mercy, thus becoming a sign in the world of conversion to God. This sign of conversion stands out in the Church's life and in its celebration of the liturgy as the faithful confess their sinfulness and ask for pardon from God and from their brothers and sisters in many ways: in services of penance, in the proclamation of the word of God, in prayers of petition, and in the penitential elements of the eucharistic celebration.

But it is in the sacrament of penance that the faithful "obtain from God's mercy pardon for having offended him and at the same time reconciliation with the Church, which they have wounded by their sins and which by charity, example, and prayer seeks their conversion."[160]

The Church carries out the ministry of the sacrament of penance through the ministry of bishops and priests. By preaching the word of God they call the faithful to conversion; in the name of Christ and by the power of the Holy Spirit they declare and grant forgiveness of sins.

In the exercise of this ministry presbyters act in communion with the bishop and share in his power and office, as the one who regulates the penitential discipline.[161]

It is altogether fitting, then, for the bishop to take part in the ministry of penance, at least in such solemn celebrations as those during Lent and on the occasion of a pastoral visitation or of other special situations in the life of the people of God.

This chapter provides a description of penitential celebrations, both those that lead up to sacramental absolution and those that take the form of a penitential service.

I. RITE FOR RECONCILIATION OF SEVERAL PENITENTS WITH INDIVIDUAL CONFESSION AND ABSOLUTION

622   Over the alb the bishop wears a pectoral cross, stole, and cope of purple or of another penitential color, and he uses the simple miter and the pastoral staff.

---

[160] See LG, no. 11: DOL 4, no. 141.

[161] See The Roman Ritual, *Rite of Penance*, English ed., 1974 (hereafter, RPen), no. 9, a: DOL 368, no. 3074. See LG, no. 26: DOL 4, no. 146.

A sufficient number of presbyters for the number of penitents should accompany the bishop; they wear a stole over a cassock and surplice or over an alb.

A deacon should assist the bishop; he wears the vestments of his order; other ministers wear an alb or other lawfully approved vesture.

623   When the faithful have assembled, they may sing a psalm, antiphon, or some other suitable song as the bishop, presbyters, and other ministers enter the church.[162]

624   When the bishop reaches the altar, he makes the proper reverence, then goes to the chair (cathedra), and the presbyters go to the seats provided for them. Once the singing has ended, the bishop, without miter, stands and greets the people. Then the bishop himself, one of the presbyters, or a deacon speaks briefly about the importance and purpose of the celebration and the order of the service.[163]

625   The bishop invites all to pray. All pray in silence for a brief period. Then the bishop sings or says the opening prayer.

626   The celebration of the word follows, comprised of one or more readings chosen to fit the occasion from the special lectionary provided in the *Rite of Penance*. If there are several readings, a psalm or some other suitable song or even a period of silence should intervene between them so that all may understand the word of God more deeply and give it their heartfelt assent. If there is only one reading, it is preferable that it be a gospel reading.[164]

627   The bishop, with miter and pastoral staff (unless he decides otherwise), gives the homily. The homily is based on the texts of the readings and should lead the penitents to examine their consciences and renew their lives.

A period of time may be spent in making an examination of conscience and in arousing true sorrow for sins. One of the presbyters or a deacon may help the faithful by brief statements or a kind of litany, taking into consideration their circumstances and age.[165]

---

[162] See RPen, no. 48.
[163] See RPen, no. 49.
[164] See RPen, no. 51.
[165] See RPen, nos. 52-53.

628   The actual rite of reconciliation follows. Putting aside the miter and pastoral staff, the bishop stands and all stand with him. Except during the Easter season or on a Sunday, the deacon invites all to kneel or bow; then all join in saying a general formulary for confession (for example, I confess to almighty God). Then, at the invitation of the deacon, all stand to respond to the intercessions provided in the *Rite of Penance* or to sing a suitable song. The Lord's Prayer is always added at the end. The bishop says the prayer that concludes the intercessions.[166]

629   Then the bishop and presbyters go to the places appointed for confessions. The penitents go to them for individual confession and confess their sins. Each one receives and accepts a fitting act of satisfaction and is absolved.
        After hearing the confession and offering suitable counsel, the confessor extends his hands, or at least his right hand, over the penitent's head and gives absolution. Everything else that is customary in individual confession is omitted.[167]

630   When the individual confessions have been completed, the bishop returns to the chair (cathedra), where, without miter, he stands, and the presbyters stand near him. All rise, and the bishop invites the assembly to offer thanks and encourages them to do good works that will proclaim the grace of repentance in the life of the entire community and each of its members. Afterward, it is fitting for all to sing a psalm or a hymn of praise and thanksgiving.[168]

631   After this song, the bishop, without miter, stands and faces the people and, with hands outstretched, says the prayer Almighty and merciful God or some other similar prayer.[169]

632   Finally, putting on the miter, the bishop greets the people, saying, The Lord be with you. Then a deacon may invite all to receive the blessing. With hands outstretched over the people, the bishop says the blessing invocations. Then, taking the pastoral staff, he says, May almighty God bless you, as he makes the sign of the cross three times over the people.
        The bishop may also use the formularies provided in nos. 1120-1121 to bestow the blessing.

---

[166] See RPen, no. 54.
[167] See RPen, no. 19 (DOL 368, no. 3084) and no. 55.
[168] See RPen, no. 56.
[169] See RPen, no. 57.

Then the deacon dismisses the assembly, saying, The Lord has freed you from your sins. Go in peace, and all reply, Thanks be to God, and leave.

II. Rite for Reconciliation of Several Penitents with General Confession and Absolution

633   For the reconciliation of several penitents with general confession and absolution, in the cases provided for in the law, everything is done as described already for the reconciliation of several penitents with individual absolution, but with the following changes.[170]

634   After the homily or as part of the homily, the bishop explains to the faithful who wish to receive general absolution that they should be properly disposed. They should repent of their sins and resolve to turn away from these sins, to make up for any scandal and harm they may have caused, and to confess individually at the proper time each of the serious sins which cannot now be confessed. Some form of satisfaction should be proposed to all, to which they may wish to add some further act of expiation.[171]

635   Then the deacon invites the penitents who wish to receive absolution to indicate this by some kind of sign.[172]

636   Then the penitents kneel or bow and say a general formulary for confession (for example, I confess to almighty God).

637   A litany or a suitable song may follow, and at the end the Lord's Prayer is added, as indicated in no. 628.

638   After receiving the miter, the bishop faces the penitents and pronounces the sacramental formulary of absolution, God, the Father of mercies.[173]

639   The bishop invites all to thank God and to acknowledge his mercy. After a suitable song or hymn, he blesses the people, and, as already indicated in no. 632, the deacon dismisses them.[174]

---

[170] See RPen, no. 60.
[171] See RPen, no. 60; see CIC, can. 962 and can. 963.
[172] See RPen, no. 61.
[173] See RPen, no. 62.
[174] See RPen, no. 63.

III. PENITENTIAL SERVICES
WITHOUT CONFESSION OR ABSOLUTION

640   Penitential services are gatherings of the people of God to hear
God's word as an invitation to conversion and renewal of life and as the
message of our liberation from sin through Christ's death and resurrection. They possess great value in preparing the faithful to celebrate the
sacrament of reconciliation.[175]

641   The bishop may preside wearing the vesture already indicated in
no. 622 or wearing simply a rochet and mozzetta, with a pectoral cross
and stole.

642   The celebration is carried out by use of the rite already described
for the reconciliation of several penitents with individual confession and
absolution, up to the Lord's Prayer that follows the recitation of the general formulary for confession and the litanic intercessions.

643   Individual confessions are omitted, and the bishop concludes the
intercessions with a suitable prayer, for example, Almighty and merciful
God (*Rite of Penance*, no. 57). Then the bishop blesses the people and,
as already indicated in no. 632, the deacon says the dismissal.[176]

---

[175] See RPen, Introduction, no. 36: DOL 368, no. 3101.

[176] See RPen, Appendix II, "Sample Penitential Services."

CHAPTER 5

SACRAMENT OF ANOINTING OF THE SICK

INTRODUCTION

644   The evangelist Mark records that the apostles sent by Christ anointed the sick with oil.[177] This is not surprising, since in biblical and Christian tradition "anointing with oil is a sign of the mercy of God, of the healing of disease, and of the enlightenment of the heart."[178]

Even though "other concerns may prevent them from going in person to visit all the sick," as Pope St. Innocent I observes,[179] bishops, the successors of the apostles, carry out this ministry through the ministry of their presbyters. In the tradition of the Latin Church, priests anoint the sick with oil that, apart from cases of necessity, is blessed by the bishop.

645   But, if possible, the bishop should preside whenever the sacrament of the anointing of the sick is celebrated at large gatherings of the faithful, for example, during a pilgrimage or at other assemblies of the sick of a diocese, city, or confraternity. This chapter provides a description of such a communal celebration.[180]

646   To ensure the pastoral effectiveness of this kind of celebration, there should be opportunity beforehand for the preparation of the sick who are to receive the sacrament of anointing, of other sick persons who may be present, and of others of the faithful who will take part in the celebration.

The full participation of those present must be fostered by every means, especially through the use of appropriate songs, in order to inspire the assembly with a sense of their unity, to enhance their shared prayer, and to express in the celebration the Easter joy that is proper to this sacrament.[181]

647   If a very large number are to be anointed, the bishop may appoint presbyters to share with him in the celebration of the sacrament.

---

[177] See Mark 6:13.

[178] See J.A. Cramer, *Catenae Graecorum Patrum in Novum Testamentum* (Oxford, 1838-1844), vol. 1, p. 324.

[179] See *Epistola* 25:8, 11: PL 20, 560.

[180] See The Roman Ritual, *Pastoral Care of the Sick: Rites of Anointing and Viaticum*, English ed., 1982 (hereafter, PCS), no. 132.

[181] See PCS, nos. 98, 108, 112.

If the anointing takes place within Mass, it is fitting that these presbyters concelebrate with the bishop.

It is also fitting that at least one deacon as well as other ministers assist the bishop.

I. Anointing of the Sick Within Mass

648   On days when ritual Masses are permitted,[182] the Mass for the sick (RM, Masses and Prayers for Various Needs and Occasions, 32. For the Sick) or the Mass from *Pastoral Care of the Sick* (nos. 135-148) may be celebrated, with the readings provided in the *Lectionary for Mass* for the anointing of the sick.[183] The vestments for the Mass are white.

If the ritual Mass is not celebrated, one of the readings may be chosen from those provided for the anointing of the sick in the *Lectionary for Mass*.

But on the days listed in nos. 1-4 of the table of liturgical days,[184] the Mass of the day is celebrated, with its proper readings. For the final blessing the formulary proper to the rite of anointing the sick is used.

649   The following should be provided:

a. *Pastoral Care of the Sick: Rites of Anointing and Viaticum;*
b. vessels with oil of the sick;
c. requisites for the washing of hands;
d. a cup large enough for communion under both kinds.

The bishop and the presbyters wear the vestments required for Mass. The deacon wears the vestments of his order; other ministers wear albs or other lawfully approved vesture.

If the presbyters do not concelebrate with the bishop, they wear a stole over a cassock and surplice or over an alb.

650   Before the entrance of the bishop, the sick are welcomed by those appointed for this and are settled in their places.[185]

651   The introductory rites and the liturgy of the word take place in the usual way. After the gospel reading, the bishop, seated and with miter

---

[182] See Appendix III of this *Ceremonial*.

[183] See LM, nos. 790-795 (Ritual Masses, Pastoral Care of the Sick and the Dying, 1. Anointing of the Sick).

[184] See Appendix II of this *Ceremonial*.

[185] See PCS, nos. 109 and 135.

and pastoral staff (unless he decides otherwise), gives the homily. He shows from the sacred text the meaning of illness in the history of salvation and of the grace given by the sacrament of anointing.

652   The celebration of the sacrament of the anointing of the sick begins after the homily and may take either of two forms, as indicated schematically in the following outlines:

A	B
LITANY	LAYING ON OF HANDS
LAYING ON OF HANDS	BLESSING OF OIL
BLESSING OF OIL	ANOINTING
ANOINTING	LITANY AND CONCLUDING PRAYER
CONCLUDING PRAYER	

The details of these forms of the rite are given in nos. 653-658.

653   After the homily, the bishop, putting aside the miter, stands and introduces the litany, as given in *Pastoral Care of the Sick*,[186] if it is to be said at this point. Then the bishop and the presbyters who are to take part in the anointing lay hands in silence on some of the sick.

654   In a celebration of this kind the bishop may bless the oil of the sick. He does this immediately after the laying on of hands by saying the prayer God of all consolation.

If the oil is already blessed, the bishop says the prayer of thanksgiving over it, Praise to you, God, the almighty Father.[187]

655   After this the bishop sits, wearing the miter. The deacon brings him the vessel or vessels with the blessed oil, and the bishop hands them to the presbyters who will join him in the anointing.

Then the bishop and the presbyters go to the sick and anoint each one on the forehead and hands, saying the sacramental formulary, Through this holy anointing, once for each person.[188]

656   After the formulary has been heard by the congregation at least once, there may be singing during the rest of the anointing.

657   When the anointing has been completed, the bishop returns to the chair and the presbyters to their seats for the washing of hands.

---

[186] See PCS, no. 138.

[187] See PCS, no. 140.

[188] See PCS, no. 141.

658   Afterward the bishop, standing without miter and with hands out-stretched, says the concluding prayer of the rite of anointing, choosing the most suitable text from those provided in *Pastoral Care of the Sick*.[189] (If the litany has not already been said, the bishop introduces it immediately after the washing of hands and then says one of the concluding prayers.)

659   The Mass then continues in the usual way with the preparation of the gifts. The sick and all others present may receive communion under both kinds.

660   At the end of Mass, in place of the usual blessing, the bishop may use one of the solemn blessings provided in *Pastoral Care of the Sick*.[190] In this case the bishop, taking the miter, greets the people, saying, The Lord be with you. Then a deacon may invite the people to receive the blessing. With hands outstretched over the people, the bishop says the invocations of the blessing. He then takes the pastoral staff and says, May almighty God bless you, as he makes the sign of the cross three times over the people.
    The bishop may also use the formularies provided in nos. 1120-1121 to bestow the blessing.

II. ANOINTING OF THE SICK OUTSIDE MASS

661   The bishop wears over an alb a pectoral cross, stole, and white cope and he uses the miter and pastoral staff. Presbyters who may join him wear a stole over a cassock and surplice or over an alb. A deacon wears the vestments of his order.

662   Before the entrance of the bishop, the sick are welcomed by those appointed for this and are settled in their places.[191]

663   As a suitable song is sung, the bishop enters the church, reverences the altar, then goes to the chair. When the singing has ended, he greets the sick people and the others present.

664   Next there is a liturgy of the word, in the same manner and with the same texts as already indicated in nos. 648 and 651 for an anointing within Mass.

---

[189] See PCS, no. 142.
[190] See PCS, no. 147.
[191] See PCS, nos. 108-130.

665   The rite of anointing takes place in the manner already described in nos. 652-657. But after the anointing and before the concluding prayer, the bishop introduces the Lord's Prayer, which all say together.

666   The bishop gives the final blessing in the manner already described in no. 660. After the blessing, the deacon dismisses the people, saying, Go in the peace of Christ, and all reply, Thanks be to God. It is recommended that the celebration conclude with a suitable song.

PART VI

SACRAMENTALS

CHAPTER 1

BLESSING OF AN ABBOT

INTRODUCTION

667   As the representative of Christ in the monastery, the abbot should act as father, teacher, and model of the Christian and monastic life. Therefore he ought not to teach or ordain or command anything which is against the law of the Lord; he should stand for what is good and holy by action more than just by word and be more concerned to serve than to rule. With moderation but with firmness he should lead his community to follow Christ, in such a way that the monks of his monastery may be a living expression of the Gospel in their prayer and in their fraternal service to one another.[1]

668   The blessing of an abbot is usually celebrated by the bishop of the place where the monastery is situated.[2] In this way the bishop has a part in one of the high points of monastic life. By example, work, and prayer, monasteries should contribute solid support to the life of the particular Church; correspondingly, the bishop should regard the monasteries of his diocese as an important part of his pastoral office, even though he must not interfere in their internal government.

669   For a good reason, and with the consent of the bishop of the place, the abbot-elect may receive the blessing from another bishop or abbot.[3]

670   Only an abbot who has been canonically elected and actually governs a monastery may receive the abbatial blessing.

671   It is most desirable that the celebration of the blessing take place in the church of the abbot's own monastery.

672   The blessing of an abbot should take place on a Sunday or major feast day; for pastoral reasons another day may be chosen.[4]

673   On days when a ritual Mass is permitted,[5] the ritual Mass for the blessing of an abbot (RM, Ritual Masses, Blessing of an Abbot or Ab-

---

[1] See *Rule of Saint Benedict*, chs. 2 and 64.

[2] See *The Roman Pontifical*, Part IV. Blessing of Persons, ch. 14, Blessing of an Abbot (hereafter, BAb), no. 2: DOL 399, no. 3278.

[3] See BAb, no. 2: DOL 399, no. 3278.

[4] See BAb, no. 1: DOL 399, no. 3277.

[5] See Appendix III of this *Ceremonial*.

bess), with its proper readings,[6] may be celebrated; the vestments for the Mass are white or of some other festive color.

But even if the ritual Mass is not celebrated, one of the readings may be chosen from those provided for this Mass.

But on the days listed in nos. 1-4 of the table of liturgical days,[7] the Mass of the day, with its proper readings, is celebrated.

674 Two religious from his monastery assist the abbot-elect.[8] If they are presbyters and are to concelebrate the Mass, they wear Mass vestments; otherwise they wear either choir dress or a surplice over the habit.

675 It is desirable that other abbots and priests present concelebrate with the bishop and abbot-elect.[9]

676 The bishop and the concelebrants wear the vestments required for Mass, but the bishop also wears a dalmatic. The abbot-elect wears Mass vestments, but in addition under the chasuble he wears a pectoral cross and a dalmatic.

The deacon wears the vestments proper to his order. Other ministers wear the alb or other lawfully approved vesture.

677 Besides the requisites for the concelebration of Mass, the following should be prepared:

   a. *The Roman Pontifical*;

   b. the Rule;

   c. pastoral staff for the abbot-elect;

   d. ring and miter for the abbot-elect, if these are to be presented to him;[10]

   e. cup large enough for communion under both kinds.

678 The blessing of the ring, pastoral staff, and miter of the abbot-elect normally take place at some convenient time before the actual blessing of the abbot-elect.[11]

679 As a rule the blessing of the abbot takes place at the chair (cathedra). To enable the faithful to participate more fully, a chair for the

---

[6] See LM, nos. 806-810 (Ritual Masses, VII. Blessing of Abbots and Abbesses).

[7] See Appendix II of this *Ceremonial*.

[8] See BAb, no. 3: DOL 399, no. 3279.

[9] See BAb, no. 4: DOL 399, no. 3280.

[10] See BAb, no. 8: DOL 399, no. 3284.

[11] See BAb, no. 7: DOL 399, no. 3284. See *The Roman Pontifical*, Appendix V, Blessing of Pontifical Insignia, p. 383.

bishop may be placed before the altar or in some other suitable place; the seats for the abbot-elect and the religious assisting him should be so arranged in the sanctuary that the religious and the faithful all have a clear view of the liturgical ceremony.[12]

DESCRIPTION OF THE RITE

680   The entrance procession is formed in the usual way. The deacon, carrying the Book of the Gospels, goes first, then concelebrating presbyters, the abbot-elect between his two assistants, then the bishop, with miter and pastoral staff, followed by the two deacons assisting him.

681   The introductory rites and the liturgy of the word, up to the end of the gospel reading, take place in the usual way.

682   The blessing begins after the gospel reading. The bishop, with miter, either goes to the special seat prepared for him or he sits at the chair (cathedra). All in the assembly also sit. The abbot-elect is escorted by his assistants to the bishop, to whom he makes a sign of reverence. One of the assistants presents the abbot-elect to the bishop, saying, Most Reverend Father, in the name of our community, and the bishop asks, Has he been duly elected? The monk replies, We know and testify that he has. The bishop replies, Thanks be to God.[13]

683   Taking the texts of the biblical readings as the starting point, the bishop briefly addresses the people, the monks, and the abbot-elect on the office and duties of an abbot.[14]

684   After the homily, the abbot-elect rises and stands in front of the bishop, who questions him in the words that begin, My dear brother. To each question the abbot-elect replies, I will. After the questioning, the bishop says, May the Lord strengthen your resolve, and all reply, Amen.[15]

685   Putting aside the miter, the bishop stands and all stand with him. The bishop, with hands joined, faces the people and invites them to pray, saying, Dearly beloved, God has chosen N.

---

[12] See BAb, no. 10: DOL 399, no. 3286.

[13] See BAb, nos. 16-18.

[14] See BAb, no. 19.

[15] See BAb, no. 20.

Then the deacon says, Let us kneel, and all kneel in their places, but the abbot-elect prostrates himself. But during the Easter season and on Sundays the deacon does not say, Let us kneel, and all in the assembly remain standing, except the abbot-elect, who prostrates himself. The cantors then begin the Litany of the Saints; they may add, at the proper places, names of other saints (for example, the patron saint, the titular of the church, the founder of the church, the patron saint of the abbot-elect, the saints of the order); they may also add petitions suitable to the occasion, since the litany takes the place of the general intercessions. After the litany, the deacon (if he had given the invitation to kneel before the litany) says, Let us stand, and all stand.[16]

686 The abbot-elect comes before the bishop and kneels. The bishop, without miter and with hands outstretched, says one of the prayers of blessing, chosen from those provided in *The Roman Pontifical*.[17]

687 After the prayer of blessing, the bishop, wearing the miter, sits, and all in the assembly also sit. The new abbot comes before the bishop, and the bishop gives him the Rule, saying, Take this Rule. Then if ring, miter, and pastoral staff are to be presented, the bishop places the ring on the ring finger of the new abbot's right hand, saying, Take this ring; in silence he puts the miter on the new abbot's head; finally, he hands the new abbot the pastoral staff, saying, Take this shepherd's staff.[18]

688 Lastly, the new abbot puts aside his pastoral staff and receives the sign of peace from the bishop and from other abbots present.

If circumstances permit, the religious and presbyters present also exchange the sign of peace with the new abbot.

689 The Mass continues in the usual way. The profession of faith is said when called for by the rubrics; the general intercessions are omitted.

690 In the liturgy of the eucharist the newly blessed abbot takes first place among the concelebrating presbyters. (But if the prelate who gave the blessing is not a bishop and if the blessing takes place in the church of the new abbot's monastery, then he himself may preside at the liturgy of the eucharist.)

691 The parents, relatives, and friends of the new abbot, as well as the members of his monastery, may receive communion under both kinds.

---

[16] See BAb, nos. 21-22.

[17] See BAb, no. 23.

[18] See BAb, nos. 24-27.

692   At the end of Mass the one who presided in the liturgy of the eucharist says, The Lord be with you, and then the blessing; the deacon dismisses the assembly in the usual way.

693   After the dismissal, as circumstances suggest, the *Te Deum* or some other suitable song may be sung. During the singing all who were in the entrance procession return in the same order to the vesting room (sacristy) and go their way in peace.

If the new abbot has jurisdiction over a territory, the *Te Deum* or some other suitable song is sung at the end of the prayer after communion. Meanwhile, the new abbot is led through the church by his assistants and he blesses all present.

After the hymn, the new abbot, wearing his miter and holding his pastoral staff, may stand at the altar or at the chair (cathedra) and address the people briefly. The Mass concludes in the usual way.[19]

---

[19] See BAb, no 32.

Chapter 2

BLESSING OF AN ABBESS

Introduction

694 An abbess, chosen by her community, should be for her nuns a model of the Christian and monastic life. Therefore she ought not to teach or ordain or command anything which is against the law of the Lord; she should stand for what is good and holy by action more than just by word and be more concerned to serve than to rule. With moderation but with firmness she should lead her community to follow Christ, in such a way that the nuns of her monastery may be a living expression of the Gospel in their prayer and in their sisterly service to one another.[20]

695 The blessing of an abbess is performed as a rule by the bishop of the place where the monastery is situated. For a good reason, and with the consent of the bishop of the place, the abbess-elect may receive the blessing from another bishop or an abbot.[21]

696 The blessing should take place on a Sunday or major feast day; for pastoral reasons another day may be chosen.[22]

697 On days when a ritual Mass is permitted,[23] the ritual Mass for the blessing of an abbess (RM, Ritual Masses, Blessing of an Abbot or Abbess), with its proper readings,[24] may be celebrated; the vestments for the Mass are white or of some other festive color.

But even if the ritual Mass is not celebrated, one of the readings may be chosen from those provided for this Mass.

But on the days listed in nos. 1-4 of the table of liturgical days,[25] the Mass of the day, with its proper readings, is celebrated.

698 The abbess-elect, assisted by two religious from her monastery, takes her place in the sanctuary (chancel), outside the enclosure, so that she may be near the bishop who gives the blessing and so that all present, nuns and faithful, may see the celebration and take part in it.

---

[20] See *Rule of Saint Benedict*, chs. 2 and 64.

[21] See *The Roman Pontifical*, Part IV. Blessing of Persons, ch. 15, Rite of Blessing of an Abbess (hereafter, BAbs), no. 2: DOL 399, no. 3288.

[22] See BAbs, no. 1: DOL 399, no. 3287.

[23] See Appendix III of this *Ceremonial*.

[24] See LM, nos. 806-810 (Ritual Masses, VII. Blessing of Abbots and Abbesses).

[25] See Appendix II of this *Ceremonial*.

The blessing usually takes place at the chair (cathedra). To enable the faithful to participate more fully, a chair for the bishop may be placed before the altar or in some other suitable place.[26]

699   It is appropriate that priests who are present concelebrate with the bishop; there should be at least one deacon in assistance and other ministers.

700   Besides the vestments and other requisites for the celebration of Mass and a dalmatic for the bishop, there should also be prepared:
   a. *The Roman Pontifical;*
   b. the Rule and, if it is to be presented, the ring;
   c. cup large enough for communion under both kinds.[27]

DESCRIPTION OF THE RITE

701   Before the celebration begins, the bishop, accompanied by the concelebrants, ministers, and clergy goes to the entrance of the enclosure. The abbess-elect, with the two nuns assisting her, leaves the enclosure and takes her place in the procession to the church immediately in front of the bishop.[28]

702   The introductory rites and the liturgy of the word, up to the end of the gospel reading, take place in the usual way.[29]

703   The blessing begins after the gospel reading. The bishop, wearing the miter, goes to the special seat prepared for him or he sits in the usual chair (cathedra). All in the assembly also sit. The abbess-elect is escorted by her assistants to the bishop, to whom she makes a sign of reverence. One of those assisting her presents the abbess-elect to the bishop, saying, Most Reverend Father, in the name of our community, as indicated in *The Roman Pontifical.*
   The bishop then asks, Has she been duly elected? The nun replies, We know and testify that she has. The bishop replies, Thanks be to God.

[26] See BAbs, nos. 3 and 5: DOL 399, nos. 3289 and 3291.
[27] See BAbs, no. 4: DOL 399, no. 3290.
[28] See BAbs, no. 6.
[29] See BAbs, no. 7.
[30] See BAbs, nos. 11-13.

704   Taking the texts of the biblical readings as the starting point, the bishop briefly addresses the people, the nuns, and the abbess-elect on the office and duties of an abbess.[31]

705   After the homily, the abbess-elect rises and stands in front of the bishop, who questions her in the words that begin, Will you persevere? To each question the abbess-elect replies, I will. After the questioning the bishop says, May the Lord strengthen your resolve, and all reply, Amen.[32]

706   Putting aside the miter, the bishop stands, and all stand with him. The bishop, with hands joined, faces the people and invites them to pray, saying, Dearly beloved, God has chosen N.
    Then the deacon says, Let us kneel, and all kneel in their places, but, where it is customary, the abbess-elect prostrates herself. But during the Easter season and on Sundays, the deacon does not say, Let us kneel, and all remain standing, except the abbess-elect, who kneels or, where it is customary, prostrates herself. The cantors then begin the Litany of the Saints; they may add, at the proper places, names of other saints (for example, the patron saint, the titular of the church, the founder of the church, the patron saint of the abbess-elect, the saints of the order); they may also add petitions suitable to the occasion, since the litany takes the place of the general intercessions. After the litany, the deacon (if he had given the invitation to kneel before the litany) says, Let us stand, and all stand.[33]

707   The abbess-elect comes before the bishop and kneels. The bishop, without miter and with hands outstretched, says one of the prayers of blessing, chosen from those provided in *The Roman Pontifical*.[34]

708   After the prayer of blessing, the bishop, wearing the miter, sits, and all in the assembly also sit. The new abbess comes before the bishop, and the bishop gives her the Rule, saying, Take this Rule.[35]

709   The ring is not presented if the abbess has already received it on the day of her profession and consecration. If the abbess has not previ-

---

[31] See BAbs, no. 14.
[32] See BAbs, no. 15.
[33] See BAbs, nos. 16-17.
[34] See BAbs, no. 18.
[35] See BAbs, no. 19.

ously received the ring, the bishop may place it on the ring finger of her right hand, saying, Take this ring.[36]

710 Then the new abbess makes a profound bow to the bishop and returns to her place with her two assistants.[37]

711 The Mass continues in the usual way. The profession of faith is said when called for by the rubrics; the general intercessions are omitted.

712 The parents, relatives, and friends of the new abbess, as well as the members of her monastery, may receive communion under both kinds.

713 After the bishop has given the final blessing, the deacon dismisses the people in the usual way.

714 After the Mass, as circumstances suggest, the *Te Deum* or some other suitable song may be sung. During the singing the bishop leads the abbess to the enclosure. If the bishop is the local Ordinary and has immediate jurisdiction over the nuns, he leads her to her place in choir and seats her there, unless the abbess has already accepted this sign of her authority immediately after her election.[38]

---

[36] See BAbs, no. 20.
[37] See BAbs, no. 21.
[38] See BAbs, no. 22.

CHAPTER 3

CONSECRATION TO A LIFE OF VIRGINITY

INTRODUCTION

715   From age-old tradition a consecrated virgin is a surpassing sign of the Church's love for Christ and an eschatological image of the world to come and of the heavenly Bride of Christ.[39]

716   Consecration to a life of virginity may be received by nuns or by women living in the world.[40]

717   It is fitting for the consecration to take place during the octave of Easter, on solemnities, especially those which celebrate the incarnation, on Sundays, or on feasts of the Blessed Virgin Mary, holy virgins, or saints distinguished in the living of the religious life.[41]

718   On a day scheduled close to the day of the rite of consecration, or at least on the day before the consecration, the candidates are presented to the bishop so that the father of the diocese may begin a pastoral dialogue with his spiritual daughters.[42]

719   As occasion offers, and especially to promote an esteem for chastity, to deepen understanding of the Church, and to encourage greater attendance of the people, the faithful should be notified of the celebration in good time.[43]

720   The minister of the rite of consecration is the diocesan bishop. But with his consent some other bishop may preside at the rite.[44]

721   On days when a ritual Mass is permitted,[45] the ritual Mass for consecration to a life of virginity (RM, Ritual Masses, V. Consecration to a

---

[39] See *The Roman Pontifical*, Part IV. Blessing of Persons, Consecration to a Life of Virginity (hereafter, CLV), Introduction, no. 1: DOL 395, no. 3253.

[40] See CLV, Introduction, no. 3: DOL 395, no. 3255.

[41] See CLV, A. Consecration to a Life of Virginity for Women Living in the World (hereafter, A), no. 1; B. Consecration to a Life of Virginity together with Religious Profession for Nuns (hereafter, B), no. 39.

[42] See CLV, A, no. 2; CLV, B, no. 40.

[43] See CLV, A, no. 4.

[44] See CLV, Introduction, no. 6: DOL 395, no. 3258.

[45] See Appendix III of this *Ceremonial*.

Life of Virginity), with its proper readings,[46] may be celebrated; the vestments for the Mass are white or of some other festive color.

But even if the ritual Mass is not celebrated, one of the readings may be chosen from those provided for this Mass.

But on the days listed in nos. 1-4 of the table of liturgical days,[47] the Mass of the day, with its proper readings, is celebrated.

I. Consecration to a Life of Virginity for Nuns

722   The consecration of nuns to a life of virginity is celebrated within Mass and ordinarily takes place in the monastery church.[48]

It is desirable that any priests present for the celebration concelebrate with the bishop. It is also desirable that at least one deacon assist the bishop and that there be several other ministers assisting him, in albs or other lawfully approved vesture.

723   Besides the vestments and other requisites for the celebration of Mass, there should also be prepared:

a. *The Roman Pontifical;*

b. veils, rings, or other insignia of consecration or religious profession to be presented in accordance with local rules or customs of the religious family;

c. chair at a suitable place in the sanctuary (chancel) for the superior, if she is to receive the religious profession of the nuns;

d. chairs in the sanctuary (chancel) for the candidates, which should be arranged in such a way that the faithful have a complete view of the liturgical rites;

e. cup large enough for communion under both kinds.

The consecration ordinarily takes place at the chair (cathedra), but to enable the faithful to take part more easily, a chair for the bishop may be placed in front of the altar or at some other convenient place.[49]

724   When the people have assembled and everything is ready, the procession moves through the church to the altar in the usual way, while the choir and people sing the entrance song of the Mass. The candidates

---

[46] See LM, nos. 811-815 (Ritual Masses, VIII. Consecration to a Life of Virginity and Religious Profession).

[47] See Appendix II of this *Ceremonial.*

[48] See CLV, B, no. 41.

[49] See CLV, B, nos. 44 and 47.

may fittingly join in the procession, accompanied by the superior and the novice mistress.[50]

725   When they come to the sanctuary (chancel), all make the customary reverence to the altar. The candidates go to their places in the body of the church, and Mass continues.[51]

726   The introductory rites and the liturgy of the word, up to the end of the gospel reading, take place in the usual way.

727   After the gospel reading, the bishop, with miter and pastoral staff, sits either in the chair (cathedra) or at the chair prepared for the occasion, as the antiphon Be wise: make ready or some other suitable song is sung. The candidates then light their lamps or candles and, accompanied by the novice mistress and other nuns assigned to this task, approach the sanctuary (chancel) and stand outside it.
      When the singing has ended, the bishop calls the candidates: he says or sings, Come, listen to me, and the candidates reply by singing the antiphon Now with all our hearts or some other suitable song. As they sing, the candidates enter the sanctuary (chancel) and take their places in such a way that everyone has a clear view of the liturgical rites. They place their candles in a candlestick or give them to the ministers.[52]

728   All sit, and the bishop gives a short homily to the candidates and the people, developing the scriptural readings and the theme of virginity as a gift and its role in the sanctification of those called to it and in the welfare of the Church and of the whole human family.[53]

729   After the homily, only the candidates stand; the bishop, using the text provided in *The Roman Pontifical*, questions them on their readiness to dedicate themselves to God and to seek perfect charity, according to the rule or constitutions of the religious community.[54]

730   Putting aside the miter and the pastoral staff, the bishop stands, and all stand with him. The bishop, with hands joined, invites all to pray, saying, Dearly beloved, let us pray.

---

[50] See CLV, B, no. 48.
[51] See CLV, B, no. 49.
[52] See CLV, B, nos. 51-52.
[53] See CLV, A, no. 16.
[54] See CLV, B, nos. 55-56.

Then the deacon says, Let us kneel, and the bishop and all present kneel, but, where it is customary, the candidates prostrate themselves.

During the Easter season and on Sundays, the deacon does not say, Let us kneel, and all except the candidates remain standing for the singing of the litany.

The cantors begin the Litany of the Saints; they may add at the proper places the names of those saints especially venerated by the religious community; they may also add petitions suitable to the occasion, since the litany takes the place of the general intercessions.[55]

731   After the litany, the bishop, standing and with hands outstretched, says the prayer Lord, hear the prayers of your Church; then the deacon (if he had given the invitation to kneel before the litany) says, Let us stand, and all stand.[56]

732   Then the bishop alone, with miter and pastoral staff, sits. If it is the custom of the community, two consecrated and professed members of the community come to the chair of the superior and, standing, act as witnesses.

Those to be professed come one by one to the superior and read the formulary of profession, which they themselves have written out beforehand.

Then one by one the newly professed may fittingly go to the altar to place on it the formulary of profession; if this can be done conveniently, each of them should sign the formulary of profession on the altar itself. After this, each goes back to her place.

Afterward, if it is the practice of the community, the newly professed may stand and sing the antiphon Uphold me, Lord or some other suitable song expressing the spirit of self-giving and joy.[57]

733   Putting aside miter and pastoral staff, the bishop rises, the congregation rises with him, and the candidates kneel. With hands outstretched over them, the bishop says or sings the solemn prayer of consecration.[58]

734   After the prayer of consecration, the bishop, wearing the miter, sits, and the people also sit. The newly consecrated stand and, accompanied by the novice mistress and another nun assigned to this task, come before the bishop. He says, once for all of them, Dearest daughters, receive,

---

[55] See CLV, B, nos. 57-59.

[56] See CLV, B, no. 60.

[57] See CLV, B, nos. 61-63.

[58] See CLV, B, no. 64.

and gives them the ring and veil, or just the ring. Meanwhile, the choir and the people may sing Psalm 45 (44), with the antiphon To you, O Lord, or some other suitable song.[59]

735   Then, as circumstances suggest, the bishop gives each of the newly consecrated a copy of *The Liturgy of the Hours*, with the words Receive the book or other suitable words, to which all the newly consecrated reply together, Amen.[60]

736   As circumstances suggest, the newly consecrated may sing together the antiphon I am espoused to him.[61]

737   Then, if it is customary or as circumstances suggest, there may be a ceremony to mark the fact that the newly professed religious have been admitted as lifelong members of the religious family. This can take the form of a suitable statement by the bishop or the superior, or of an exchange of the sign of peace. If the second way is chosen, first the bishop offers the newly consecrated the sign of peace, then, in the manner customary in the community or in this monastery, the superior and the other nuns offer a sign of their sisterly love.
       Meanwhile, the choir and the people may sing Psalm 84 (83), with the antiphon How lovely is your dwelling place, or some other suitable song.[62]

738   After this, the newly consecrated return to their places in the sanctuary (chancel) and the Mass continues. The profession of faith is said when called for by the rubrics; the general intercessions are omitted.[63]
       During the song for the preparation of the gifts (offertory song), some of the newly consecrated may bring to the altar the bread and the wine and water for the eucharistic sacrifice.[64]
       In Eucharistic Prayers I-IV the special intercessions (interpolations) for the newly consecrated are to be added (RM, Ritual Masses, V. Consecration to a Life of Virginity).[65]
       The bishop now gives the sign of peace in some suitable form to those newly consecrated.[66]

---

[59] See CLV, B, nos. 65-67.
[60] See CLV, B, no. 68.
[61] See CLV, B, no. 69.
[62] See CLV, B, no. 70.
[63] See CLV, B, no. 50.
[64] See CLV, B, no. 73.
[65] See CLV, B, no. 74.
[66] See CLV, B, no. 75.

739   After the bishop has received the body and blood of Christ, the newly consecrated virgins come to the altar to receive communion under both kinds. The other nuns as well as the parents, relatives, and friends of the newly consecrated may also receive communion in the same way.[67]

740   When the prayer after communion has been said, the newly consecrated stand before the altar. The bishop, wearing the miter, gives the greeting The Lord be with you. A deacon may then give the invitation to pray for God's blessing. With hands outstretched over the newly consecrated virgins, the bishop sings or says the blessing invocations. Then, taking the pastoral staff, he blesses the whole congregation by making the sign of the cross three times and saying, May almighty God bless you.
    The bishop may also impart the blessing by using one of the formularies given in nos. 1120-1121.

741   After the blessing by the bishop, those newly consecrated may take their candles. The choir and the people sing a suitable song or a canticle of praise, and the procession is formed as at the beginning to escort the newly consecrated virgins to the door of the enclosure.[68]

II. Consecration to a Life of Virginity for Women Living in the World

742   It is at the discretion of the bishop and by his authority that women living in the world are admitted to this consecration, and often they take part in the good works of the diocese. It is therefore fitting that the rite of consecration take place in the cathedral, unless local circumstances or custom suggests otherwise.[69]

743   Everything is done as in the rite for nuns, but with the exceptions indicated in The Roman Pontifical and in the following paragraphs.

744   It is appropriate for two women—either consecrated themselves or chosen from the laity—to accompany the candidates to the altar.[70]

---

[67] See CLV, B, no. 76.
[68] See CLV, B, no. 80.
[69] See CLV, A, no. 3.
[70] See CLV, A, no. 10.

745 For the questioning of the candidates after the homily on the intention to consecrate themselves to God, a proper text is provided in *The Roman Pontifical.*[71]

746 Immediately after the litany and its concluding prayer, each candidate comes to the bishop, kneels before him, places her joined hands in his, and then states her resolve to live a life of virginity: Father, receive my resolution. If this rite is not acceptable, some other rite authorized by the conference of bishops may be used in its stead.[72]

747 The sign of peace is not exchanged after the presentation of the insignia of consecration, but at its usual place in Mass.[73]

---

[71] See CLV, A, no. 17.
[72] See CLV, A, no. 22.
[73] See CLV, A, no. 34.

Chapter 4

PERPETUAL PROFESSION OF MEN RELIGIOUS

Introduction

748   "The Church not only raises religious profession to the dignity of being a canonical state by its law, but by its liturgy shows that it is a state consecrated to God. For the Church itself, by the authority committed to it by God, receives the vows of those making profession; by its public prayer it entreats God that help and grace be given to them; it puts them in God's hands and bestows on them a spiritual blessing, as it conjoins their offering to the eucharistic sacrifice."[74]

This ecclesial significance of religious profession is visibly expressed when the bishop, who is also a father and pastor for religious, even exempt religious, presides at the rite of perpetual religious profession. The rite should be celebrated within Mass and with appropriate solemnity and the participation of the faithful.

749   The rite of profession ordinarily takes place in the church of the religious community. But for pastoral reasons or in order to promote esteem for the religious life, to give edification to the people of God, or to permit larger attendance, the rite may take place in the cathedral, a parish church, or some other notable church, as may seem fitting. This is particularly the case when religious from two or more institutes wish to celebrate their profession at the same eucharistic sacrifice. The superiors of the communities involved are to be present at such a communal celebration and, if they are priests, it is fitting that they concelebrate with the bishop, along with other priests present to take part in the rite. The bishop should be assisted by at least one deacon, and other ministers should take part in the rite. Those making profession will pronounce their vows before their respective superiors.[75]

750   It is fitting that the rite of perpetual profession take place on a Sunday or a solemnity of the Lord, of the Blessed Virgin Mary, or of a saint distinguished in the living of the religious life.[76]

751   On days when a ritual Mass is permitted,[77] the ritual Mass for religious profession (RM, Ritual Masses, VI. Religious Profession), with

---

[74] LG, no. 45: DOL 4, no. 156.

[75] See The Roman Ritual, *Rite of Religious Profession*, English ed., 1975, Part I, Rite of Religious Profession for Men, ch. III, Rite of Perpetual Profession during Mass (hereafter, RPM), nos. 44-46.

[76] See RPM, no. 40; see CIC, can. 657, §3.

[77] See Appendix III of this *Ceremonial.*

its proper readings,[78] may be celebrated; the vestments for the Mass are white or of some other festive color.

But even if the ritual Mass is not celebrated, one of the readings may be chosen from those provided for this Mass.

But on the days listed in nos. 1-4 of the table of liturgical days,[79] the Mass of the day, with its proper readings, is celebrated.

The formulary for the final blessing proper to the ritual Mass of profession may always be used.

752   Besides the vestments and other requisites for the concelebration of Mass, the following should be prepared:

a. ritual for religious profession;

b. insignia of religious profession, if these are to be presented in accordance with the rules or customs of the religious community;

c. cup large enough for communion under both kinds;

d. in a lay institute, a chair in a suitable part of the sanctuary (chancel) for the superior;

e. chairs in the sanctuary (chancel) for those making profession, arranged in such a way that the faithful have a complete view of the liturgical rites.[80]

The rite of profession takes place at the chair (cathedra) or in front of the altar or at some other convenient place.

DESCRIPTION OF THE RITE

753   The entrance procession takes place in the usual way. Those to be professed may fittingly join in the procession, accompanied by the novice master, and in lay institutes by the superior. When they come to the sanctuary (chancel), all those in the procession make the customary reverence to the altar and go to their places.[81]

754   The introductory rites and the liturgy of the word, up to the end of the gospel reading, take place in the usual way.

755   After the gospel reading, the bishop, with miter and pastoral staff, sits in the chair (cathedra) or at the chair provided for the occasion. All

---

[78] See LM, nos. 811-815 (Ritual Masses, VIII. Consecration to a Life of Virginity and Religious Profession).

[79] See Appendix II of this *Ceremonial*.

[80] See RPM, nos. 50 and 48.

[81] See RPM, no. 51.

in the assembly sit, but those to be professed remain standing, and the calling or request takes place.

The deacon or the novice master calls each of those to be professed by name. They answer, Present, or make some other reply according to local usage or the custom of the religious community. The bishop then questions them on their intent, in the way indicated in the ritual.

The calling and questioning may be replaced by a request from those to be professed: one of them, in the name of all, may request admission to profession, using the formulary provided in the ritual or some other suitable words.

At the end all present reply, Thanks be to God, or express their approval in some other suitable way.[82]

756   Those to be professed then sit. The bishop, seated and with miter and pastoral staff (unless he decides otherwise), gives the homily, developing the scriptural readings and the theme of religious profession as God's gift and call for the sanctification of those chosen and for the good of the Church and the whole human family.[83]

757   After the homily, those to be professed stand, and the bishop questions them on their readiness to dedicate themselves to God and to seek perfect charity, according to the rule or constitutions of their religious community. This is done by means of the questions and responses provided in the *Rite of Religious Profession* or in the particular ritual of the community. At the end of the questions the bishop confirms the intention of those to be professed, saying, May God who has begun, or some other suitable words.[84]

758   Putting aside the miter and the pastoral staff, the bishop stands, and all stand with him. With hands joined, he invites all to pray, saying, Dear friends in Christ. Then the deacon says, Let us kneel, and the bishop and all present kneel in their places. Those to be professed prostrate themselves or kneel, according to the custom of the place or of the religious community. But during the Easter season and on Sundays, the deacon does not say, Let us kneel, and all remain standing, except those to be professed, who prostrate themselves.

The cantors begin the Litany of the Saints; they may add at the proper places the names of those saints especially venerated in the religious community or by the faithful; or, as circumstances suggest, they

---

[82] See RPM, nos. 48, 53-55.

[83] See RPM, no. 56.

[84] See RPM, nos. 57-59.

may also add petitions suitable to the occasion, since the litany takes the place of the general intercessions.[85]

759   After the litany, the bishop stands and, with hands outstretched, says the prayer Lord, grant the prayers of your people; then the deacon (if he had given the invitation to kneel before the litany) says, Let us stand, and all stand.[86]

760   The bishop, with miter and pastoral staff, sits. If it is the custom of the community, two professed members come to the chair of the superior and, standing, act as witnesses.

Those to be professed come one by one to the superior and read the formulary of profession, which they themselves have written out beforehand.

Then one by one the newly professed may fittingly go to the altar to place on it the formulary of profession; if this can be done conveniently, each of them should sign the formulary of profession on the altar itself. After this, each goes back to his place.[87]

761   Afterward, if it is the practice of the community, the newly professed may stand and sing the antiphon Uphold me, Lord or some other suitable song.[88]

762   Then the newly professed kneel; the bishop, putting aside miter and pastoral staff, stands and, with hands outstretched over the newly professed, says the solemn prayer of blessing.[89]

763   After the blessing of the professed, if it is the custom of the religious community to present insignia of religious profession, the newly professed rise and come before the bishop. Seated and with miter, the bishop presents the insignia to each in silence or with a formulary provided in the particular ritual of the religious community. Meanwhile all sit, and the choir and people sing the antiphon How happy, Lord with Psalm 84 (83), or some other suitable song.[90]

764   When the presentation of insignia is completed or after the prayer of solemn blessing, if it is customary or seems opportune, there may be a ceremony to mark the fact that the newly professed religious have been admitted as lifelong members of the institute or religious family. This

---

[85] See RPM, nos. 60-62.
[86] See RPM, no. 63.
[87] See RPM, nos. 64-65.
[88] See RPM, no. 66.
[89] See RPM, no. 67.
[90] See RPM, no. 68.

can take the form of a suitable statement by the bishop or by the superior. It may also take the form of an exchange of the sign of peace, by which the bishop, the superior, and the other members of the religious community express their fraternal love for the newly professed. Meanwhile the choir and the people sing the antiphon See how good it is with Psalm 133 (132), or some other suitable song.

765   Afterward, the newly professed return to their places, and the Mass continues.[91]

The profession of faith is said when called for by the rubrics; the general intercessions are omitted.

During the song for the preparation of the gifts (offertory song), some of the newly professed may bring to the altar the bread and the wine and water for the eucharistic sacrifice.[92]

In Eucharistic Prayers I-IV the special intercessions (interpolations) for the newly professed are to be added (RM, Ritual Masses, VI. Religious Profession, 2. Perpetual Profession).[93]

The bishop gives the sign of peace to the newly professed.[94]

766   After the bishop has received the body and blood of Christ, the newly professed religious come to the altar to receive communion, which may be given to them under both kinds. Then their confreres, parents, and relatives may also receive communion in the same way.[95]

767   When the prayer after communion has been said, the newly consecrated religious stand before the altar. Then the bishop, with the miter, says the greeting The Lord be with you. A deacon may give the invitation Bow your heads and pray for God's blessing, and the bishop, with hands outstretched over the newly professed, says the blessing invocations. He then takes the pastoral staff and says, And may almighty God bless you all, as he makes the sign of the cross three times over the people.[96]

The bishop may also impart the blessing by using one of the formularies given in nos. 1120-1121.

768   After the blessing, the deacon dismisses the people, saying, The Mass is ended, go in peace (or one of the other formulas), and all reply, Thanks be to God.

---

[91] See RPM, no. 71.

[92] See RPM, no. 72.

[93] See RPM, no. 73.

[94] See RPM, no. 74.

[95] See RPM, no. 75.

[96] See RPM, nos. 76-77.

CHAPTER 5

PERPETUAL PROFESSION OF WOMEN RELIGIOUS

INTRODUCTION

769   The life dedicated to God by the bonds of religious life has always held a place of high honor in the eyes of the Church, which from the earliest centuries has surrounded the act of religious profession with liturgical rites.

The same holds true today: the Church itself, by the authority committed to it by God, receives the vows of those making profession; by its public prayer it entreats God that help and grace be given to them; it puts them in God's hands and bestows on them a spiritual blessing, as it conjoins their offering to the eucharistic sacrifice.[97]

This aspect of the Church's life has one of its chief manifestations when the bishop, as high priest from and on whom the life of the faithful in his diocese in some way derives and depends,[98] presides at a celebration within the Mass for the perpetual profession of women religious of the diocese.

770   The rite of profession ordinarily takes place in the church of the religious community. But for pastoral reasons or in order to promote esteem for the religious life, to give edification to the people of God, or to permit larger attendance, the rite may take place in the cathedral, a parish church, or some other notable church, as may seem fitting. This is particularly the case when religious from two or more institutes wish to celebrate their profession at the same eucharistic sacrifice, with the bishop presiding. Those making profession will pronounce their vows before their respective superiors.[99]

It is fitting that priests who are present to take part in the rite concelebrate with the bishop. The bishop should be assisted by at least one deacon, and other ministers should take part in the rite.

771   It is fitting that the rite of perpetual profession take place on a Sunday or a solemnity of the Lord, of the Blessed Virgin Mary, or of a saint distinguished in the living of the religious life.[100]

---

[97] See LG, no. 45: DOL 4, no. 156.

[98] See SC, art. 41: DOL 1, no. 41.

[99] See The Roman Ritual, *Rite of Religious Profession*, Part II, Rite of Religious Profession for Women, ch. III, Rite of Perpetual Profession during Mass (hereafter, RPW), nos. 50-51.

[100] See RPW, no. 43; see CIC, can. 657, §3.

772   On days when a ritual Mass is permitted,[101] the ritual Mass for religious profession (RM, Ritual Masses, VI. Religious Profession), with its proper readings,[102] may be celebrated; the vestments for the Mass are white or of some other festive color.

But even if the ritual Mass is not celebrated, one of the readings may be chosen from those provided for this Mass.

But on the days listed in nos. 1-4 of the table of liturgical days,[103] the Mass of the day, with its proper readings, is celebrated.

The formulary for the final blessing proper to the ritual Mass of profession may always be used.

773   Besides the vestments and other requisites for the concelebration of Mass, the following should be prepared:

a. ritual for religious profession;

b. insignia of religious profession, if these are to be presented in accordance with the rules or customs of the religious community;

c. cup large enough for communion under both kinds;

d. at a convenient place in the sanctuary (chancel), a chair for the superior who is to receive the profession of the sisters;

e. chairs in the sanctuary (chancel) for those making profession, arranged in such a way that the faithful have a complete view of the liturgical rites.

The rite of profession takes place at the chair (cathedra) or in front of the altar or at some other convenient place.

DESCRIPTION OF THE RITE

774   The entrance procession takes place in the usual way. Those to be professed may fittingly join in the procession, accompanied by the superior and the novice mistress. When they come to the sanctuary (chancel), all those in the procession make the customary reverence to the altar and go to their places.[104]

775   The introductory rites and the liturgy of the word, up to the end of the gospel reading, take place in the usual way.

---

[101] See Appendix III of this *Ceremonial*.

[102] See LM, nos. 811-815 (Ritual Masses, VIII. Consecration to a Life of Virginity and Religious Profession).

[103] See Appendix II of this *Ceremonial*.

[104] See RPW, nos. 55-56.

776   After the gospel reading, the bishop, with miter and pastoral staff, sits in the chair (cathedra) or at the chair provided for the occasion. All in the assembly sit, but those to be professed remain standing, and the calling or request takes place.

The deacon or the novice mistress calls each of those to be professed by name. They answer, Present, or make some other reply according to local usage or the custom of the religious community. The bishop then questions them on their intent, in the way indicated in the ritual.

The calling and questioning may be replaced by a request from those to be professed: one of them, in the name of all and facing toward the superior, may request admission to profession, using the formulary provided in the ritual or some other suitable words.

At the end all present reply, Thanks be to God, or express their approval in some other suitable way.[105]

777   Those to be professed then sit. The bishop, seated and with miter and pastoral staff (unless he decides otherwise), gives the homily, developing the scriptural readings and the theme of religious profession as God's gift and call for the sanctification of those chosen and for the good of the Church and the whole human family.[106]

778   After the homily, those to be professed stand, and the bishop questions them on their readiness to dedicate themselves to God and to seek perfect charity, according to the rule or constitutions of the religious community. This is done by means of the questions and responses provided in the *Rite of Religious Profession* or in the particular ritual of the community. At the end of the questions the bishop confirms the intention of those to be professed, saying, May God who has begun, or some other suitable words.[107]

779   Putting aside the miter and the pastoral staff, the bishop stands, and all stand with him. With hands joined, he invites all to pray, saying, Dear friends in Christ. The deacon says, Let us kneel, and the bishop and all present kneel in their places. Those to be professed prostrate themselves or kneel, according to the custom of the place or of the religious community. But during the Easter season and on Sundays, the deacon does not say, Let us kneel, and all remain standing, except those to be professed, who prostrate themselves.

The cantors begin the Litany of the Saints; they may add at the proper places the names of those saints especially venerated in the reli-

---

[105] See RPW, nos. 58, 59, 60.
[106] See RPW, no. 61.
[107] See RPW, nos. 62-64.

gious community or by the faithful; or, as circumstances suggest, they may also add petitions suitable to the occasion, since the litany takes the place of the general intercessions.[108]

780   After the litany, the bishop stands and, with hands outstretched, says the prayer Lord, grant the prayers of your people; then the deacon (if he had given the invitation to kneel before the litany) says, Let us stand, and all stand.[109]

781   The bishop, with miter and pastoral staff, sits. If it is the custom of the community, two professed members come to the chair of the superior and, standing, act as witnesses.

Those to be professed come one by one to the superior and read the formulary of profession, which they themselves have written out beforehand.

Then one by one the newly professed may fittingly go to the altar to place on it the formulary of profession; if this can be done conveniently, each of them should sign the formulary of profession on the altar itself. After this, each goes back to her place.[110]

782   Afterward, if it is the practice of the community, the newly professed may stand and sing the antiphon Uphold me, Lord or some other suitable song expressing the spirit of self-giving and joy.[111]

783   Then the newly professed kneel; the bishop, putting aside miter and pastoral staff, stands and, with hands outstretched over the newly professed, says the solemn prayer of blessing.[112]

784   After the blessing of the professed, if it is the custom of the religious community to present insignia of religious profession, the newly professed rise and come before the bishop. Seated and with miter, the bishop presents the insignia to each in silence or with a formulary provided in the particular ritual of the religious community. For example, if the insignia are rings, the newly professed religious rise and go to the bishop, who presents a ring to each, saying the appropriate formulary. But if a large number have been professed, the bishop may say the formulary of presentation once for all; then each religious goes to the bishop to receive the ring.

---

[108] See RPW, nos. 65-67.

[109] See RPW, no. 68.

[110] See RPW, nos. 69-70.

[111] See RPW, no. 71.

[112] See RPW, no. 72.

Meanwhile all sit, and the choir and people sing the antiphon I am betrothed to the Son with Psalm 45 (44), or some other suitable song.[113]

785 When the presentation of insignia is completed or after the prayer of solemn blessing, if it is customary or seems opportune, there may be a ceremony to mark the fact that the newly professed religious have been admitted as lifelong members of the institute or religious family. This can take the form of a suitable statement by the bishop or by the superior. It may also take the form of an exchange of the sign of peace, by which the bishop, the superior, and the other members of the religious community express their love for their newly professed sisters.

Meanwhile the choir and the people sing the antiphon How lovely is your dwelling place with Psalm 84 (83), or some other suitable song.[114]

786 Afterward, the newly professed return to their places and the Mass continues.

The profession of faith is said when called for by the rubrics; the general intercessions are omitted.

During the song for the preparation of the gifts (offertory song), some of the newly professed may bring to the altar the bread and the wine and water for the eucharistic sacrifice.[115]

In Eucharistic Prayers I-IV the special intercessions (interpolations) for the newly professed are to be added (RM, Ritual Masses, VI. Religious Profession).[116]

The bishop, in some suitable form, gives the sign of peace to the newly professed.[117]

787 After the bishop has received the body and blood of Christ, the newly professed religious come to the altar to receive communion, which may be given to them under both kinds. Then their sister religious, parents, and relatives may also receive communion in the same way.[118]

788 When the prayer after communion has been said, the newly consecrated religious stand before the altar. Then the bishop, with the miter, says the greeting The Lord be with you. A deacon may give the

---

[113] See RPW, no. 73-76.
[114] See RPW, no. 77.
[115] See RPW, no. 79.
[116] See RPW, no. 80.
[117] See RPW, no. 81.
[118] See RPW, no. 82.

invitation Bow your heads and pray for God's blessing, and the bishop, with hands outstretched over the newly professed, says the blessing invocations. He then takes the pastoral staff and says, And may almighty God bless you all, as he makes the sign of the cross three times over the people.[119]

The bishop may also impart the blessing by using one of the formularies given in nos. 1120-1121.

789   After the blessing, the deacon dismisses the people, saying, The Mass is ended, go in peace (or one of the other formulas), and all reply, Thanks be to God.

---

[119] See RPW, nos. 83-84, 160.

Chapter 6

INSTITUTION OF READERS AND ACOLYTES

Introduction

790   The ministries of reader and acolyte are to be preserved in the Latin Church. These ministries may be assigned to lay Christians and are no longer to be considered as reserved to candidates for the sacrament of orders.

Unless they have already done so, candidates for ordination as deacons and presbyters are to receive these ministries and are to exercise them for a suitable time in order to be better disposed for the future service of the word and of the altar.[120]

791   An interval determined by the Holy See or by the conference of bishops is to be observed between the conferring of the ministries of reader and acolyte whenever more than one ministry is to be conferred on the same person.[121]

792   These ministries are conferred by the Ordinary (the bishop and, in clerical institutes, the major superior), either within Mass or within a celebration of the word.[122]

793   In the celebration of the rite of institution, the bishop is to be assisted in the calling of the candidates by a deacon or a presbyter, and by other necessary ministers.

The rite is carried out at the chair (cathedra) or the celebrant's chair, unless a special chair is provided for the occasion in order to facilitate the participation of the people.

When the rite is celebrated within Mass, the bishop wears the vestments required for Mass, and he uses the miter and pastoral staff. If the rite is celebrated outside Mass, the bishop may wear an alb with pectoral cross, stole, and cope of suitable color; or he may wear a rochet and mozzetta with pectoral cross and stole, in which case he does not use the miter or pastoral staff.

---

[120] See MQ, nos. III, IV, XI: AAS 64 (1972), pp. 531-533; DOL 340, nos. 2928, 2929, 2936.
[121] See MQ, no. X: DOL 340, no. 2935.
[122] See MQ, no. IX: DOL 340, no. 2934.

I. Institution of Readers

794 The reader is appointed for a function proper to him, that of reading the word of God in the liturgical assembly. Accordingly, he is to proclaim the readings from Sacred Scripture, except for the gospel reading in the Mass and other sacred celebrations.[123]

In addition, the reader is entrusted with the special office of instructing children and adults in the faith and of preparing them to receive the sacraments worthily.[124]

795 For the celebration of the rite the following should be prepared:

a. when the ministry is to be conferred within Mass, the vestments required for the celebration of Mass; otherwise, the vesture indicated in no. 804;

b. *The Roman Pontifical;*

c. Bible;

d. chair for the bishop;

e. chairs for the candidates, arranged in such a way in a convenient place in the sanctuary (chancel) that the faithful have a complete view of the liturgical rites;

f. when the rite is to be celebrated within Mass, a cup large enough for communion under both kinds.

Institution of Readers within Mass

796 The Mass for the ministers of the Church (RM, Masses and Prayers for Various Needs and Occasions, I. For the Church, 8. For the Ministers of the Church), with the proper readings for the rite of institution, may be celebrated.[125]

But on the days listed in nos. 1-9 of the table of liturgical days, the Mass of the day is celebrated.

When the Mass for the ministers of the Church is not celebrated, one of the readings may be chosen from those provided in the *Lectionary for Mass* for the rite of institution, except on the days listed in nos. 1-4 of the table of liturgical days.[126]

---

[123] See MQ, no. V: DOL 340, no. 2930.

[124] See *The Roman Pontifical*, Part II. Institution of Readers and Acolytes, ch. 5, Institution of Readers (hereafter, IR), no. 4, the bishop's words concluding his homily.

[125] See LM, nos. 780-784 (Ritual Masses, IV. Ministries, 1. Institution of Readers).

[126] See Appendix II of this *Ceremonial.*

797   The introductory rites and the liturgy of the word, up to the end of the gospel reading, take place in the usual way.

798   After the gospel reading, the bishop, with miter and, as circumstances suggest, pastoral staff, sits in the chair (cathedra) or at the chair provided for the occasion. All in the assembly also sit, and the deacon or presbyter appointed to this task calls the candidates: Those to be instituted in the ministry of reader, please come forward. The candidates are called by name and each one answers, Present, and goes to the bishop, before whom he makes a sign of reverence; then the candidates return to their places.[127]

799   The bishop then gives the homily, in which he explains to the people the biblical texts just proclaimed and the ministry of the reader. He concludes by addressing the candidates, using the words provided in *The Roman Pontifical* or other suitable words.[128]

800   Then, putting aside the miter and pastoral staff, the bishop stands, and all stand with him. The candidates kneel before the bishop and, with hands joined, he invites the people to pray: Brothers and sisters, let us ask God our Father. All pray in silence for a brief period. Then, with hands outstretched, the bishop says the prayer of blessing over the candidates: Lord God, source of all goodness and light.[129]

801   All then sit and the bishop, wearing the miter, also sits. Each candidate goes to the bishop, who gives him the Bible, saying, Take this book of holy Scripture. Meanwhile Psalm 19 (18) or some other suitable song is sung, especially if there are many candidates.[130]

802   Then the Mass proceeds in the usual way, either with the profession of faith, when called for by the rubrics, or with the general intercessions, which include special intentions for the newly instituted readers.

803   The new readers, as well as their families and friends, may receive communion under both kinds.

---

[127] See IR, no. 3.

[128] See IR, no. 4.

[129] See IR, nos. 5-6.

[130] See IR, no. 7.

Institution of Readers within a Celebration of the Word

804   The bishop may wear an alb with pectoral cross, stole, and cope of suitable color; or he may wear a rochet and mozzetta with pectoral cross and stole, in which case he does not use the miter or pastoral staff.

805   Before the calling of the candidates and their sign of reverence to the bishop, the celebration may begin with the singing of an antiphon or some other suitable song; then the opening prayer of the Mass for the ministers of the Church may be said. The liturgy of the word is carried out as at Mass and with suitable responsorial psalms or other songs between the readings.

806   The rite of institution itself is carried out in the manner indicated in nos. 799-801.

807   The celebration is concluded with intercessions and the Lord's Prayer. Then the bishop blesses all present in the manner indicated in nos. 1120-1121, and the deacon pronounces the dismissal formula, saying, Go in peace, and all reply, Thanks be to God, then leave.

II. INSTITUTION OF ACOLYTES

808   The acolyte is appointed in order to aid the deacon and to minister to the priest. It is his duty therefore to attend to the service of the altar and to assist the deacon and the priest in liturgical celebrations, especially in the celebration of Mass; he is also to distribute communion as a special minister of the eucharist. In extraordinary circumstances an acolyte may be entrusted with publicly exposing the blessed sacrament for adoration by the faithful and afterward replacing it, but not with blessing the people with the blessed sacrament.[131]

809   The institution of acolytes takes place only within Mass.

810   For the celebration of the rite the following should be prepared:
   a. requisites for the celebration of Mass;
   b. *The Roman Pontifical*;
   c. vessel with the bread or wine to be consecrated;
   d. chair for the bishop;

---

[131] See MQ, no. VI: DOL 340, no. 2931.

e. chairs for the candidates, arranged in such a way in a convenient place in the sanctuary (chancel) that the faithful have a complete view of the liturgical rites;

f. cup large enough for communion under both kinds.

811   The Mass for the ministers of the Church (RM, Masses and Prayers for Various Needs and Occasions, I. The Church, 8. For the Ministers of the Church), with the proper readings for the rite of institution, may be celebrated;[132] the vestments for the Mass are white or of some other festive color.

But on the days listed in nos. 1-9 of the table of liturgical days, the Mass of the day is celebrated.

When the Mass for the ministers of the Church is not celebrated, one of the readings may be chosen from those provided in the *Lectionary for Mass* for the rite of institution, except on the days listed in nos. 1-4 of the table of liturgical days.[133]

812   The introductory rites and the liturgy of the word, up to the end of the gospel reading, take place in the usual way.

813   After the gospel reading, the bishop, with miter and, as circumstances suggest, pastoral staff, sits in the chair (cathedra) or at the chair provided for the occasion. All in the assembly also sit, and the deacon or presbyter appointed to this task calls the candidates: Those to be instituted in the ministry of acolyte, please come forward. The candidates are called by name and each one answers, Present, and goes to the bishop, before whom he makes a sign of reverence; then the candidates return to their places.[134]

814   The bishop then gives the homily, in which he explains to the people the biblical texts just proclaimed and the ministry of the acolyte. He concludes by addressing the candidates, using the words provided in *The Roman Pontifical* or other suitable words.[135]

815   Then, putting aside the miter and pastoral staff, the bishop stands, and all stand with him. The candidates kneel before the bishop, who,

---

[132] See LM, nos. 785-789 (Ritual Masses, IV. Ministries, 2. Institution of Acolytes).

[133] See Appendix II of this *Ceremonial*.

[134] See *The Roman Pontifical*, Part II. Institution of Readers and Acolytes, ch. 6, Institution of Acolytes (hereafter, IA), no. 3.

[135] See IA, no. 4.

with hands joined, invites the people to pray: Brothers and sisters, let us pray to the Lord. All pray in silence for a brief period. Then, with hands outstretched, the bishop says the prayer of blessing over the candidates: God of mercy, through your only Son.[136]

816   All then sit and the bishop, wearing the miter, also sits. Each candidate goes to the bishop, who gives him a vessel with the bread or wine to be consecrated, saying, Take this vessel.[137] Meanwhile a suitable song is sung, especially if there are many candidates.

817   Then the Mass proceeds in the usual way, either with the profession of faith, when called for by the rubrics, or with the general intercessions, which include special intentions for the newly instituted acolytes.

818   At the preparation of the gifts, the acolytes (or some of them, if there are too many) present the paten with the bread and the cup with the wine.[138]

819   The acolytes, as well as their family and friends, may receive communion under both kinds. The acolytes receive communion immediately after the deacons.

820   In the Mass of institution the bishop may direct the acolytes as special ministers to help in giving communion.[139]

---

[136] See IA, nos. 5-6.
[137] See IA, no. 7.
[138] See IA, no. 8.
[139] See IA, no. 10.

Chapter 7

FUNERALS AT WHICH THE BISHOP PRESIDES*

INTRODUCTION

821   It is altogether fitting that, if at all possible, the bishop, who is a herald of faith and a minister of comfort, preside at funerals that are celebrated with a large number of the faithful taking part, and especially at the funeral of another bishop or a presbyter.

822   For the celebration of a funeral the following are to be made ready:

a. *In the vesting room (sacristy) or some other convenient place, vestments of the color used at funerals:*
   — for the bishop: alb, stole, pectoral cross, cope for processions and celebrations of the word, chasuble for Mass, simple miter, pastoral staff;
   — for concelebrants: Mass vestments;
   — for deacons: albs, stoles, (dalmatics);
   — for other ministers: albs, or other lawfully approved vesture.

b. *At the home of the deceased (or the funeral home):*
   — The Roman Ritual;
   — cross and candlesticks for the procession;
   — vessel of holy water with sprinkler;
   — censer and incense boat with spoon.

c. *In the sanctuary (chancel):*
   — the requisites for Mass or for a celebration of the word of God.

d. *Near the place where the coffin rests:*
   — Easter candle;
   — requisites for the rite of final commendation (unless these have been brought in the procession to the church from the home of the deceased).

823   Apart from the marks of distinction arising from a person's liturgical function or holy orders, and those honors due to civil authorities according to liturgical law, no special honors are to be paid in the celebration of a funeral to any private persons or classes of persons, whether in the ceremonies or by external display.

---

   * The notes for this chapter correspond to the arrangement of the rites and their content as given in the Latin *editio typica* of the *Ordo exsequiarum*. Since the arrangement and content of the rites in the Latin *editio typica* have been adapted and supplemented in the ICEL edition of the *Order of Christian Funerals* and in the particular rituals currently in use within the conferences of bishops, the bishop's master of ceremonies and others involved in the liturgical preparation for funerals will need to refer to the particular ritual book approved within the territory of their conference of bishops.

It is fitting that the custom be continued of placing the coffin in the position that the deceased held in the liturgical assembly, so that the body of an ordained minister lies facing the assembly and the body of a layperson lies facing the altar.

824   In the celebration of funerals a dignified simplicity should be observed. The Easter candle should be placed near the coffin. A Book of the Gospels, a bible, or a cross may be placed on the coffin. If the deceased is an ordained minister, insignia of his order may, depending on local custom, be placed on the coffin.

There should be no flowers on the altar, and the music of the organ or other instruments is permitted only to assist the singing.

DESCRIPTION OF THE RITES

825   Particularly for the funeral of another bishop and as local customs and practical considerations permit, the first type of celebration provided in The Roman Ritual is preferable. This consists of three stations, namely, at the home of the deceased, at the church, and at the cemetery, with two intervening processions. For such a celebration it is recommended that the bishop preside even for the station at the home of the deceased and for the first procession.

Should the bishop not go to the home of the deceased, but the first station is to be celebrated there, a presbyter is to be appointed as celebrant; the bishop waits at the church, either at the chair (cathedra) or in the vesting room (sacristy).

826   When the bishop is to preside at the home of the deceased and in the procession to the church, he vests in some convenient place, putting on an alb, pectoral cross, stole, and cope of the color customary for funerals; he also wears a simple miter and carries the pastoral staff. Before the first station any concelebrants of the Mass should vest in the required Mass vestments.

Deacons and other ministers also wear their proper vesture.

827   At the home of the deceased the bishop cordially greets those present, speaking to them of the consolation that comes from faith. Then, as circumstances suggest, a psalm is said or sung responsorially, after which the bishop, without miter or pastoral staff, says a prayer selected from those provided in The Roman Ritual.[140]

---

[140] See RF, nos. 33-34, 167-169; see OCF, nos. 107, 398, 399.

828 In a procession transferring the body of the deceased to the church, usually the censerbearer, carrying a censer with incense burning, goes first; then a crossbearer between two acolytes carrying candlesticks; then the clergy and deacons, in cassock and surplice; then presbyters, in choir dress; then concelebrants, if there are any present; then the bishop, with miter and pastoral staff and accompanied by two deacons; finally, the ministers who assist with the book and the pastoral staff precede the coffin.

During the procession psalms or other suitable songs are sung, in keeping with the provisions of The Roman Ritual.[141]

829 If there is no station at the home of the deceased, the rites pertaining to that station are carried out at the door of the church by the bishop or a presbyter.

830 For the entrance into the church and the beginning of Mass, only one song is usually sung, as indicated in *The Roman Missal* (*Sacramentary*); but if pastoral considerations so require, one of the responsories provided in The Roman Ritual[142] may be added.

831 Upon reaching the altar, the bishop reverences it and, as circumstances suggest, may incense it. He then goes to the chair (cathedra) and replaces the cope with a chasuble (he may also do this, if it seems more convenient, immediately upon reaching the altar and before reverencing it).

During this time the coffin is put in a convenient place before the altar, so that the body lies in the position proper to the deceased person in the liturgical assembly, as already indicated in no. 823.

832 The funeral Mass is celebrated in the same way as other Masses.

In Eucharistic Prayers II and III the intercessions (interpolations) for the deceased are added.

833 Following the prayer after communion or, if there has been no Mass, following the liturgy of the word, the bishop, even if he has not celebrated the Mass, vested in chasuble or cope, as the case may be, and with the miter and pastoral staff, goes to the coffin. Facing the people, and assisted by a deacon and ministers with holy water and incense, he carries out the rite of final commendation and farewell.[143]

---

[141] See RF, no. 35; see OCF, nos. 127, 347.

[142] See RF, nos. 37, 47, 187-191; see OCF, no. 403.

[143] See RF, no. 46; see OCF, nos. 170-171.

But if the burial place is in the church itself, the rite of final commendation may be carried out there; as the procession proceeds to this burial place, the songs indicated in The Roman Ritual are sung.[144]

834   At the coffin the bishop, without miter or pastoral staff, gives the invitation Before we go our separate ways or something similar. All pray briefly in silence. Then the bishop sprinkles the body with holy water and incenses it, as the song Saints of God or some other responsory indicated in The Roman Ritual is sung. The sprinkling and incensing may also be done after the song. The bishop says the prayer Into your hands or some other suitable prayer.[145]

835   If the coffin is carried from the church to the cemetery, the bishop either waits at the chair (cathedra) as the coffin is borne out of the church, or he returns immediately to the vesting room (sacristy). But if he himself goes in the procession to the cemetery, this procession is formed in the same way as the procession from the home to the church, and suitable psalms and antiphons are sung, as indicated in The Roman Ritual.[146]

836   Upon reaching the cemetery, the bishop, without the miter or pastoral staff, blesses the grave, if it has not been blessed; and after saying the prayer for the committal provided in The Roman Ritual, he may, in keeping with local custom, sprinkle the grave and the coffin with holy water and incense them.[147]

837   Depending on local custom, the burial may take place immediately or at the end of the rite. As the coffin is placed in the burial place, or at some other opportune moment, the bishop may say the words of committal provided in The Roman Ritual.[148]

838   The bishop may then introduce the intercessions or prayer of the faithful; the deacon gives the intentions and the bishop says the concluding prayer God of holiness and power or another such prayer provided in The Roman Ritual. Depending on local custom, after the prayer the verse Eternal rest may be recited, and some suitable song may be sung.[149]

---

[144] See RF, nos. 50, 166; see OCF, no. 176.

[145] See RF, nos. 48, 192; see OCF, no. 175. .

[146] See RF, nos. 52, 157; see OCF, no. 176.

[147] See RF, nos. 53, 193-195; see OCF, nos. 216-218.

[148] See RF, no. 55; see OCF, no. 219.

[149] See RF, nos. 56, 196-199; see OCF, nos. 220-222.

839   If the bishop is not the celebrant, he presides at the liturgy of the word, still wearing the cope. He does the same if instead of a funeral Mass, there is a celebration of the word as provided in The Roman Ritual.

In funerals of children or of adults that are celebrated according to one of the other types provided in The Roman Ritual, the bishop follows the directives already given, but with the necessary modifications.

CHAPTER 8

LAYING OF A FOUNDATION STONE
OR
COMMENCEMENT OF WORK ON THE BUILDING
OF A CHURCH

INTRODUCTION

840   When the building of a new church begins, it is desirable to celebrate a rite to ask God's blessing for the success of the work and to remind the people that the structure built of stone will be a visible sign of the living Church, God's building that is formed of the people themselves.[150]

In accordance with liturgical tradition, this rite consists of the blessing of the site of the new church and the blessing and laying of the foundation stone.

When there is to be no foundation stone because of the particular architecture of the building, the rite of the blessing of the site of the new church should still be celebrated, in order to dedicate the beginning of the work to God.[151]

841   The rite for the laying of a foundation stone or for beginning a new church may be celebrated on any day except during the Easter triduum. But a day should be chosen when the people can attend in large numbers.[152]

842   The bishop of the diocese is rightly the one to celebrate the rite. If he cannot do so himself, he should entrust the function to another bishop or a presbyter, especially to one who is his associate and assistant in the pastoral care of the diocese or of the community for which the new church is to be built.[153]

843   Notice of the day and hour of the celebration should be given to the people in good time. The parish priest (pastor) or others concerned should instruct the people on the meaning of the rite and the reverence to be shown toward the church that is to be built for them.

---

[150] See 1 Corinthians 3:9; LG, no. 6; see DOL 4, no. 138.

[151] See The Roman Pontifical, *Dedication of a Church and an Altar*, ch. 1, Laying of a Foundation Stone or Commencement of Work on the Building of a Church (hereafter, LFS), no. 1: DOL 547, no. 4361.

[152] See LFS, no. 2: DOL 547, no. 4362.

[153] See LFS, no. 3: DOL 547, no. 4363.

It is also desirable that the people be asked to give their generous and willing support to the building of the new church.[154]

844   Insofar as possible, the area for the erection of the church should be marked out clearly. It should be possible to walk about without difficulty.[155]

845   In the place where the altar will be located a wooden cross of suitable height is to be fixed in the ground.[156]

846   For the celebration of the rite the following should be prepared:
   a. *Dedication of a Church and an Altar* and *Lectionary for Mass*;
   b. chair for the bishop;
   c. if there is to be one, the foundation stone (which by tradition is a rectangular cornerstone), together with cement and the tools for setting the stone in the foundation;
   d. vessel of holy water with sprinkler;
   e. censer and incense boat with spoon;
   f. processional cross and torches for the ministers.
   Sound equipment should be set up so that the assembly can clearly hear the readings, prayers, and instructions.[157]

847   The vestments for the celebration of the rite are white or of some other festive color. The following should be prepared:
   a. for the bishop: alb, pectoral cross, stole, cope, miter, and pastoral staff;
   b. for deacons: albs, stoles, and, as circumstances suggest, dalmatics;
   c. for other ministers: albs or other lawfully approved vesture.[158]

APPROACH TO THE CONSTRUCTION SITE

848   The assembly of the people and the approach to the construction site take place, according to circumstances of time and place, in one of the two ways described here.[159]

---

[154] See LFS, no. 4: DOL 547, no. 4364.
[155] See LFS, no. 5: DOL 547, no. 4365.
[156] See LFS, no. 6: DOL 547, no. 4366.
[157] See LFS, no. 7: DOL 547, no. 4367.
[158] See LFS, no. 8: DOL 547, no. 4368.
[159] See LFS, no. 9.

A. First Form: Procession

849   At a convenient hour the people assemble in a suitable place, from which they will go in procession to the site.[160]

850   The bishop, in his vestments and with miter and pastoral staff (or, as circumstances suggest, with rochet, mozzetta, pectoral cross, and stole, and in this case without the miter or pastoral staff), proceeds with the ministers to the place where the people are gathered. Putting aside the pastoral staff and miter, he greets the people, saying, The grace of our Lord Jesus Christ, or some other similar words.
   Then the bishop briefly instructs the people on their participation in the celebration and explains to them the meaning of the rite.[161]

851   When the bishop has finished the instruction, he says, Let us pray. All pray in silence for a brief period. The bishop then continues, Lord, you built a holy Church.[162]

852   When the bishop has finished the prayer, he receives the miter and pastoral staff. As circumstances suggest, a deacon then says, Let us go forth in peace. The procession is formed in the usual way, the censer-bearer carrying a censer with burning incense, and the crossbearer, between two acolytes carrying lighted torches, lead; the clergy follow; then the bishop with the deacons assisting him and other ministers; and lastly the faithful. As the procession proceeds, Psalm 84 (83), with the antiphon My soul is yearning, or some other suitable song is sung. After the procession, the reading of the word of God takes place, as described in nos. 855-857.[163]

Second Form: Station at the Construction Site of the New Church

853   If the procession cannot take place or seems inappropriate, the people gather at the construction site of the new church. When the people have assembled, the acclamation Eternal peace or some other suitable song is sung. Meanwhile the bishop, in his vestments and with miter and pastoral staff (or, as circumstances suggest, with rochet, mozzetta, pectoral cross, and stole, and in this case without the miter or staff), approaches the people. Putting aside the miter and pastoral staff, he greets the people, saying, The grace of our Lord Jesus Christ, or some other

---

[160] See LFS, no. 10.
[161] See LFS, nos. 11-12.
[162] See LFS, no. 13.
[163] See LFS, no. 14.

similar words. The people reply, And also with you, or in some other suitable way.

Then the bishop briefly instructs the people on their participation in the celebration and explains to them the meaning of the rite.[164]

854   When the bishop has finished the instruction, he says, Let us pray. All pray in silence for a brief period. The bishop then continues, Lord, you built a holy Church.[165]

READING OF THE WORD OF GOD

855   The bishop is seated and puts on the miter. Then one or more passages of Sacred Scripture are read, chosen preferably from those provided in the *Lectionary for Mass* for the ritual Mass for the dedication of a church, with an appropriate intervening responsorial psalm or some other suitable song.[166]

856   When the readings are finished, the bishop, seated and with miter and pastoral staff (unless he decides otherwise), gives the homily, in which he explains the biblical readings and the significance of the rite, namely, that Christ is the cornerstone of the Church, and that the temple to be built by the living Church of the community of believers will be at the same time the house of God and the house of the people of God.[167]

857   After the homily, according to the custom of the place, the document of the blessing of the foundation stone and of the beginning of the building of the church may be read; it is signed by the bishop and by representatives of those who are going to work on the building of the church and, together with the stone, is enclosed in the foundation.[168]

BLESSING OF THE SITE OF THE NEW CHURCH

858   When the homily is finished, the bishop, putting aside miter and staff, rises and blesses the site of the new church. With hands outstretched, he says the prayer Lord, you fill the entire world. Then he

---

[164] See LFS, nos. 15-16.

[165] See LFS, no. 17.

[166] See LFS, nos. 18-21; see also LM, no. 816 (Ritual Masses, IX. Dedication or Blessing of a Church or Altar, 1. Dedication of a Church).

[167] See LFS, no. 22.

[168] See LFS, no. 23.

puts on the miter and sprinkles the new site with holy water. To do this he may stand in the middle of the site or, escorted by the assisting deacons, may go in procession around the foundations, in which case Psalm 48 (47), with the antiphon The walls of Jerusalem, or some other suitable song is sung.[169]

BLESSING AND LAYING OF THE FOUNDATION STONE

859　When the site has been blessed, if a foundation stone is to be laid, it is blessed and placed in position in the manner described in nos. 860-861; otherwise the conclusion of the rite takes place immediately, in the way indicated in nos. 862-863.[170]

860　The bishop with the deacons assisting him goes to the place where the foundation stone is to be laid, and, taking off the miter, he blesses the stone, saying the prayer Father, the prophet Daniel. As circumstances suggest, he may then sprinkle the stone with holy water and incense it. Afterward, he puts on the miter again.[171]

861　Then the bishop lays the stone on the foundation in silence, or, as circumstances suggest, while saying, With faith in Jesus Christ, or similar words. A stonemason then fixes the stone in with mortar. Meanwhile, as circumstances suggest, the acclamation The house of the Lord or some other suitable song is sung.[172]

CONCLUDING RITE

862　When the singing has finished, the bishop takes off the miter and invites the people to pray the general intercessions, in the way provided in the Dedication of a Church and an Altar or in some similar way. The bishop then introduces the Lord's Prayer, after which he says the prayer God of love.[173]

863　When the bishop has received the miter and pastoral staff, he blesses the people in the usual way, as indicated in nos. 1120-1121. The deacon dismisses them, saying, Go in peace, and all reply, Thanks be to God.[174]

---

[169] See LFS, nos. 24-25.
[170] See LFS, no. 26.
[171] See LFS, no. 27.
[172] See LFS, nos. 28-29.
[173] See LFS, no. 30.
[174] See LFS, no. 31.

CHAPTER 9

DEDICATION OF A CHURCH

INTRODUCTION

864   From early times the name "church" has also been given to the building in which the Christian community gathers to hear the word of God, to pray together, to celebrate the sacraments, and to participate in the eucharist.

When a church is erected as a building destined solely and permanently for assembling the people of God and for carrying out sacred functions, it is fitting that it be dedicated to God with a solemn rite, in accordance with the ancient custom of the Church. But if a church is not to be dedicated, it is at least to be blessed, by the celebration of the rite of blessing described in nos. 954-971 of this *Ceremonial*.[175] When a church is dedicated, such appointments as its baptismal font, cross, images and statues, organ, bells, stations of the cross are to be considered as blessed and duly erected or installed; they therefore need no further blessing, erection, or installation.

865   Every church to be dedicated must have a titular. This may be the Blessed Trinity; our Lord Jesus Christ, invoked according to a mystery of his life or a title already accepted in the liturgy; the Holy Spirit; the Blessed Virgin Mary, likewise invoked according to some appellation already accepted in the liturgy; one of the angels; or, finally, a saint inscribed in the Roman Martyrology or in a duly approved Appendix to the Martyrology. A blessed may not be the titular without an indult of the Apostolic See.

A church should have one titular only, unless it is named after saints who are listed together in the Calendar.[176]

866   The tradition in the Roman liturgy of placing relics of martyrs or other saints beneath the altar should be preserved, if possible.[177] But the following should be noted:

  a. such relics should be of a size sufficient for them to be recognized as parts of human bodies; hence excessively small relics of one or more saints must not be placed beneath the altar;

---

[175] See The Roman Pontifical, *Dedication of a Church and an Altar*, ch. 2, Dedication of a Church (hereafter, DC), nos. 1-2: DOL 547, nos. 4369-4370.

[176] See DC, no. 4: DOL 547, no. 4372.

[177] See GIRM, no. 266: DOL 208, no. 1656.

b. the greatest care must be taken to determine whether the relics in question are authentic; it is better for an altar to be dedicated without relics than to have relics of doubtful authenticity placed beneath it;

c. a reliquary must not be placed upon the altar or set into the table of the altar; it must be placed beneath the table of the altar, as the design of the altar permits.[178]

867 Since the bishop has been entrusted with the care of the particular Church, it is his responsibility to dedicate to God new churches built in his diocese.

If he cannot himself preside at the rite, he should entrust this function to another bishop, especially to one who is his associate and assistant in the pastoral care of the community for which the church has been built, or, in altogether special circumstances, to a presbyter, to whom he shall give a special mandate.[179]

868 A day should be chosen for the dedication of the new church when the people can attend in large numbers, especially a Sunday. Since the theme of the dedication pervades this entire rite, the dedication of a new church may not take place on days on which it is altogether improper to disregard the mystery then being commemorated: the Easter Triduum, Christmas, Epiphany, Ascension, Pentecost, Ash Wednesday, the weekdays of Holy Week, and All Souls.[180]

869 The celebration of the eucharist is inseparably bound up with the rite of the dedication of a church; when a church is dedicated, therefore, the liturgical texts of the day are omitted, and texts proper to the rite are used for both the liturgy of the word and the liturgy of the eucharist.

It is fitting that the bishop concelebrate the Mass with the presbyters who take part with him in the rite of dedication and those who have been given charge over the parish or community for which the church has been built.[181]

870 The office of the dedication of a church is celebrated, beginning with Evening Prayer I. When the rite of depositing relics takes place, it is highly recommended that a vigil be kept at the relics of the martyr

---

[178] See DC, no. 5: DOL 547, no. 4373.
[179] See DC, no. 6: DOL 547, no. 4374.
[180] See DC, no. 7: DOL 547, no. 4375.
[181] See DC, nos. 8-9: DOL 547, nos. 4376-4377.

or saint that are to be placed beneath the altar; the best way of doing this is to have the office of readings, taken from the respective common or proper. This vigil should be properly adapted to encourage the people's participation, but the requirements of the General Instruction of the Liturgy of the Hours are to be respected.[182]

871   In order that the people may take part fully in the rite of dedication, the rector of the church to be dedicated and others experienced in the pastoral ministry are to instruct them on the import of the celebration and its spiritual, ecclesial, and evangelizing power.[183]

872   It is for the bishop and for those in charge of the celebration of the rite:

a. to decide the manner of entrance into the church (see nos. 879-891);

b. to determine the manner of handing over the new church to the bishop (see nos. 883, 888, 891);

c. to decide whether to have the depositing of the relics of the saints. The decisive consideration is the spiritual good of the community; the prescription in no. 866 must be followed.

It is for the rector of the church to be dedicated, helped by those who assist him in the pastoral work, to decide and prepare everything concerning the readings, singing, and other pastoral aids to foster the fruitful participation of the people and to ensure a dignified celebration.[184]

873   For the celebration of the rite the following should be prepared:

a. *In the place of assembly:*

— *Dedication of a Church and an Altar;*

— processional cross;

— if relics of the saints are to be carried in procession, the items indicated in no. 876, a;

b. *In the vesting room (sacristy) or in the sanctuary (chancel) or in the body of the church as each situation requires:*

— *The Roman Missal (Sacramentary);*

— *Lectionary for Mass;*

— vessel of water to be blessed and sprinkler;

— vessels with the holy chrism;

---

[182] See DC, no. 10: DOL 547, no. 4378.

[183] See DC, no. 20: DOL 547, no. 4388.

[184] See DC, no. 19: DOL 547, no. 4387.

— towels for wiping the table of the altar;

— if needed, a waxed linen cloth or waterproof covering of the same size as the altar;

— basin and pitcher of water, towels, and all that is needed for washing the bishop's hands and those of the presbyters after they have anointed the walls of the church;

— linen apron (gremial);

— brazier for burning incense or aromatic spices; or grains of incense and small candles (wax tapers) to burn on the altar;

— censer and incense boat with spoon;

— large enough cup, corporal, purificators, and hand towel;

— bread and wine and water for the celebration of Mass;

— altar cross, unless there is already a cross in the sanctuary or the cross that is carried in the entrance procession is to be placed near the altar;

— humeral veil, if there is to be an inauguration of a blessed sacrament chapel;

— altar cloth, candles, and candlesticks;

— small candle to be handed to the deacon by the bishop;

— flowers, as circumstances suggest.[185]

874 It is praiseworthy to keep the ancient custom of hanging on the walls of the church crosses made of stone, brass, or other suitable material or of having the crosses carved on the walls. Thus twelve or four crosses should be provided, depending on the number of anointings, and fixed here and there at a suitable height on the walls of the church. Beneath each cross a small bracket should be fitted and in it a small candlestick is placed, with a candle to be lighted.[186]

875 The vestments for the Mass of the dedication are white or of some other festive color. The following should be prepared:

— for the bishop: alb, pectoral cross, stole, dalmatic, chasuble, miter, pastoral staff, and pallium, if the bishop has the right to wear one;

— for the concelebrating presbyters: vestments for concelebrating Mass;

— for the deacons: albs, stoles, and dalmatics;

— for other ministers: albs or other lawfully approved vesture.[187]

---

[185] See DC, no. 21: DOL 547, no. 4389.

[186] See DC, no. 22: DOL 547, no. 4390.

[187] See DC, no. 23: DOL 547, no. 4391.

876 If relics of the saints are to be placed beneath the altar, the following should be prepared:

a. *In the place of assembly:*
– reliquary containing the relics, placed between flowers and lights. When the simple entrance is used, the reliquary may be placed in a suitable part of the sanctuary (chancel) before the rite begins;
– for the deacons who will carry the relics to be deposited: albs, red stoles, if the relics are those of a martyr, or white in other cases, and, if available, dalmatics. If the relics are carried by presbyters, then in place of dalmatics, chasubles should be prepared. The relics may also be carried by other ministers, vested in albs or in cassocks and surplices or in other lawfully approved vesture.

b. *In the sanctuary (chancel):*
– small table on which the reliquary is placed during the first part of the dedication rite.

c. *In the vesting room (sacristy):*
– sealant or cement to close the cover of the aperture. In addition, a stonemason should be on hand to close the depository of the relics at the proper time.[188]

877 A record of the dedication of the church is to be drawn up in duplicate, signed by the bishop, the rector of the church, and representatives of the local community; one copy is to be kept in the diocesan archives, the other in the archives of the church.

Where the depositing of relics takes place, a third copy of the record should be made, to be placed at the proper time in the reliquary.

In this record mention should be made of the day, month, and year of the church's dedication, the name of the bishop who celebrated the rite, also the titular of the church and, where applicable, the names of the martyrs or saints whose relics have been deposited beneath the altar.

Moreover, in a suitable place in the church, an inscription should be placed, stating the day, month, and year when the dedication took place, the titular of the church, and the name of the bishop who celebrated the rite.[189]

878 In order that the importance and the dignity of the particular Church may stand out with greater clarity, the anniversary of the dedi-

---

[188] See DC, no. 24: DOL 547, no. 4392.
[189] See DC, no. 25: DOL 547, no. 4393.

cation of its cathedral is to be celebrated, with the rank of a solemnity in the cathedral itself, with the rank of a feast in other churches of the diocese, on the date on which the dedication of the church recurs. If this date is always impeded, the celebration is assigned to the nearest open date.[190]

The anniversary of a church's dedication is celebrated with the rank of a solemnity.[191]

ENTRANCE INTO THE CHURCH

879 The entry into the church is made, according to circumstances of time and place, in one of the three ways described here.[192]

First Form: Procession

880 The door of the church to be dedicated should be closed. At a convenient hour the people assemble in a neighboring church or other suitable place from which the procession may proceed to the church. The relics of the martyrs or saints, if they are to be put beneath the altar, are prepared in the place where the people assemble.[193]

881 The bishop, the concelebrating presbyters, the deacons, and ministers, each in appropriate vestments, proceed to the place where the people are assembled.

Putting aside the pastoral staff and miter and facing the people, the bishop says, In the name of the Father. He then greets the people, saying, The grace and peace of God, or other suitable words, taken preferably from Sacred Scripture. The people reply, And also with you, or in some other suitable way. Then the bishop addresses the people, using the words provided in the *Dedication of a Church and an Altar* or some similar words of instruction.[194]

882 When he has finished addressing the people, the bishop receives the miter and pastoral staff, and the procession to the church to be dedicated begins. No lights are used, apart from those surrounding the relics of the saints, nor is incense used either in the procession or in the Mass before the rite of the incensation and lighting of the altar and the

---

[190] See DC, no. 26: DOL 547, no. 4394. See Appendix II: I, 4b and II, 8b of this *Ceremonial*.

[191] See DC, no. 27: DOL 547, no. 4393. See Appendix II: I, 4b of this *Ceremonial*.

[192] See DC, no. 28.

[193] See DC, no. 29.

[194] See DC, no. 30.

church (see nos. 905-907). The crossbearer leads the procession, without the usual candlebearers on either side; the ministers follow; then the deacons or presbyters with the relics of the saints, ministers or the faithful accompanying them on either side with lighted torches; then the concelebrating presbyters; then the bishop, followed by two deacons; then the ministers who assist with the book and the miter; and lastly, the faithful.[195]

As the procession proceeds, Psalm 122 (121), with the antiphon Let us go rejoicing to the house of the Lord, or some other suitable song is sung.[196]

883   At the threshold of the church the procession comes to a halt. Representatives of those who have been involved in the building of the church (members of the parish or of the diocese, contributors, architects, workers) hand over the building to the bishop, offering him, according to the place and circumstances, either the legal documents for possession of the building, or the keys, or the plan of the building, or the book in which the progress of the work is described and the names of those in charge of it and the names of the workers are recorded. One of the representatives addresses the bishop and the community in a few words, pointing out, when appropriate, what the new church expresses in its art and in its own special design. The bishop then calls upon the presbyter to whom the pastoral care of the church has been entrusted to open the door.[197]

884   When the door is unlocked, the bishop invites the people to enter the church, using the words provided in *Dedication of a Church and an Altar,* Go within his gates giving thanks, or some other similar words. Then, preceded by the crossbearer, the bishop and the assembly enter the church. As the procession enters, Psalm 24 (23), with the antiphon Lift high the portals, or some other suitable song is sung.[198]

885   The bishop, without kissing the altar, goes to the chair (cathedra); the concelebrants, deacons, and ministers go to the places assigned to them in the sanctuary (chancel). The relics of the saints are placed in a suitable part of the sanctuary (chancel) between lighted torches. Water is then blessed with the rite described in no. 892.[199]

---

[195] See DC, no. 31.
[196] See DC, no. 32.
[197] See DC, no. 33.
[198] See DC, no. 34.
[199] See DC, no. 35.

Second Form: Solemn Entrance

886   If the procession cannot take place or seems inappropriate, the people assemble at the door of the church to be dedicated, where the relics of the saints have been placed beforehand.

   Preceded by the crossbearer, the bishop and the concelebrating presbyters, the deacons, and the ministers, each in appropriate vestments, approach the church door where the people are assembled. In the interest of the authenticity of the rite, the door should be closed, and the bishop, concelebrants, deacons, and ministers should approach the door from outside. But if this cannot be done, the door of the church is left open, and the bishop and those accompanying him go to it from the church.[200]

887   Putting aside the pastoral staff and miter, the bishop greets the people saying, The grace and peace, or other suitable words, taken preferably from Sacred Scripture. The people reply, And also with you, or in some other suitable way. Then the bishop addresses the people, saying, Brothers and sisters in Christ, or something similar.[201]

888   When the bishop has finished addressing the people, he puts on the miter and, as circumstances suggest, Psalm 122 (121), with the antiphon Let us go rejoicing, or some other suitable song is sung. Then representatives of those who have been involved in the building of the church (members of the parish or of the diocese, contributors, architects, workers) hand over the building to the bishop, offering him, according to the place and circumstances, either the legal documents for possession of the building, or the keys, or the plan of the building, or the book in which the progress of the work is described and the names of those in charge of it and the names of the workers are recorded. One of the representatives addresses the bishop and the community in a few words, pointing out, when appropriate, what the new church expresses in its art and in its own special design. If the door is closed, the bishop then calls upon the presbyter to whom the pastoral care of the church has been entrusted to open the door.[202]

889   The bishop takes the pastoral staff and invites the people to enter the church, using the words provided in *Dedication of a Church and an Altar*, Go within his gates giving thanks, or some other similar words.

---

[200] See DC, nos. 36-37.
[201] See DC, no. 38.
[202] See DC, nos. 39-40.

Then, preceded by the crossbearer, the bishop and the assembly enter the church. As the procession enters, Psalm 24 (23), with the antiphon Lift high the portals, or some other suitable song is sung. The bishop, without kissing the altar, goes to the chair (cathedra); the concelebrants, deacons, and ministers go to the places assigned to them in the sanctuary (chancel). The relics of the saints are placed in a suitable part of the sanctuary (chancel) between lighted torches. Water is then blessed with the rite described in no. 892.[203]

Third Form: Simple Entrance

890   If the solemn blessing cannot take place, the simple entrance is used. When the people are assembled, the bishop and the concelebrating presbyters, the deacons, and the ministers, each in appropriate vestments and preceded by the crossbearer, go from the vesting room (sacristy) through the main body of the church to the sanctuary (chancel).

If there are relics of the saints to be put beneath the altar, these are brought in the entrance procession to the sanctuary (chancel) from the vesting room (sacristy) or the chapel where, since the vigil, they have been exposed for the veneration of the people. For a good reason, before the celebration begins, the relics may be placed between lighted torches in a suitable part of the sanctuary (chancel).

As the procession proceeds, the entrance song God in his holy dwelling, or Psalm 122 (121), with the antiphon Let us go rejoicing, or some other suitable song is sung.[204]

891   When the procession reaches the sanctuary (chancel), the relics of the saints are placed between lighted torches in a suitable place. The concelebrating presbyters, the deacons, and the ministers go to the places assigned to them; the bishop, without kissing the altar, goes to the chair. Then, putting aside the pastoral staff and miter, he greets the people, saying, The grace and peace, or other suitable words, taken preferably from Sacred Scripture. The people reply, And also with you, or in some other suitable way.

Then representatives of those who have been involved in the building of the church (members of the parish or of the diocese, contributors, architects, workers) hand over the building to the bishop, offering him, according to the place and circumstances, either the legal documents for possession of the building, or the keys, or the plan of the building, or

---

[203] See DC, nos. 41-42.
[204] See DC, nos. 43-45.

the book in which the progress of the work is described and the names of those in charge of it and the names of the workers are recorded. One of the representatives addresses the bishop and the community in a few words, pointing out, when appropriate, what the new church expresses in its art and in its own special design.[205]

BLESSING AND SPRINKLING OF WATER

892   When the entrance rite is completed, the bishop blesses water with which to sprinkle the people as a sign of repentance and as a reminder of their baptism, and to purify the walls and the altar of the new church. The ministers bring the vessel with the water to the bishop, who stands at the chair (cathedra). The bishop invites all to pray, saying, Brothers and sisters in Christ, or other similar words. All pray in silence for a brief period. Then the bishop says the prayer God of mercy.[206]

893   The bishop, accompanied by the deacons, passes through the main body of the church, sprinkling the people and the walls with holy water; then, when he has returned to the sanctuary (chancel), he sprinkles the altar. Meanwhile, the antiphon I saw water flowing, or, during Lent, I will pour clean water, or some other suitable song is sung.[207]

894   After the sprinkling, the bishop returns to the chair (cathedra) and, when the singing is finished, stands and with hands joined, says, May God, the Father of mercies. Then the Gloria is sung, and when it is finished the bishop, following the usual rite, sings or says the opening prayer of the Mass.[208]

LITURGY OF THE WORD

895   The bishop is seated, wearing the miter. The proclamation of the word of God is fittingly carried out in this way: two readers, one of whom carries the Lectionary for Mass, and the psalmist (cantor) come to the bishop. The bishop, standing with the miter on, takes the Lectionary and shows it to the people, saying, May the word of God. Then the bishop hands

---

[205] See DC, nos. 46-47.
[206] See DC, no. 48.
[207] See DC, no. 49.
[208] See DC, nos. 50-52.

the *Lectionary* to the first reader. The readers and the psalmist proceed to the ambo, carrying the *Lectionary* for all to see.[209]

896   The readings are arranged in this way: the first is always taken from the Book of Nehemiah 8:1-4a, 5-6, 8-10, and it is followed by the singing of Psalm 19 (18):8-9, 10, 15, with the response Your words, Lord, are spirit and life. The second reading and the gospel reading are taken from the texts in the *Lectionary for Mass* for the rite of the dedication of a church (Ritual Masses, IX. Dedication of a Church or Altar, 1. Dedication of a Church). Neither lights nor incense is carried for the gospel reading.[210]

897   After the gospel reading, the bishop sits, with miter and pastoral staff, and gives the homily, in which he explains the biblical readings and the meaning of the rite by which the church building is dedicated to God and the growth of the Church is fostered.[211]

898   After the homily, the bishop puts aside the pastoral staff and miter; all stand and the profession of faith is sung or recited. The general intercessions are omitted, since in their place the Litany of the Saints is sung.[212]

PRAYER OF DEDICATION AND THE ANOINTINGS

Litany of the Saints

899   After the profession of faith, the bishop invites the people to pray, saying, Let us ask, or other similar words.
      Then the Litany of the Saints is sung, with all responding. On Sundays and also during the Easter season, all stand; on other days all kneel, and the deacon says, Let us kneel.
      At the proper place in the litany, the cantors add the names of other saints (the titular of the church, the patron saint of the place, and the saints whose relics are to be deposited, if this is to take place) and petitions suitable to the occasion and to the faithful taking part.
      When the litany is finished, the bishop, standing and with hands outstretched, says the prayer Lord, may the prayers of the Blessed Virgin Mary. Then, if the people have been kneeling, the deacon says, Let

---

[209] See DC, no. 53.
[210] See DC, no. 54.
[211] See DC, no. 55.
[212] See DC, no. 56.

us stand. All rise. The bishop receives the miter and proceeds to the depositing of the relics.

When there is no depositing of the relics of the saints, the bishop immediately says the prayer of dedication, as indicated in no. 901.[213]

Depositing of the Relics

900   If relics of the martyrs or other saints are to be placed beneath the altar, the bishop approaches the altar. A deacon or presbyter brings the relics to the bishop, who places them in a suitably prepared aperture. Meanwhile, Psalm 15 (14), with the antiphon Saints of God or The bodies of the saints, or some other suitable song is sung.

During the singing a stonemason closes the aperture, and the bishop returns to the chair (cathedra).[214]

Prayer of Dedication

901   Then the bishop, without miter and standing at the chair (cathedra) or near the altar and with hands outstretched, sings or says in a clear voice, Father in heaven.[215]

Anointing of the Altar and of the Walls of the Church

902   Then the bishop, removing the chasuble if necessary and putting on a linen apron (gremial), goes to the altar with the deacon and other ministers, one of whom carries the vessel with the holy chrism. The bishop proceeds to anoint the altar and the walls of the church.

If the bishop wishes to associate some of the concelebrating presbyters with him in anointing the walls, after the anointing of the altar he hands them vessels of holy chrism and goes with them to carry out the anointing.

But the bishop may give the task of anointing the walls to the presbyters alone.[216]

903   The bishop, with the miter and standing before the altar, says in a clear voice, We now anoint. Then he pours holy chrism on the middle of the altar and on each of its four corners, and it is recommended that he anoint the entire table of the altar.

---

[213] See DC, nos. 57-60.
[214] See DC, no. 61.
[215] See DC, no. 62.
[216] See DC, no. 63.

When the altar has been anointed, the bishop anoints the walls of the church, signing with holy chrism the suitably distributed twelve or four crosses. He may have the assistance of two or four presbyters.

If the anointing of the walls is given to the presbyters, after the bishop has anointed the altar, they anoint the walls of the church, signing the crosses with holy chrism. Meanwhile Psalm 84 (83), with the antiphon See the place or Holy is the temple, or some other suitable song is sung.[217]

904   When the altar and walls have been anointed, the bishop returns to the chair (cathedra), sits, and washes his hands. Then the bishop takes off the linen apron (gremial) and puts on the chasuble. The presbyters also wash their hands after they have anointed the walls.[218]

Incensation of the Altar and the Church

905   After the rite of anointing, a brazier is placed on the altar for burning incense or aromatic gums, or, if desired, a heap of incense mixed with small candles or wax tapers is made on the altar. The bishop puts incense into the brazier, or he lights the heap of incense with a small candle handed to him by a minister; then he says, Lord, may our prayer ascend.

Then the bishop puts incense into several censers. He himself incenses the altar, then returns to the chair (cathedra), puts on the miter, is incensed, and sits. Ministers, walking through the church, incense the people and the walls. Meanwhile, Psalm 138 (137), with the antiphon An angel stood or From the hand of the angel, or some other suitable song is sung.[219]

Lighting of the Altar and the Church

906   After the incensation, a few ministers wipe the table of the altar with towels and, if necessary, cover it with a waterproof covering. They then cover the altar with an altar cloth and, if circumstances suggest, decorate it with flowers. They arrange in a suitable manner the candles needed for the celebration of Mass and, if necessary, the cross.[220]

907   Then the deacon goes to the bishop, who stands and gives the deacon a small lighted candle and says in a clear voice, Light of Christ. The

[217] See DC, no. 64.
[218] See DC, no. 65.
[219] See DC, nos. 66-68.
[220] See DC, no. 69.

bishop then sits. The deacon goes to the altar and lights the candles for the celebration of the eucharist. Then the festive lighting takes place: as a sign of rejoicing, all the candles, including those at the places where the anointings were made, and the other lamps of the church are lit. Meanwhile, the Canticle of Tobias, with the antiphon Your light will come or, during Lent, Jerusalem, city of God, or some other suitable song is sung, especially one in honor of Christ, the light of the world.[221]

LITURGY OF THE EUCHARIST

908   The deacons and the ministers prepare the altar in the usual way. Then some of the congregation bring the bread and the wine and water for the celebration of the Lord's sacrifice. The bishop receives the gifts at the chair (cathedra). While the gifts are being brought, the antiphon Lord God or some other suitable song may be sung.

In Eucharistic Prayer I the special form of Father, accept this offering is said. In Eucharistic Prayer III the proper intercessions (interpolations) for the dedication of a church are said.

Everything else is done in the usual way, up to and including the communion.[223]

909   Eucharistic Prayer I or III is said, with the proper preface, which is an integral part of the rite of the dedication of a church.

In Eucharistic Prayer I the special form of Father, accept this offering is said. In Eucharistic Prayer III the proper intercessions (interpolations) for the dedication of a church are said.

Everything else is done in the usual way, up to and including the communion.[223]

INAUGURATION OF THE BLESSED SACRAMENT CHAPEL

910   The inauguration of a chapel where the blessed sacrament is to be reserved may be appropriately carried out in this way: after the communion a pyx containing the blessed sacrament is left on the side of the altar. The bishop goes to the chair (cathedra), and all pray in silence for a brief period. Then the bishop says the prayer after communion.[224]

911   When the prayer is completed, the bishop returns to the altar, and, kneeling, incenses the blessed sacrament. Afterward, when he has

---

[221] See DC, nos. 70-71.
[222] See DC, nos. 72-73.
[223] See DC, nos. 75-78.
[224] See DC, no. 79.

received the humeral veil, he takes the pyx, which he covers with the veil. Then a procession is formed in which the blessed sacrament, preceded by the crossbearer and acolytes carrying lighted torches and censer, is carried through the main body of the church to the chapel of reservation.

As the procession proceeds, Psalm 147 (146):12-20, with the antiphon Praise the Lord, Jerusalem, or some other suitable song is sung.[225]

912 When the procession comes to the chapel of reservation, the bishop places the pyx on the altar or in the tabernacle, the door of which remains open. Then he puts incense into the censer and, kneeling, incenses the blessed sacrament. Finally, after a brief period during which all pray in silence, the deacon puts the pyx into the tabernacle or closes the tabernacle door. A minister lights the lamp that will burn perpetually before the blessed sacrament.[226]

913 If the chapel where the blessed sacrament is reserved can be seen clearly by the congregation, the bishop immediately imparts the blessing of the Mass. Otherwise the procession returns to the sanctuary by the shortest route, and the bishop imparts the blessing either at the altar or at the chair (cathedra), and the Mass concludes in the manner indicated in no. 915.[227]

914 If there is no inauguration of a blessed sacrament chapel, when the communion of the congregation has finished, the bishop says the prayer after communion, and the Mass is concluded in the manner indicated in no. 915.[228]

BLESSING AND DISMISSAL

915 For the final blessing, the bishop uses the formulary provided for this rite in Dedication of a Church and an Altar.

The deacon dismisses the people in the usual way.

---

[225] See DC, no. 80.
[226] See DC, no. 81; see CIC, can. 940.
[227] See DC, no. 82.
[228] See DC, no. 83.

CHAPTER 10

DEDICATION OF A CHURCH ALREADY IN GENERAL USE FOR SACRED CELEBRATIONS

916   In order to bring out fully the symbolism and the significance of the rite, the opening of a new church and its dedication should take place at one and the same time. For this reason care should be taken that, as far as possible, Mass is not celebrated in a new church before it is dedicated.

Nevertheless, in the case of the dedication of a church where the sacred mysteries are already being celebrated regularly, the rite set out in nos. 864-915 must be used.

Moreover, a clear distinction exists in regard to these churches. In the case of those just built, the reason for a dedication is obvious. In the case of those standing for some time, the following requirements must be met for them to be dedicated:

— that the altar has not already been dedicated, since it is rightly forbidden both by custom and by liturgical law to dedicate a church without dedicating the altar, for the dedication of the altar is the principal part of the whole rite;

— that there be something new or notably altered about the edifice, relative either to its structure (for example, a total restoration) or of its status in law (for example, the church's being ranked as a parish church).

917   All the directives already given in nos. 864-878 apply to this rite, unless they are clearly extraneous to the situation for which this rite provides or unless other directions are given.

This rite differs from that described in Chapter 9 chiefly on these points:

a. The rite of opening the doors of the church (see no. 884 or no. 889) is omitted, since the church is already open to the community; consequently, the entrance takes the form of the simple entrance, described in nos. 890-891. However, in the case of dedicating a church closed for a long time and now being reopened for sacred celebrations, the rite of opening the doors may be carried out, since in this case it retains its point and significance.

b. The rite of handing over the church to the bishop (see no. 883 or no. 888 or no. 891) is either to be followed, omitted, or adapted, as the case may be, in a way consistent with the condition of the church being dedicated (for example, it will be right to retain it in a church built recently; to omit it in dedicating an older church where nothing has been changed in the structure; to adapt it in dedicating an older church completely restored).

c. The rite of sprinkling the church walls with holy water (see nos. 892-894), purificatory by its nature, is omitted.

d. All the rites belonging to the first proclamation of the word of God in a church (see no. 896) are omitted; thus the liturgy of the word takes place in the usual way. A different, pertinent reading is chosen in place of Nehemiah 8:1-4a, 5-6, 8-10 and its responsorial psalm, Psalm 19 (18):8-9, 10, 15 (see no. 896).[229]

---

[229] See The Roman Pontifical, *Dedication of a Church and an Altar*, ch. 3, Dedication of a Church Already in General Use for Sacred Celebrations: DOL 547, nos. 4396-4397.

CHAPTER 11

DEDICATION OF AN ALTAR

INTRODUCTION

918   At the altar the sacrifice of the cross is made present under sacramental signs. It is also the table of the Lord, and the people of God are called together to share in it. The altar is, as well, the center of the thanksgiving that the eucharist accomplishes.[230]

919   It is desirable that in every church there be a fixed altar and that in other places set apart for sacred celebrations there be either a fixed or a movable altar.[231]

   In accordance with received custom in the Church and the biblical symbolism connected with an altar, the table of a fixed altar should be of stone, indeed of natural stone. But, at the discretion of the conference of bishops, any becoming, solid, and finely wrought material may be used in erecting an altar.[232]

920   It is fitting to maintain the practice of placing beneath the altar relics of the saints, even those who are not martyrs (see no. 866).

921   The altar is of its very nature dedicated to the one God, for the eucharistic sacrifice is offered to the one God. This is the sense in which the Church's practice of dedicating altars to God in honor of the saints must be understood. St. Augustine expresses it well: "It is not to any of the martyrs, but to the God of the martyrs, though in memory of the martyrs, that we raise our altars."[233]

   In places where altars are customarily dedicated to God in honor of the saints, the practice may be continued, but it should be made clear to the people that the altar is dedicated to God alone. In new churches statues and pictures of saints may not be placed above the altar.

   Likewise, when relics of saints are exposed for veneration, they should not be placed on the table of the altar.[234]

922   Since an altar becomes sacred principally by the celebration of the eucharist, in conformity to this truth the celebration of Mass on a new

---

[230] See GIRM, no. 259: DOL 208, no. 1649.

[231] See The Roman Pontifical, *Dedication of a Church and an Altar*, ch. 4, Dedication of an Altar (hereafter, DA), no. 6: DOL 547, no. 4403.

[232] See DA, no. 9: DOL 547, no. 4406.

[233] Augustine, *Contra Faustum* XX, 21: PL 42, 384.

[234] See DA, no. 10: DOL 547, no. 4407.

altar before it has been dedicated should be carefully avoided, so that the Mass of dedication may also be the first eucharist celebrated on the altar.[235]

923   Since the bishop has been entrusted with the care of the particular Church, it is his responsibility to dedicate to God new altars built in his diocese.

If he cannot himself preside at the rite, he should entrust this function to another bishop, especially to one who is his associate and assistant in the pastoral care of the community for which the new altar has been erected, or, in altogether special circumstances, to a presbyter, to whom he shall give a special mandate.[236]

924   A day should be chosen for the dedication of a new altar when the people can attend in large numbers, especially a Sunday, unless pastoral considerations suggest otherwise. However, the rite of the dedication of an altar may not be celebrated during the Easter Triduum, on Ash Wednesday, the weekdays of Holy Week, and All Souls.[237]

925   The celebration of the eucharist is inseparably bound up with the rite of dedication of an altar. The Mass for the dedication of an altar is celebrated (RM, Ritual Masses, Dedication of an Altar). On Christmas, Epiphany, Ascension, Pentecost, and on the Sundays of Advent, Lent, and the Easter season, the texts for the Mass of the day are said, with the exception of the prayer over the gifts and the preface, which are closely interwoven with the rite itself.[238]

926   It is fitting that the bishop concelebrate the Mass with the presbyters present, especially with those who have been given charge over the parish or the community for which the altar has been erected.[239]

927   It is for the bishop and those in charge of the celebration of the rite to decide whether to have the depositing of relics of the saints; in so doing, they are to follow what is laid down in no. 866 and they are to take as the decisive consideration the spiritual good of the community and a proper sense of the liturgy.[240]

---

[235] See DA, no. 13: DOL 547, no. 4410.
[236] See DA, no. 12: DOL 547, no. 4409.
[237] See DA, no. 14: DOL 547, no. 4411.
[238] See DA, no. 15: DOL 547, no. 4412.
[239] See DA, no. 16: DOL 547, no. 4413.
[240] See DA, no. 25: DOL 547, no. 4422.

928 The people are to be informed in good time about the dedication of the new altar and they are to be properly prepared to take an active part in the rite. Accordingly, they should be taught what each rite means and how it is carried out. In this way the people will be imbued with the rightful love that is owed to the altar.[241]

It is for the rector of the church in which the altar is to be dedicated, helped by those who assist him in the pastoral work, to decide and prepare everything concerning the readings, singing, and other pastoral aids to foster the fruitful participation of the people and to ensure a dignified celebration.[242]

929 For the celebration of the rite the following should be prepared:

a. *The Roman Missal (Sacramentary), Lectionary for Mass, Dedication of a Church and an Altar;*

b. the processional cross and the Book of the Gospels to be carried in the procession;

c. vessel with water to be blessed and sprinkler;

d. vessel with the holy chrism;

e. towels for wiping the table of the altar;

f. if needed, a waxed linen cloth or other waterproof covering of the same size as the altar;

g. basin and pitcher of water, towels, and all that is needed for washing the bishop's hands;

h. linen apron (gremial);

i. brazier for burning incense or aromatic spices; or grains of incense and small candles (wax tapers) to burn on the altar;

j. censer and incense boat with spoon;

k. large enough cup, corporal, purificators, and hand towel;

l. bread and wine and water for the celebration of Mass;

m. altar cross, unless there is already a cross in the sanctuary (chancel), or the cross that is carried in the entrance procession is to be placed near the altar;

n. altar cloth, candles, and candlesticks;

o. flowers, as circumstances suggest.[243]

930 The vestments for the Mass of dedication are white or of some other festive color. The following should be prepared:

---

[241] See DA, no. 26: DOL 547, no. 4423.

[242] See DA, no. 25: DOL 547, no. 4422.

[243] See DA, no. 27: DOL 547, no. 4424.

a. for the bishop: alb, pectoral cross, stole, chasuble, miter, pastoral staff, and pallium, if the bishop has the right to wear one;

b. for the concelebrating presbyters: vestments for concelebrating Mass;

c. for the deacons: albs, stoles, and, if opportune, dalmatics;

d. for other ministers: albs or other lawfully approved vesture.[244]

931 If relics of the saints are to be placed beneath the altar, the following should be prepared:

a. *In the place from which the procession begins*:
— reliquary containing the relics, placed between flowers and lights. But, as circumstances dictate, the reliquary may be placed in a suitable part of the sanctuary (chancel) before the rite begins;
— for the deacons who will carry the relics to be deposited: albs, red stoles, if the relics are those of a martyr, or white in other cases, and, if available, dalmatics. If the relics are carried by presbyters, then, in place of dalmatics, chasubles should be prepared. The relics may also be carried by other ministers, vested in albs or in cassocks and surplices or in other lawfully approved vesture.

b. *In the sanctuary (chancel)*:
— small table on which the reliquary is placed during the first part of the dedication rite.

c. *In the vesting room (sacristy)*:
— sealant or cement to close the cover of the aperture. In addition, a stonemason should be on hand to close the depository of the relics at the proper time.[245]

932 It is fitting to observe the custom of enclosing in the reliquary a parchment on which is recorded the day, month, and year of the dedication of the altar, the name of the bishop who celebrated the rite, the titular of the church, and the names of the martyrs or saints whose relics are deposited beneath the altar.[246]

A record of the dedication is to be drawn up in duplicate, signed by the bishop, the rector of the church, and representatives of the local community; one copy is to be kept in the diocesan archives, the other in the archives of the church.[247]

---

[244] See DA, no. 28: DOL 547, no. 4425.
[245] See DA, no. 29: DOL 547, no. 4426.
[246] See DA, no. 30: DOL 547, no. 4427.
[247] See no. 877 of this *Ceremonial*.

Entrance into the Church

933   When the people are assembled, the bishop and the concelebrating presbyters, the deacons, and the ministers, each in appropriate vestments, and preceded by the crossbearer, go from the vesting room (sacristy) through the main body of the church to the sanctuary (chancel).[248]

934   If there are relics of saints to be placed beneath the altar, these are brought in the entrance procession to the sanctuary (chancel) from the vesting room (sacristy) or the chapel where, since the vigil, they have been exposed for the veneration of the people. For a good reason, before the celebration begins, the relics may be placed between lighted torches in a suitable part of the sanctuary (chancel).[249]

935   As the procession proceeds, Psalm 43 (42), with the entrance antiphon O God our shield or I will go to the altar of God, or some other suitable song is sung.[250]

936   When the procession reaches the sanctuary (chancel), the relics of the saints are placed between lighted torches in a suitable place. The concelebrating presbyters, the deacons, and the ministers go to the places assigned to them; the bishop, without kissing the altar, goes to the chair (cathedra). Then, putting aside the pastoral staff and miter, he greets the people, saying, The grace and peace, or some other suitable words, taken preferably from Sacred Scripture. The people reply, And also with you, or in some other suitable way.[251]

Blessing and Sprinkling of Water

937   When the entrance rite is completed, the bishop blesses water with which to sprinkle the people as a sign of repentance and as a reminder of their baptism, and to purify the altar. The ministers bring the vessel with the water to the bishop, who stands at the chair. The bishop invites all to pray, using the words Brothers and sisters in Christ or other suitable words. All pray in silence for a brief period. Then the bishop says the prayer God of mercy.[252]

---

[248] See DA, no. 31.
[249] See DA, no. 32.
[250] See DA, no. 33.
[251] See DA, no. 34.
[252] See DA, no. 35.

938   When the invocation over the water is finished, the bishop, accompanied by the deacons, passes through the main body of the church, sprinkling the people with holy water; then, when he has returned to the sanctuary (chancel), he sprinkles the altar. Meanwhile, the antiphon I saw water, or, during Lent, the antiphon I will pour clean water, or some other suitable song is sung.[253]

939   After the sprinkling, the bishop returns to the chair (cathedra) and, when the singing is finished, standing with hands joined, says, May God, the Father of mercies.
      Then the *Gloria* is sung except on a Sunday of Advent or Lent.
      When the *Gloria* is finished, the bishop, in the usual way, sings or says the opening prayer of the Mass.[254]

LITURGY OF THE WORD

940   In the liturgy of the word everything takes place in the usual way. The readings and the gospel are taken, in accordance with the rubrics, either from those provided in the *Lectionary for Mass* for the ritual Mass for the dedication of an altar or from those of the Mass of the day.[255]

941   After the gospel reading, the bishop, as a rule seated and with miter and pastoral staff, gives the homily, in which he explains the biblical readings and the meaning of the rite.[256]

942   The profession of faith is always said. The general intercessions are omitted, since in their place the Litany of the Saints is sung.[257]

PRAYER OF DEDICATION AND THE ANOINTINGS

Litany of the Saints

943   After the profession of faith, the bishop invites the people to pray, saying, Let our prayers, or other similar words.[258]

---

[253] See DA, no. 36.

[254] See DA, nos. 37-39.

[255] DA, no. 40; see LM, nos. 817-822 (Ritual Masses, IX. Dedication or Blessing of a Church or Altar, 2. Dedication of an Altar).

[256] See DA, no. 41.

[257] See DA, no. 42.

[258] See DA, no. 43.

Then the Litany of the Saints is sung, with all responding. On Sundays and also during the Easter season all stand; on other days all kneel, and the deacon says, Let us kneel.[259]

At the proper place in the litany the cantors add the names of other saints (the titular of the church, the patron saint of the place, and the saints whose relics are to be deposited, if this is to take place) and petitions suitable to the occasion and to the faithful taking part.[260]

When the litany is finished, the bishop, standing and with hands outstretched, says the prayer Lord, may the prayers of the Blessed Virgin Mary. Then, if the people have been kneeling, the deacon says, Let us stand. All rise. The bishop receives the miter and proceeds to the depositing of the relics.

When there is no depositing of the relics of the saints, the bishop immediately says the prayer of dedication, as indicated in no. 945.[261]

Depositing of the Relics

944   If relics of the martyrs or other saints are to be placed beneath the altar, the bishop approaches the altar. A deacon or presbyter brings the relics to the bishop, who places them in a suitably prepared aperture. Meanwhile, Psalm 15 (14), with the antiphon Saints of God or The bodies of the saints, or some other suitable song is sung.

During the singing a stonemason closes the aperture, and the bishop returns to the chair (cathedra).[262]

Prayer of Dedication

945   The bishop, without miter and standing at the altar with hands outstretched, sings or says the prayer Father, we praise you.[263]

Anointing of the Altar

946   Then the bishop, removing the chasuble if necessary and putting on a linen apron (gremial), goes to the altar with the deacon or another minister, who carries the vessel with the holy chrism. Standing before the altar and wearing the miter, the bishop says in a clear voice: We now anoint this altar. Then he pours holy chrism on the middle of the altar

---

[259] See DA, no. 44.
[260] See DA, no. 45.
[261] See DA, no. 46.
[262] See DA, no. 47.
[263] See DA, no. 48.

and on each of its four corners, and it is recommended that he anoint the entire table.[264]

During the anointing, outside the Easter season, Psalm 45 (44), with the antiphon God, your God, or some other suitable song is sung; during the Easter season, Psalm 118 (117), with the antiphon The stone which the builders rejected, or some other suitable song is sung.[265]

When the altar has been anointed, the bishop returns to the chair (cathedra), sits, washes his hands, then takes off the linen apron (gremial).[266]

Incensation of the Altar

947   After the rite of anointing, a brazier is placed on the altar for burning incense or aromatic gums, or, if desired, a heap of incense mixed with small candles or wax tapers is made on the altar. The bishop puts incense into the brazier, or he lights the heap of incense with a small candle handed to him by a minister; then he says, Lord, may our prayer ascend.

Then the bishop puts incense into the censer, blesses it, and incenses the altar; he returns to the chair (cathedra), puts on the miter, is incensed, and then sits. A minister incenses the people. Meanwhile, Psalm 138 (137), with the antiphon An angel stood or From the hand of the angel, or some other suitable song is sung.[267]

Covering and Lighting of the Altar

948   After the incensation, a few ministers wipe the table of the altar with towels and, if necessary, cover it with a waterproof covering. They then cover the altar with an altar cloth and, if circumstances suggest, decorate it with flowers. They arrange in a suitable manner the candles needed for the celebration of Mass and, if necessary, the cross.[268]

949   Then the deacon goes to the bishop, who stands and gives the deacon a small lighted candle and says in a clear voice, Light of Christ. The bishop then sits. The deacon goes to the altar and lights the candles for the celebration of the eucharist.[269]

---

[264] See DA, no. 49.

[265] See DA, nos. 50-51.

[266] See DA, no. 52.

[267] See DA, no. 53.

[268] See DA, no. 54.

[269] See DA, no. 55.

950   Then the festive lighting takes place: as a sign of rejoicing, all the lamps around the altar are lit. Meanwhile, the antiphon In you, O Lord or some other suitable song is sung, especially one in honor of Christ, the light of the world.[270]

LITURGY OF THE EUCHARIST

951   The deacons and the ministers prepare the altar in the usual way. Then some of the congregation bring the bread and the wine and water for the celebration of the Lord's sacrifice. The bishop receives the gifts at the chair (cathedra). While the gifts are being brought, the antiphon If you are bringing your gift or Moses consecrated the altar or some other suitable song may be sung.[271]

When all is ready, the bishop goes to the altar, removes the miter, and kisses the altar. The Mass proceeds in the usual way; however, the gifts and the altar are not incensed.[272]

952   The prayer over the gifts, Lord, send your Spirit upon this altar, and the proper preface, which are also provided in Dedication of a Church and an Altar, are always said, since they are an integral part of the rite of dedication of an altar.[273]

Eucharistic Prayer I or Eucharistic Prayer III is said.

953   At the end of Mass the bishop gives the final blessing, using the formulary provided in Dedication of a Church and an Altar. Then the deacon dismisses the people in the usual way.[274]

---

[270] See DA, no. 56.

[271] See DA, no. 57.

[272] See DA, no. 58.

[273] See DA, nos. 59-60.

[274] See DA, nos. 63-64.

CHAPTER 12

BLESSING OF A CHURCH

INTRODUCTION

954   Since sacred edifices, that is, churches, are permanently set aside for the celebration of the divine mysteries, it is right for them to receive a dedication to God. This is done according to the rite for dedicating a church, a rite impressive for its striking ceremonies and symbols.

But if the church does not receive dedication, it should at least receive a blessing, according to the rite described in this chapter.

Private oratories, chapels, or other sacred edifices set aside only temporarily for divine worship because of special conditions, more properly receive a blessing, according to the rite described in this chapter.[275] When a church, private oratory, or chapel is blessed, all such things as the cross, images, organ, stations of the cross are counted as blessed and installed by the one rite of blessing and do not therefore need a special blessing or installation.

955   As to the structure of the liturgy, the choice of a titular, and the pastoral preparation of the people, what has been said already in nos. 864-871 and no. 877 on the dedication of a church is to be followed, with the necessary modifications.[276]

956   A church or an oratory is blessed by the bishop of the diocese or by a presbyter delegated by him. A church or an oratory may be blessed on any day, apart from the Easter Triduum. As far as possible, a day should be chosen when the people can be present in large numbers, especially a Sunday, unless pastoral considerations suggest otherwise.[277]

957   On the days mentioned in nos. 1-4 of the table of liturgical days,[278] the Mass of the day is celebrated; but on other days either the Mass of the day or the Mass of the titular of the church or oratory is celebrated.

958   For the rite of the blessing of a church or an oratory, all things needed for the celebration of Mass are prepared. But even though the altar may have already been blessed or dedicated, it should be left bare

---

[275] See The Roman Pontifical, *Dedication of a Church and an Altar*, ch. 5, Blessing of a Church (hereafter, BC), no. 1: DOL 547, no. 4428.

[276] See BC, no. 2: DOL 547, no. 4429.

[277] See BC, nos. 2-3: DOL 547, nos. 4429-4430.

[278] See Appendix II of this *Ceremonial*.

until the beginning of the liturgy of the eucharist. In a suitable place in the sanctuary the following also should be prepared:

a. vessel of water to be blessed and sprinkler;

b. censer and incense boat with spoon;

c. *Dedication of a Church and an Altar;*

d. altar cross, unless there is already a cross in the sanctuary, or the cross that is carried in the entrance procession is to be placed near the altar;

e. altar cloths, candles, candlesticks, and flowers, if opportune.[279]

959   When the altar is to be consecrated at the same time as the church is to be blessed, all those things should be prepared that are listed in no. 929 and, if relics of the saints are to be deposited beneath the altar, in no. 931.[280]

960   The vestments for the Mass of the blessing of a church are white or of some other festive color. The following should be prepared:

a. for the bishop: alb, pectoral cross, stole, chasuble, miter, pastoral staff;

b. for concelebrating presbyters: vestments for concelebrating Mass;

c. for the deacons: albs, stoles, and dalmatics;

d. for other ministers: albs or other lawfully approved vesture.[281]

DESCRIPTION OF THE RITE

961   When the people are assembled, while the entrance song is being sung, the bishop and the concelebrating presbyters, the deacons, and the ministers, each in appropriate vestments and preceded by the cross-bearer, go from the vesting room (sacristy) through the main body of the church to the sanctuary (chancel).

When the procession arrives at the sanctuary (chancel), the bishop, without kissing or incensing the altar, goes immediately to the chair (cathedra); the others go to the places assigned to them.[282]

962   The bishop puts aside the pastoral staff and miter, and when the singing is finished, he greets the people, saying, The grace and peace,

---

[279] See BC, no. 5: DOL 547, no. 4432.

[280] See BC, no. 6: DOL 547, no. 4433.

[281] See BC, no. 7: DOL 547, no. 4434.

[282] See BC, no. 8.

or other suitable words, taken preferably from Sacred Scripture. The people reply, And also with you, or make some other suitable reply.[283]

963   Then the bishop blesses water with which to sprinkle the people as a sign of repentance and as a reminder of their baptism, and to purify the walls of the new church or oratory. The ministers bring the vessel with the water to the bishop, who stands at the chair (cathedra). The bishop invites all to pray, saying, Brothers and sisters, or another similar invitation. All pray in silence for a brief period. Then the bishop says the prayer God of mercy.[284]

964   When the invocation over the water is finished, the bishop, accompanied by the deacons, passes through the main body of the church, sprinkling the people and the walls with holy water; then, when he has returned to the sanctuary (chancel), he sprinkles the altar, unless it is already blessed or dedicated. Meanwhile, the antiphon I saw water flowing or, during Lent, the antiphon I will pour clean water, or some other suitable song is sung.
    After the sprinkling, the bishop returns to the chair (cathedra) and, when the singing is finished, stands and with hands joined says, May God, the Father of mercies.[285]

965   Then, except on the Sundays or weekdays of Advent and Lent, the *Gloria* is sung, and when it is finished the bishop says the opening prayer of the Mass.[286]

966   The Mass proceeds in the usual way, but with the following special provisions:

    — the readings are taken, in accordance with the rubrics, either from the texts provided in the *Lectionary for Mass* for the ritual Mass for the dedication of a church or for the Mass of the day;

    — neither lights nor incense is carried for the gospel reading;

    — after the gospel reading, the bishop gives the homily, in which he explains the biblical readings and the meaning of the rite;

    — the profession of faith is said when called for by the rubrics;

[283] See BC, no. 9.
[284] See BC, nos. 10-11.
[285] See BC, nos. 12-13.
[286] See BC, nos. 14-15.

the general intercessions are said in the usual way (unless the altar is to be dedicated; see no. 968).[287]

967 Then the bishop goes to the altar, if it is to be blessed. Meanwhile, the antiphon May the children of the Church or some other suitable song is sung.

When the singing is finished, the bishop, standing and without miter, speaks to the people, using the words Brothers and sisters, provided in *Dedication of a Church and an Altar*, or other similar words. All pray in silence for a brief period. Then, with hands outstretched, the bishop sings or says in a clear voice the prayer Blessed are you, Lord our God.

Then he puts incense into several censers and incenses the altar. Then, receiving the miter, he returns to the chair (cathedra), is incensed, then sits. Ministers, walking through the church, incense the people and the main body of the church.[288]

968 If the altar is to be dedicated, the profession of faith is said, the general intercessions are omitted, and the provisions of nos. 943-950 are observed.

But if the altar is to be neither blessed nor dedicated (for example, because an altar already blessed or dedicated has been transferred to the new church), after the general intercessions the Mass proceeds in the manner indicated in no. 969.[289]

969 After the general intercessions, the bishop sits and receives the miter. Ministers cover the altar with an altar cloth, and, if circumstances suggest, decorate it with flowers. They arrange in a suitable manner the candles needed for the celebration of Mass and, if necessary, the cross.

When the altar is ready, some of the congregation bring the bread and the wine and water for the celebration of the Lord's sacrifice. The bishop receives the gifts at the chair (cathedra). While the gifts are being brought, the antiphon If you are bringing, or the antiphon Moses consecrated the altar, or some other suitable song may be sung.[290]

970 When all is ready, the bishop goes to the altar, removes the miter, and kisses the altar. The Mass proceeds in the usual way; however, the

---

[287] See BC, nos. 16-19; see LM, no. 816 (Ritual Masses: IX. Dedication or Blessing of a Church or Altar, 1. Dedication of a Church).

[288] See BC, nos. 20-21.

[289] See BC, no. 22.

[290] See BC, nos. 23-24.

gifts and the altar are not incensed. But if the altar was not blessed or dedicated in this celebration, the incensation takes place in the usual way.[291]

If a chapel of the blessed sacrament is to be inaugurated, when the communion of the congregation is finished, everything takes place as already described in nos. 910-913.[292]

971   For the final blessing the bishop uses the formulary provided in *Dedication of a Church and an Altar.*

The deacon dismisses the people in the usual way.[293]

---

[291] See BC, no. 25.

[292] See BC, no. 26.

[293] See BC, nos. 27-28.

CHAPTER 13

BLESSING OF AN ALTAR

INTRODUCTION

972   A movable altar is one that is not attached to the floor and so can be moved from place to place. A movable altar also deserves religious respect, because it is a table set aside solely and permanently for the eucharistic banquet. Consequently, before a movable altar is put to use, if it is not dedicated, it should at least be blessed.[294]

973   A movable altar may be constructed of any solid material that the traditions and cultures of different regions determine to be suitable for liturgical use.[295]

974   To erect a movable altar, what is laid down in the liturgical books is to be followed, with the necessary modifications. However, it is not permissible to place the relics of saints in the base of a movable altar.[296]

975   It is appropriate that a movable altar be blessed by the bishop of the diocese or by the presbyter who is rector of the church.[297]

976   A movable altar may be blessed on any day except Good Friday and Holy Saturday. As far as possible, a day should be chosen when the people can be present in large numbers, especially a Sunday, unless pastoral considerations suggest otherwise.[298]

977   In the rite of blessing a movable altar, the Mass of the day is celebrated. But in the liturgy of the word, except on those days listed in nos. 1-9 of the table of liturgical days, one or two readings may be taken from those provided in the *Lectionary for Mass* for the dedication of an altar.[299]

978   The altar should be left bare until the beginning of the liturgy of the eucharist. Hence a cross (if need be), an altar cloth, candles, and every-

---

[294] See The Roman Pontifical, *Dedication of a Church and an Altar*, ch. 6, Blessing of an Altar (hereafter, BA), no. 1: DOL 547, no. 4428. See GIRM, nos. 261, 265: DOL 208, nos. 1651, 1655.

[295] See GIRM, no. 264: DOL 208, no. 1654.

[296] See BA, no. 3: DOL 547, no. 4437.

[297] See BA, no. 4: DOL 547, no. 4438.

[298] See BA, no. 5: DOL 547, no. 4439.

[299] See Appendix II of this *Ceremonial*; see LM, nos. 817-822 (Ritual Masses, IX. Dedication or Blessing of a Church or Altar, 2. Dedication of an Altar).

thing necessary to prepare the altar should be on hand at a convenient place in the sanctuary (chancel).[300]

DESCRIPTION OF THE RITE

979   During Mass everything takes place in the usual way. When the general intercessions are finished, the bishop goes to bless the altar. Meanwhile, the antiphon May the children of the Church or some other suitable song is sung.[301]

980   When the singing is finished, the bishop, standing and without miter, speaks to the people, using the words Brothers and sisters, our community, provided in *Dedication of a Church and an Altar*, or other similar words. All pray in silence for a brief period; then, with hands outstretched, the bishop sings or says in a clear voice the prayer Blessed are you, Lord our God.[302]

The bishop then sprinkles the altar with holy water and incenses it. Then he returns to the chair (cathedra), receives the miter, is incensed, then sits. A minister incenses the people.[303]

981   Ministers cover the altar with an altar cloth and, if circumstances suggest, decorate it with flowers. They arrange in a suitable manner the candles needed for the celebration of Mass, and, if necessary, the cross.[304]

982   When the altar is ready, some of the congregation bring the bread and the wine and water for the celebration of the Lord's sacrifice. The bishop receives the gifts at the chair (cathedra). While the gifts are being brought, the antiphon If you are bringing or some other suitable song may be sung.[305]

983   When all is ready, the bishop goes to the altar, removes the miter, and kisses the altar. The Mass proceeds in the usual way; however, the gifts and the altar are not incensed.[306]

---

[300] See BA, no. 7: DOL 547, no. 4441.

[301] See BA, no. 8.

[302] See BA, no. 9.

[303] See BA, no. 10.

[304] See BA, no. 11.

[305] See BA, no. 12.

[306] See BA, no. 13.

CHAPTER 14

BLESSING OF A CHALICE (CUP) AND PATEN

INTRODUCTION[307]

984   The chalice (cup) and paten for offering, consecrating, and receiving the bread and wine[308] have as their sole and permanent purpose the celebration of the eucharist and are therefore "sacred vessels."[309]

985   The intention to devote these vessels entirely to the celebration of the eucharist is expressed in the presence of the community through a special blessing, which is preferably imparted within Mass.[310]

986   Any priest may bless a chalice (cup) and paten, provided these have been made in conformity with the norms given in the General Instruction of the Roman Missal, nos. 290-295.[311]

987   If only a chalice (cup) or only a paten is to be blessed, the text of *Dedication of a Church and an Altar* should be modified accordingly.[312]

DESCRIPTION OF THE RITE

988   The Mass of the day is celebrated. In the liturgy of the word, apart from the days listed in nos. 1-9 in the table of liturgical days,[313] one or two readings may be taken from those provided in the *Lectionary for Mass*.[314]

989   After the reading of the word of God, the homily is given, in which the bishop explains the biblical readings and the meaning of the blessing of a chalice (cup) and paten that are used in the celebration of the eucharist.[315]

---

[307] See The Roman Pontifical, *Dedication of a Church and an Altar*, ch. 7, Blessing of a Chalice and Paten (hereafter, BCP).

[308] See GIRM, no. 261: DOL 208, no. 1651.

[309] See BCP, no. 1: DOL 547, no. 4442.

[310] See BCP, no. 2: DOL 547, no. 4443.

[311] See BCP, no. 3: DOL 547, no. 4444.

[312] See BCP, no. 4: DOL 547, no. 4445.

[313] See Appendix II of this *Ceremonial*.

[314] See BCP, nos. 5-7; see LM, nos. 823-826 (Ritual Masses, IX. Dedication or Blessing of a Church or Altar, 3. Blessing of a Chalice and Paten).

[315] See BCP, no. 9.

990   When the general intercessions are finished, ministers or representatives of the community that is presenting the chalice (cup) and paten place them on the altar. The bishop, with the deacons assisting him, then goes to the altar, as the antiphon I will take the cup of salvation or some other suitable song is sung.[316]

991   When the singing is finished, the bishop says, Let us pray. All pray in silence for a brief period. The bishop then continues with the prayer Lord, with joy we place on your altar.[317]

992   Afterward, a minister places a corporal on the altar. Some of the congregation bring the bread and the wine and water for the celebration of the Lord's sacrifice. The bishop places the bread on the newly blessed paten and pours the wine and water into the chalice (cup) and offers them in the usual way.

      Meanwhile, the antiphon I will take the cup or some other suitable song is sung.[318]

993   When he has said the prayer Lord God, we ask you to receive us, the bishop may incense the gifts and the altar. The Mass then proceeds in the usual way.[319]

994   If the circumstances of the celebration permit, it is appropriate that the congregation receive the blood of Christ from the newly blessed chalice (cup).[320]

---

[316] See BCP, no. 10.
[317] See BCP, no. 11.
[318] See BCP, no. 12.
[319] See BCP, no. 13.
[320] See BCP, no. 14.

CHAPTER 15

BLESSING OF A BAPTISTERY
OR OF A NEW BAPTISMAL FONT

INTRODUCTION

995   The baptistery, or the area where the baptismal font is located, should be reserved for the sacrament of baptism and should be worthy to serve as the place where Christians are reborn in water and the Holy Spirit. The baptistery may be situated in a chapel either inside or outside the church or in some other part of the church easily seen by the faithful; it should be large enough to accommodate a good number of people.[321]

The baptismal font, or the vessel in which on occasion the water is prepared for the celebration of the sacrament in the sanctuary, should be spotlessly clean and of pleasing design.[322]

996   It is appropriate that the rite of blessing be carried out by the bishop of the diocese or by the parish priest (pastor) or rector of the church.

997   If this rite of blessing is combined with the celebration of baptism, either at the Easter Vigil or at another time, the provisions of nos. 356-367, 427, 430, 440-448 of this *Ceremonial* are to be followed. But instead of the usual formulary for the blessing of the water, the bishop, with hands outstretched and facing the font, says the prayer Lord God, Creator of the world. After the blessing of the font, the celebration of baptism proceeds in the usual way.[323]

998   The blessing of a baptismal font without the celebration of baptism may take place at any hour and on any day except Ash Wednesday, during Holy Week, and All Souls. The day chosen should preferably be one on which a large number of the faithful can gather for the celebration.[324]

999   The following should be prepared for the rite of blessing a baptistery or a new baptismal font:

---

[321] See RBC, *Christian Initiation*, General Introduction, no. 25: DOL 294, no. 2274.

[322] See RBC, *Christian Initiation*, General Introduction, no. 19: DOL 294, no. 2268.

[323] See RM, Easter Vigil, Blessing of Water; RBC, no. 54; RCIA, no. 215 (U.S. ed., no. 222).

[324] See The Roman Ritual, *Book of Blessings*, English ed., 1987, ch. 25, Order for the Blessing of a Baptistery or of a New Baptismal Font (hereafter, OBBF), Introduction, no. 840.

a. *Book of Blessings, Lectionary for Mass;*

b. censer and incense boat;

c. vessel to receive the newly blessed water, and sprinkler;

d. Easter candle, candlestand for the Easter candle placed in the middle of the baptistery or near the font;

e. chairs for the bishop and the other ministers;

f. vestments, either white or of some other festive color:
   – for the bishop: alb, pectoral cross, stole, cope (or chasuble if he is to celebrate Mass), miter, pastoral staff;
   – for presbyters: vestments for the celebration of Mass;
   – for deacons: albs, stoles, and, as circumstances suggest, dalmatics;
   – for other ministers: albs or other lawfully approved vesture.

INTRODUCTORY RITES

1000 When the people have gathered, a procession is formed to go from the vesting room (sacristy) through the body of the church to the baptistery. The procession is led by a censerbearer carrying a censer with burning incense; an acolyte bearing the Easter candle follows; then the ministers, deacons, presbyters, and the bishop, all wearing their proper liturgical vestments.[325]

1001 During the procession Psalm 36 (35), with the antiphon You will drink or Lord, you are the source of life, or some other suitable song is sung.[326]

1002 When the procession reaches the baptistery, all go and stand in their assigned places. The Easter candle is placed in the candlestand prepared for it at the center of the baptistery or near the font. When the singing has ended, the bishop puts aside the miter and pastoral staff and greets those present with the words The grace of our Lord Jesus Christ or other suitable words, taken mainly from Sacred Scripture. All reply, And also with you, or make some other suitable reply. Then the bishop prepares those present for the celebration, using the words My dear brothers and sisters or other suitable words.[327]

---

[325] See OBBF, nos. 844 and 861.

[326] See OBBF, no. 862.

[327] See OBBF, nos. 863-864.

1003 After his introductory remarks, the bishop, with hands joined, says, Let us pray. All pray briefly in silence; then, with hands outstretched, the bishop says the prayer O God, by the sacrament of rebirth.[328]

LITURGY OF THE WORD

1004 After the introductory rites, the bishop sits and puts on the miter. Then one or more texts of Sacred Scripture are read, taken from those provided in the Lectionary for Mass for use in the celebration of the sacraments of Christian initiation.[329] Between the readings there is a responsorial psalm related to the reading that preceded it or an interval of silence. The gospel reading always holds the place of honor.

1005 After the reading of the word of God, the bishop in the homily explains the biblical texts so that those present may better understand the importance of baptism and the symbolism of the font.[330]

BLESSING OF THE NEW FONT

1006 Putting aside the miter, the bishop invites the people to pray, using the words Brothers and sisters, the time has come or some similar words. All pray briefly in silence; then, facing the font and with hands outstretched, the bishop says the prayer Lord God, Creator of the world.[331]

1007 After the invocation over the font, a baptismal song may be sung, for example, The Lord's voice resounding, The Father's voice calls us, or This is the fountain of life, as the font is being incensed. Then, as circumstances suggest, the bishop, standing with miter and facing the people, may receive the renewal of their baptismal faith, and afterward sprinkle them with water taken from the font.[332]

---

[328] See OBBF, no. 865.

[329] See LM, nos. 751-760 (Ritual Masses, I. Christian Initiation, 1. Order of Catechumens and Christian Initiation of Adults, Christian Initiation apart from the Easter Vigil, and 2. Christian Initiation of Children).

[330] See OBBF, no. 867.

[331] See OBBF, nos. 868-869.

[332] See OBBF, nos. 870-872.

Concluding Rite

1008   The intercessions are then said, either in the form usual in the celebration of Mass or in the form provided in the *Book of Blessings*.

The bishop then introduces the Lord's Prayer, using the words of
invitation provided in the ritual, Remembering that our baptism, or some
other similar words.

After the Lord's Prayer, the bishop says the prayer O God, who
endowed these waters.[333]

1009   The bishop blesses the people in the usual way, as provided in
nos. 1120-1121. The deacon dismisses the people with the words Go in
peace, and all reply, Thanks be to God.

1010   If this blessing is celebrated within Mass, the Mass of the day or,
depending on the rubrics, a votive Mass may be celebrated and one of
the readings may be taken from those provided in the *Lectionary for Mass*
for the ritual Mass for the celebration of the sacraments of Christian initiation (Ritual Masses, I. Christian Initiation, 1. Order of Catechumens
and Christian Initiation of Adults, Christian Initiation apart from the Easter
Vigil, and 2. Christian Initiation of Children).

---

[333] See OBBF, no. 874.

CHAPTER 16

BLESSING OF A NEW CROSS FOR PUBLIC VENERATION

INTRODUCTION

1011 Of all sacred images, the "figure of the precious, life-giving cross of Christ"[334] is preeminent, because it is the symbol of the entire paschal mystery. The cross is the image most cherished by the Christian people and the most ancient; it represents Christ's suffering and victory, and at the same time, as the Fathers of the Church have taught, it points to his Second Coming.

1012 The blessing of a new cross may be celebrated at any hour and on any day except Ash Wednesday, the Easter Triduum, and All Souls. But the preferred day is one that permits a large attendance of the faithful; they should receive proper preparation for their active participation in the rite.[335]

1013 The order presented in this chapter is meant for only two situations:

a. the solemn blessing of a cross erected in a public place, separate from a church;

b. the blessing of the principal cross that occupies a central place in the body of the church where the worshiping community assembles; in this case the rite of blessing begins at the point described here in no. 1020.

1014 The following should be prepared for the rite:

a. *Book of Blessings, Lectionary for Mass;*

b. censer and incense boat with spoon;

c. candlesticks for the acolytes;

The vestments for the celebration of the rite are white or of some other festive color:

— for the bishop: alb, pectoral cross, stole, cope, miter, pastoral staff;

— for deacons: albs, stoles, and, as circumstances suggest, dalmatics;

— for other ministers: albs or other lawfully approved vesture.

---

[334] See Council of Nicaea II, Act. 7: Mansi 13, 378; Denzinger-Schönmetzer, *Enchiridion symbolorum, definitionum et declarationum de rebus fidei et morum,* ed. XXXIV, no. 601.

[335] See The Roman Ritual, *Book of Blessings,* ch. 28, Order for the Blessing of a New Cross for Public Veneration (hereafter, OBNC), no. 964.

DESCRIPTION OF THE RITE

1015 When feasible, it is preferable for the community of the faithful to go in procession from the church or another location to the site where the cross that is to be blessed has been erected. When a procession either is not feasible or seems inadvisable, the faithful simply assemble at the site of the cross.[336]

When the people have gathered, the bishop, vested in alb, pectoral cross, stole, and cope, and with miter and pastoral staff, goes to them, accompanied by the ministers. Putting aside miter and pastoral staff, he greets the faithful in the words The grace of Jesus Christ or other suitable words. The people reply, And also with you, or make some other suitable reply.

1016 Then, using if he so chooses the words provided in the *Book of Blessings*, the bishop briefly addresses the faithful, in order to prepare them for the celebration and to explain the meaning of the rite.

After his introductory remarks, the bishop invites all to pray. After a brief period of silent prayer, the bishop, with hands outstretched, says the opening prayer, Lord, your Son reconciled us to you.[337]

1017 After the opening prayer, the bishop again takes the miter and pastoral staff, and the deacon may say, Let us proceed in peace. The procession to the site of the cross is then formed. During the procession Psalm 98 (97), with the antiphon We should glory in the cross, or some other suitable song is sung.[338]

When there is no procession, the opening prayer is followed immediately by the reading of the word of God.

1018 After the opening prayer, the bishop puts on the miter and sits for the proclamation of the word of God. There may be one or two readings, each followed by a responsorial psalm related to it. The texts may be taken from those given in the *Lectionary for Mass* (Votive Masses, Holy Cross).[339]

1019 The bishop then gives the homily, in which he explains both the biblical texts and the power of the cross of Christ.

---

[336] See OBNC, no. 966.

[337] See OBNC, nos. 967-968.

[338] See OBNC, no. 971.

[339] See LM, nos. 969-975 (Votive Masses, Holy Cross); OBNC, nos. 973-975.

1020   After the homily, the bishop, putting aside the miter and stand-ing before the cross, blesses it, saying the prayer Blessed are you, Lord God or the prayer Lord God, Father all-holy.

After the prayer, he puts incense into the censer, stands before the cross, and incenses it, as all sing the antiphon We worship you, or the antiphon Through the sign of the cross, or some other suitable song in honor of the cross.[340]

1021   After the incensation,* the bishop, the ministers, and the faithful venerate the new cross, if this can be done conveniently. One by one in procession all go to the cross and kneel before it or kiss it or offer some other sign of reverence in keeping with local custom.†

But if this procedure is impossible because of the large number in attendance or for some other good reason, the bishop speaks a few words, inviting the people to venerate the cross either by observing an interval of silent prayer or by some appropriate acclamation.[341]

1022   The veneration of the cross is followed by intercessions, either in the form usual at Mass or in the form provided in the *Book of Blessings*. The intercessions are concluded by the Lord's Prayer, sung or recited by all, and the prayer of the bishop.

Then, taking the miter and pastoral staff, the bishop blesses the people in the usual way, and the deacon assisting him dismisses them, saying, Go in peace, and all reply, Thanks be to God. Then a song in honor of the cross of Christ may be sung.[342]

---

[340] See OBNC, nos. 977-979.

* OBNC, no. 980, begins *Cantu expleto* ("After the singing"), not *Thurificatione completa* ("After the incensation").

† The rubrics for OBNC do not mention kneeling or kissing.

[341] See OBNC, no. 980.

[342] See OBNC, nos. 981-983.

CHAPTER 17

BLESSING OF BELLS

INTRODUCTION

1023 It is the longstanding custom of the Latin Church, which should be continued, to bless bells before they are hung in the belfry or campanile.

It is fitting that the rite of blessing be carried out by the bishop of the diocese or by the parish priest (pastor) or rector of the church.[343]

Depending on the place and the particular circumstances, bells are blessed within a celebration of the word of God.*

1024 The blessing of bells may be celebrated at any hour and on any day except Ash Wednesday, the Easter Triduum, and All Souls. But the preferred day is one that permits a large attendance of the faithful, especially a Sunday.[344]

1025 The bells should be hung or set up in the place chosen for the blessing in such a way that it will be easy to walk around the bells or ring them, if this suits the occasion.

The following should be prepared for the rite:

a. *Book of Blessings, Lectionary for Mass;*

b. vessel of holy water with sprinkler;

c. processional cross and torches for the ministers;

d. censer and incense boat;

The vestments for the celebration of this rite are white or of some other festive color. The following vestments should be prepared:

— for the bishop: alb, pectoral cross, stole, cope, miter, pastoral staff;

— for deacons: albs, stoles, and, as circumstances suggest, dalmatics;

— for other ministers: albs or other lawfully approved vesture.

DESCRIPTION OF THE RITE

1026 When the community has gathered, the bishop, with miter and pastoral staff, goes in procession to the chair or to the site of the bells

---

[343] See The Roman Ritual, *Book of Blessings,* ch. 30, Order for the Blessing of Bells (hereafter, OBB), no. 1036.

* No. 1035 of OBB also suggests that the bells may be blessed within Mass after the homily.

[344] See OBB, no. 1035.

276

to be blessed; a crossbearer between two ministers with lighted torches leads; then come the other ministers, deacons, presbyters, and the bishop. During the procession a suitable song is sung.

1027   After the singing, the bishop, putting aside miter and pastoral staff, greets the people, saying, The grace of our Lord; then he briefly addresses the faithful, in order to prepare them for the celebration.[345]

1028   After this, the bishop puts on the miter and sits for the proclamation of the word of God. There may be one or two readings, taken from those provided in the Book of Blessings; the first reading is followed by a responsorial psalm related to it.[346]

1029   After the reading of the word of God, the bishop gives the homily, in which he explains the biblical readings and the meaning and use of bells in the tradition and life of the Church.[347]

1030   After the homily, the bishop puts aside the miter and pastoral staff and, standing before the bells, says the prayer of blessing, either We praise you, Lord, Father all-holy or Lord, from the beginning of time. He then sprinkles the bells with holy water and incenses them. During this time Psalm 149, with the antiphon Sing to the Lord, or some other suitable song is sung.[348]

1031   The singing is followed by intercessions, either in the form usual at Mass or in the form provided in the Book of Blessings.[349] The intercessions are concluded by the Lord's Prayer, sung or recited by all, and the prayer of the bishop.*
     Then, taking the miter and pastoral staff, the bishop blesses the people in the usual way or with the formulary provided in the Book of Blessings. The assisting deacon dismisses them, saying, Go in peace, and all reply, Thanks be to God.

---

[345] See OBB, nos. 1038-1039. (The text of this Ceremonial differs at many points from the rite as given in OBB, most notably in the omission of the sign of the cross to begin the rite.)

[346] See OBB, nos. 1040-1042.

[347] See OBB, no. 1043.

[348] See OBB, nos. 1046-1048.

[349] See OBB, no. 1044.

* The Latin and English editions of OBB, nos. 1044-1046, provide no prayer concluding the intercessions as indicated in the Latin of this Ceremonial; a prayer of blessing, not the Lord's Prayer or a concluding prayer, follows the intercessions.

As circumstances suggest, before they depart, the bishop and the people may ring the newly blessed bells in jubilation.[350]

1032 If the blessing of bells is to be celebrated within Mass,[351] the following provisions should be observed:

a. the Mass of the day is celebrated;

b. except on solemnities, feasts, and Sundays, the readings may be taken either from the Mass of the day or from those provided in the *Book of Blessings* for the blessing of bells;

c. the blessing takes place after the homily, according to the rite set out in no. 1030;

d. the bells are not to be rung until after the Mass.

---

[350] See OBB, nos. 1049-1050.
[351] See OBB, nos. 1035 and 1051.

CHAPTER 18

ORDER OF CROWNING AN IMAGE
OF THE BLESSED VIRGIN MARY

INTRODUCTION

1033   Special honor is paid to images of the Blessed Virgin Mary by the practice of placing a crown upon the head of the image of the Mother of God and, when she is depicted with Christ, also upon the head of her Son. By means of this rite the faithful proclaim that the Blessed Virgin, who was raised body and soul to the glory of heaven, is rightly regarded and invoked as Queen. She is the Mother and faithful companion of Christ, the King of creation, who by the shedding of his precious blood acquired as his heritage dominion over all peoples.

1034   It is the responsibility of the bishop of the diocese, together with the local community, to decide on the opportuneness of crowning an image of the Blessed Virgin Mary. But it should be noted that it is proper to crown only those images to which the faithful come with a confidence in the Mother of the Lord so strong that the images are of great renown and their sites centers of a genuine liturgical cultus and of Christian vitality.
   The faithful who desire the crowning of an image of the Blessed Virgin Mary should be so instructed about the rite that they have a clear understanding and correct interpretation of its meaning.[352]

1035   The crown that will be placed on the image should be fashioned out of material of a kind that will symbolize the singular dignity of the Blessed Virgin. But opulence and lavish display are to be avoided; this would ill-suit the soberness of Christian worship or be in shocking contrast to the standard of living of the faithful in the region.[353]

1036   It is fitting that the diocesan bishop carry out the rite; if he is unable to do so, he should entrust this responsibility to another bishop or to a presbyter, particularly one associated with him in the pastoral care of the faithful in whose church the image to be crowned is venerated.
   But if an image is crowned in the name of the pope, the directives of the authorizing papal brief are to be followed.[354]

---

[352] See the *Order of Crowning an Image of the Blessed Virgin Mary* (hereafter, CIBVM), Introduction, no. 6.

[353] See CIBVM, no. 7.

[354] See CIBVM, no. 8.

1037 The rite of crowning is fittingly held on solemnities and feasts of the Blessed Virgin Mary or on other festive days. But the rite is not to be held on the principal solemnities of the Lord nor on days having a penitential character.

Depending on circumstances, the crowning of an image of the Blessed Virgin Mary may take place within Mass, within the liturgy of the hours at evening prayer, or within a celebration of the word of God suited to the occasion.[355]

1038 In addition to the requisites for the liturgical celebration with which the crowning is joined, the following should be prepared for the rite:

a. *Order of Crowning an Image of the Blessed Virgin Mary;*

b. *Lectionary for Mass;*

c. crown or crowns, ready in a convenient place;

d. vessel of holy water with sprinkler;

e. censer and incense boat with spoon.

The vestments for the rite are white or of some other festive color, except when a Mass requiring another color is celebrated.

When Mass is to be celebrated, the following are to be prepared:

— for the bishop: alb, pectoral cross, stole, chasuble, miter, pastoral staff;

— for deacons: albs, stoles, and, as circumstances suggest, dalmatics;

— for other ministers: albs or other lawfully approved vesture.[356]

I. Crowning of an Image of the Blessed Virgin Mary Within Mass

1039 Liturgical norms permitting, it is appropriate to celebrate the Mass of the Queenship of the Blessed Virgin Mary (22 August) or the Mass corresponding to the title represented by the image to be crowned.[357]

1040 In the Mass everything up to and including the gospel reading is done in the usual way. After the gospel reading, the bishop gives the homily, in which he explains both the biblical readings and the maternal and regal role of the Blessed Virgin Mary in the mystery of the Church.[358]

---

[355] See CIBVM, nos. 9-10.

[356] See CIBVM, nos. 11-12.

[357] See CIBVM, no. 13.

[358] See CIBVM, no. 14.

Thanksgiving and Invocation

1041   After the homily, ministers bring the crown (crowns) with which the image (images) of (Christ and) Mary is (are) to be crowned. Putting aside the miter, the bishop rises, and, while standing at the chair (cathedra), says the prayer Blessed are you, Lord. If an image of the Blessed Virgin Mary alone is to be crowned, he uses the words who by crowning this image of the Mother of your Son rather than the words printed in brackets, who by crowning this image of Christ and his Mother.[359]

Crowning

1042   After the prayer, the bishop sprinkles the crown (crowns) with holy water and in silence places the crown on the image of the Blessed Virgin Mary. But if the Blessed Virgin Mary is depicted with the infant Jesus, the image of Christ is crowned, then the image of his Mother.

   After the crown (crowns) has (have) been placed on the image (images), the antiphon Mary, Virgin for ever or some other suitable song is sung.

   During the singing, the bishop incenses the image (images), then returns to the chair (cathedra).

   After the singing, the Mass continues with the general intercessions in the manner provided in the *Order of Crowning* or in some similar manner.

   As circumstances suggest, after the incensation of the gifts, the altar, and the cross, the bishop may also incense the image (images) of (Christ and) the Blessed Virgin Mary.[360]

1043   The Mass continues in the usual way. After Mass, the antiphon Hail, holy Queen or *Ave, Regina caelorum* or, during the Easter season, the antiphon Queen of heaven, rejoice, or some other suitable song in honor of the Blessed Virgin Mary is sung.[361]

II. CROWNING OF AN IMAGE OF THE BLESSED VIRGIN MARY WITHIN EVENING PRAYER

1044   Liturgical norms permitting, it is appropriate to celebrate evening prayer of the Queenship of the Blessed Virgin Mary (22 August) or eve-

[359] See CIBVM, no. 15.
[360] See CIBVM, nos. 16-19.
[361] See CIBVM, no. 20.

ning prayer corresponding to the title represented by the image to be crowned.

1045 Evening prayer begins in the usual way. After the hymn,* the bishop may give a brief instruction to the people for the purpose of preparing them for the celebration. The singing of the psalms with their antiphons follows.

Following the psalmody, a longer reading is appropriate, chosen from those given in the *Lectionary for Mass* for feasts of the Blessed Virgin Mary. The bishop then gives the homily.[362]

1046 After the homily, all may reflect in silence on the word of God. Then the short responsory Holy Mary is Queen or a song with a similar theme is sung.[363]

1047 After the singing, the bishop, putting aside the miter, rises and all rise with him. While standing at the chair (cathedra), he blesses the crown (crowns), saying the prayer Blessed are you, Lord, and then sprinkles the crown (crowns) with holy water.[364] He then goes to the image (images) and in silence places the crown (crowns) on the image (images).[365]

1048 After the crown (crowns) has (have) been placed on the image (images), all stand and the Canticle of Mary is sung with one of the antiphons provided in the *Order of Crowning*. During the singing, the bishop first incenses the altar and cross, then the image (images).[366]

1049 After the canticle, evening prayer continues with the intercessions, in one of the formularies provided in the *Order of Crowning*. After the Lord's Prayer, the bishop says the prayer God of mercy, unless the office of the day requires a different prayer. The bishop next blesses the people in the usual way, and the deacon says the formulary of dismissal, Go in peace, and all reply, Thanks be to God. Then an antiphon or some other suitable song in honor of the Blessed Virgin Mary may be sung.[367]

---

* No. 22 of CIBVM reads: "after the opening verse and before the hymn."

[362] See CIBVM, nos. 21-25.

[363] See CIBVM, no. 26.

[364] See CIBVM, no. 27.

[365] See CIBVM, no. 28.

[366] See CIBVM, no. 29. (No. 29 of the CIBVM provides for the incensing of the ministers and the people as well.)

[367] See CIBVM, nos. 30-31.

III. Crowning of an Image of the Blessed Virgin Mary Within a Celebration of the Word of God

1050   The bishop vests in the vesting room (sacristy) or other suitable place, putting on an alb, pectoral cross, stole, and white cope or one of some other festive color, and taking the miter and pastoral staff. He enters the church in the usual way as Psalm 45 (44), with the antiphon The queen stands, or some other suitable song is sung. When he has reached the altar, the bishop puts aside the miter and pastoral staff and reverences the altar. Then he goes to the chair (cathedra), where, after the singing, he greets the people, saying, The grace of our Lord Jesus Christ, or some other similar greeting.[368]

1051   The bishop then gives a brief instruction to the people for the purpose of preparing them for the rite and explaining its significance. After the brief instruction, he invites the people to pray; all pray briefly in silence, and the bishop then continues with the prayer O God, since you have given.[369]

1052   After the prayer, all sit. The bishop puts on the miter and the celebration of the word of God begins and is carried out in the usual way. The readings are chosen from those given in the Lectionary for Mass for feasts of the Blessed Virgin Mary, but preferably from the readings for 22 August, the Queenship of the Blessed Virgin Mary. There should be suitable responsorial psalms or intervals of silence between the readings. The gospel reading always holds the place of honor.[370]

1053   After the readings, the bishop gives the homily, and everything else is done in the way already indicated in nos. 1041-1042.
    Then there are intercessions either in the form of a litany as provided in the Order of Crowning or in some other suitable manner.
    After the litany, the bishop blesses the people in the usual way, and the deacon says the formulary of dismissal.
    In conclusion, an antiphon appropriate to the liturgical season or some other suitable song is sung.[371]

---

[368] See CIBVM, nos. 32-33.
[369] See CIBVM, nos. 34-35.
[370] See CIBVM, no. 36.
[371] See CIBVM, nos. 37-43.

CHAPTER 19

BLESSING OF A CEMETERY

INTRODUCTION

1054 The Church considers the cemetery to be a holy place and there-fore wishes and urges that new cemeteries, established either by the Catholic community or by the civil authority in Catholic regions, be blessed and that a cross be erected as a sign to all of Christian hope in the resurrection.

"Neither place, nor language, nor their manner of civil life sets the followers of Christ apart from other people,"[372] with whom they seek to live in harmony. Christians therefore offer prayers to the heavenly Fa-ther for all and when they pray to him they include all, both those "who have died in the peace of Christ and all the dead whose faith is known to God alone."[373]

1055 The blessing of a cemetery may be celebrated at any hour and on any day except Ash Wednesday and the days of Holy Week. But the pre-ferred day is one that permits a large attendance of the faithful, and es-pecially a Sunday, since this weekly remembrance of Easter markedly expresses the paschal meaning death has for Christians.[374]

1056 This rite should preferably be celebrated by the bishop of the dio-cese, but he may entrust the responsibility to another bishop or to a pres-byter, particularly one who assists him in the pastoral care of the faithful who have established the cemetery, for example, to the parish priest (pas-tor) or the rector of the cemetery.[375] By adaptation of the provisions of no. 877 of this *Ceremonial*, a document recording the celebration of the blessing should be drawn up and one copy deposited in the diocesan curia, the other in the archives of the cemetery.

1057 The following should be prepared for the rite of blessing a ceme-tery:

a. *Book of Blessings, Lectionary for Mass;*

b. processional cross and torches to be carried by ministers in the procession to the cemetery;

---

[372] *Epistula ad Diognetum*, 5: F.X. Funk, ed., *Didascalia et constitutiones apostolorum*, 2 vols. (1905), vol. 1, p. 397.

[373] See RM, Order of Mass, Eucharistic Prayer IV.

[374] See The Roman Ritual, *Book of Blessings*, ch. 35, Order for the Blessing of a Cemetery (hereafter, OBC), no. 1117.

[375] See OBC, no. 1116.

c. vessel of holy water with sprinkler; censer and incense boat;

d. if the altar of the cemetery chapel is to be dedicated or blessed, the requisites for the dressing of the altar and everything else needed for a dedication or blessing;

e. if the eucharistic sacrifice is to be celebrated in the cemetery after the blessing, everything needed for the celebration of Mass.

The vestments for the celebration of this rite are of an appropriate color. The following vestments should be prepared:

— for the bishop: alb, pectoral cross, stole, cope or chasuble as required, miter, pastoral staff;

— for concelebrating presbyters: vestments for the celebration of Mass;

— for deacons: albs, stoles, and, as circumstances suggest, dalmatics;

— for other ministers: albs or other lawfully approved vesture.

APPROACH TO THE CEMETERY

1058　When feasible, a procession of the community from the church or other suitable place to the cemetery is preferable. When a procession is not feasible or not in keeping with circumstances, the faithful simply gather at the entrance of the cemetery.

Vested in alb, stole, and cope (or in chasuble if Mass is to be celebrated at the cemetery and the circumstances so suggest), and with miter and pastoral staff, the bishop with the ministers goes to the gathered people.

Putting aside the miter and pastoral staff, he greets them with the words The grace of our Lord Jesus Christ or with some similar greeting. The people reply, And also with you, or make some other suitable reply.[376]

1059　The bishop then prepares those present for the celebration, using the instruction Brothers and sisters in Christ or something similar. After the brief instruction, he invites the people to pray; all pray briefly in silence, and the bishop then continues with the prayer Lord, you have made your people a pilgrim Church.[377]

1060　After the prayer, when there is a procession, the deacon says, Let us proceed in peace. The procession to the cemetery is then formed; a

---

[376] See OBC, no. 1120.

[377] See OBC, no. 1121-1122.

crossbearer leads, walking between two ministers carrying lighted torches; the other ministers and the bishop, with miter and pastoral staff, follow; then the faithful. During the procession Psalm 118 (117), with the antiphon Lord, let my inheritance or another of those provided in the *Book of Blessings*, or some other suitable song is sung.

When there is no procession, the bishop, again taking miter and pastoral staff, with the ministers and the faithful enters the cemetery immediately after the opening prayer, as all sing Psalm 134 (133), with the antiphon I heard a voice, or some other suitable song.[378]

READING OF THE WORD OF GOD

1061   The procession moves to the place where the cemetery cross has been erected, and there the reading of the word of God takes place; if this is not convenient, the procession moves to the cemetery chapel or to another suitable place for the readings.[379]

1062   One or more texts of Sacred Scripture are read. But when the celebration of the liturgy of the eucharist is to follow, at least two readings are taken from the *Lectionary for Mass* (Masses for the Dead); one of these is a gospel reading, and there is a relevant responsorial psalm between these readings.[380]

1063   After the readings, the bishop in the homily explains both the biblical texts and the paschal meaning of death for the Christian.[381]

BLESSING OF THE CROSS AND THE CEMETERY GROUNDS

1064   After the homily, the bishop, without miter, stands before the cross erected at the center of the cemetery and blesses the cross as well as the cemetery grounds, saying the prayer God of all consolation. After the prayer, he places incense in the censer and incenses the cross. He then sprinkles the cemetery and those present with holy water. He may sprinkle the cemetery either as he stands at the center or by walking around the grounds. In the second case Psalm 51 (50), with the antiphon The bones that were broken, or some other suitable song is sung.[382]

---

[378] See OBC, nos. 1123-1125.

[379] See OBC, no. 1126.

[380] See OBC, no. 1127; LM, nos. 1011-1016 (Masses for the Dead).

[381] See OBC, no. 1128.

[382] See OBC, nos. 1129-1130.

Liturgy of the Eucharist
or Intercessions

1065　After the completion of the blessing, when the eucharistic sacrifice is to be offered for the dead, the bishop, if he is to be the celebrant, puts on a chasuble and goes to the altar prepared for Mass. Along with the ministers he makes the proper reverence to the altar, then kisses it.

　　The deacon assisting him or other ministers put the corporal, purificator, cup, and *The Roman Missal (Sacramentary)* in place on the altar; then they bring the bread and the wine and water to the bishop, and Mass proceeds in the usual way.[383]

1066　When the altar of a cemetery chapel is to be dedicated or blessed, everything is done, with the necessary adaptations, as already indicated for such a dedication (nos. 943-950) or blessing (nos. 979-983).[384]

1067　When the eucharist is not to be celebrated, after the sprinkling of the cemetery with holy water, the rite is concluded with intercessions. These may take the form usual at Mass or the form provided in the *Book of Blessings*. The intercessions are followed by the Lord's Prayer, sung or recited by all. Then, with miter and pastoral staff, the bishop blesses the people in the usual way,* and the deacon dismisses them, saying, Go in the peace of Christ, and all reply, Thanks be to God, then leave.[385]

*Dedication of a Cemetery Celebrated
by Several Christian Communities Together*

1068　Sometimes either the civil government or a Christian community made up of both Catholics and other Christians separated from us may establish a cemetery specifically for the burial of the deceased members of the Christian communities. In such a case it is most desirable that the formal opening of the cemetery be marked by an ecumenical celebration, the parts of which are planned by all the parties involved. Everything in the celebration that relates to Catholics is regulated by the local Ordinary.[386]

---

[383] See OBC, no. 1131.

[384] See OBC, no. 1132.

* Invocations in the form of a solemn blessing are provided in OBC, no. 1135.

[385] See OBC, nos. 1133-1136.

[386] See OBC, no. 1118.

Catholic Participation in the Dedication of a Cemetery
That Belongs to a Non-Christian Religion or Is Purely Secular

1069 If the Catholic community is invited to take part in the opening of a cemetery that belongs to a non-Christian religion or is purely secular, the Church does not refuse its presence or prayer for all the dead. The local Ordinary has responsibility for regulating the participation of Catholics.

When given the opportunity to do so, the Catholic priest and the faithful should choose scriptural readings, psalms, and prayers that plainly express the Church's teaching on death and the destiny of the human person, in whom there is a natural desire for the living and true God.[387]

---

[387] See OBC, no. 1119.

PUBLIC PRAYER AFTER THE DESECRATION OF A CHURCH*

INTRODUCTION

1070 Crimes committed in a church affect and do injury to the entire Christian community, which the church building in a sense symbolizes and represents.

The crimes in question are those that do grave dishonor to sacred mysteries, especially to the eucharistic species, and are committed to show contempt for the Church, or are crimes that are serious offenses against the dignity of the person and of society.

A church, therefore, is desecrated by actions that are gravely injurious in themselves and a cause of scandal to the faithful. In the judgment of the local Ordinary, they are so serious and so offensive to the sanctity of the church building that divine worship may be celebrated in the church only after penitential reparation for the wrong done.[388]

1071 Reparation for the desecration of a church is to be carried out with a penitential rite celebrated as soon as possible. Until that time neither the eucharist nor any other sacrament or rite is to be celebrated in the church. But through preaching and devotional exercises the faithful should be prepared for the penitential rite of reparation, and for their own inner conversion they should celebrate the sacrament of penance.

To symbolize the theme of penance, the altar of the church should be stripped bare, and all customary signs of joy and gladness should be put away, for example, lights, flowers, and other such articles.

1072 It is fitting that the bishop of the diocese preside at the rite of reparation. This will demonstrate that not only the immediate community but the entire diocesan Church joins in the rite and is ready for repentance and conversion.

As circumstances suggest, the bishop together with the rector of the church of the local community will decide whether the rite should be carried out with a celebration of the eucharistic sacrifice or with a celebration of the word of God.

---

* The Latin edition of this rite has not as yet been completed or issued by the Holy See. This rite may be published in the future as a supplementary part of the *Book of Blessings*.

[388] See The Roman Ritual, *Public Prayer*. The rite described in chapter 20 must be followed not only in the case of the desecration of a church but also in the case of any other sacred place that has been desecrated: see CIC, can. 1205-1213.

1073 The penitential rite may be celebrated on any day except the Easter Triduum, Sundays, or solemnities. But nothing precludes celebration of this rite on the vigil of a Sunday or solemnity; rather, such an arrangement has the advantage of avoiding spiritual harm to the faithful.

1074 The following are to be prepared for the celebration of the penitential rite:

a. The Roman Ritual, *Lectionary for Mass*;

b. vessel of water to be blessed and sprinkler;

c. censer and incense boat with spoon;

d. processional cross, torches for the ministers;

e. altar cloth, candles, other requisites for dressing the altar;

f. when Mass is to be celebrated, the requisites for its celebration.

The vestments for the penitential rite are violet or of some other penitential color in keeping with local custom, unless a Mass requiring some other color is to be celebrated.

The following are to be prepared:

— for the bishop: alb, pectoral cross, stole, cope or chasuble, miter, pastoral staff;

— for concelebrants: vestments for Mass;

— for deacons: albs, stoles, and, as circumstances suggest, dalmatics;

— for other ministers: albs or other lawfully approved vesture.

I. Penitential Rite Within Mass

1075 The rite most suitable for use in reparation for the desecration of a church is one in which the penitential service is aptly joined to the celebration of the eucharist. A new church is most properly dedicated through a celebration of the eucharist, and a desecrated church should be restored to divine service in the same way.

1076 Because of the communion binding priests to their bishop, in the celebration of the penitential rite the bishop should concelebrate with the presbyters present, especially those who carry out the pastoral ministry in the church that has been desecrated.

1077 The proper texts required for the celebration of the Mass are all indicated in their place in The Roman Ritual. But the Mass celebrated may also be one that is best suited to the reparation of the wrong done, for example, one of the votive Masses of the holy eucharist in a case of profanation of the blessed sacrament (RM, Votive Masses, Holy Eucharist) or the Mass for promoting harmony in a case of a violent clash in the church building between members of the community (RM, Masses and Prayers for Various Needs and Occasions, IV. For Particular Needs, 42. For Promoting Harmony).

ENTRANCE INTO THE CHURCH

1078   The gathering of the faithful and the entrance into the church may be carried out in either of two ways, as the circumstances of time and place suggest.

First Form: Procession

1079   At the time scheduled, the people gather in a nearby church or other convenient place, from which a procession, led by a crossbearer, will make its way to the desecrated church. The bishop, with miter and pastoral staff, the concelebrants, deacons, and other ministers, all in their proper liturgical vesture, go to the place where the people have gathered. Putting aside miter and pastoral staff, the bishop greets the people.

1080   The bishop gives a brief instruction to prepare the faithful for the celebration of the rite. He next invites them to pray and, after a brief pause for silent prayer, says the opening prayer.

1081   The deacon may then say, Let us go forth in peace, and the procession to the desecrated church is formed. The crossbearer, between two acolytes carrying lighted candles, leads, followed by the ministers, the concelebrating presbyters, the bishop, with miter and pastoral staff and accompanied by deacons, then the faithful.
      During the procession the Litany of the Saints is sung, with invocations of the patron of the place or the titular of the church added at the appropriate place. Before the invocation Jesus, Son of the living God, an invocation related to the rite of reparation is added, as well as other invocations pertinent to the needs of the community.

1082   When he has entered the church, the bishop goes directly to the chair, without reverencing the altar. The concelebrants, deacons, and ministers take their assigned places. Putting aside the miter and pastoral staff, the bishop blesses water and carries out the sprinkling in the manner to be indicated in nos. 1085-1086.

Second Form: Simple Entrance

1083 If a procession is not feasible or seems inadvisable, the faithful gather in the church. Led by a crossbearer between two acolytes with lighted candles, the bishop, with miter and pastoral staff, the concelebrating presbyters, deacons, and ministers, all in their proper liturgical vesture, proceed from the vesting room (sacristy) through the body of the church to the sanctuary (chancel). During this time Psalm 130 (129), with an antiphon, or some other suitable song is sung.

1084 When the procession has reached the sanctuary (chancel), the concelebrants, deacons, and ministers go to their assigned places. Without reverencing the altar, the bishop goes directly to the chair and, putting aside the miter and pastoral staff, greets the people.

Blessing and Sprinkling of Water

1085 After the entrance rite, the bishop blesses water with which to sprinkle the people as a reminder of their baptism and as a sign of penance, and to sprinkle the altar and walls of the desecrated church as a sign of purification. Ministers bring water to the bishop as he stands at the chair. He invites all to pray, and, after a pause for silent prayer, says the prayer for the blessing of water.

1086 After the invocation over the water, the bishop, escorted by deacons, sprinkles the altar with the holy water and, if he wishes, passes through the body of the church, sprinkling the people and the walls. During this time an antiphon is sung.

1087 When the sprinkling is finished, the bishop returns to the chair and, with hands joined, invites those present to pray. After a brief pause for silent prayer, the bishop, with hands outstretched, says the opening prayer.

Liturgy of the Word

1088 In the liturgy of the word the readings, responsorial psalms, and verse before the gospel reading are taken from those provided in the *Lectionary for Mass* for the Mass for forgiveness of sins,[389] unless other read-

---

[389] See LM, nos. 948-952 (Masses for Various Occasions, IV. For Particular Needs, 27. For Forgiveness of Sins).

ings are chosen that in view of the circumstances are more pertinent. After the gospel reading, the bishop, seated and with miter and pastoral staff (unless he decides otherwise), gives the homily, in which he explains the biblical readings, the restored dignity of the church building, and the need of the local Church to grow in holiness.

1089 If the Litany of the Saints has been sung, the general intercessions are omitted. If not, the general intercessions should be carried out in such a way that besides the usual intentions a fervent petition is added for conversion and pardon. This may be patterned on the examples provided in The Roman Ritual.

LITURGY OF THE EUCHARIST

1090 After the general intercessions, the bishop puts on the miter and sits. The deacon and the ministers cover the altar with an altar cloth and, as circumstances suggest, may place flowers around it; they also arrange candlesticks with the candles required for Mass and, if necessary, an altar cross.

When the altar has been prepared, some members of the faithful present the bread and the wine and water for the celebration of the eucharist. The bishop receives the gifts at the chair. During the presentation of the gifts an antiphon or some other suitable song may be sung.

The deacon and the ministers then place a corporal, purificator, cup, and The Roman Missal (Sacramentary) on the altar.

When everything is ready, the bishop, putting aside the miter, goes to the altar and kisses it. The Mass continues in the usual way. After the prayer Lord God, we ask you to receive, the bishop incenses the gifts and the altar.

Then the prayer over the gifts is said.

1091 In a case of desecration of the eucharistic species, the concluding rites of the Mass are replaced by exposition and benediction of the blessed sacrament, in the manner to be indicated in no. 1105.

To impart the final blessing in the usual manner, the bishop may use one of the formularies for the solemn blessing; after the blessing, the deacon dismisses the faithful in the usual way.

II. PENITENTIAL RITE WITHIN A CELEBRATION OF THE WORD

1092 When there is to be only a celebration of the word of God, everything is done in the way already indicated in nos. 1079-1089. Then there is prayer for God's mercy by means of the form of intercession provided in The Roman Ritual or some other similar form. Then the ministers or members of the faithful place an altar cloth upon the altar and, as circumstances suggest, flowers around it; during this time there is a festive illumination of the body of the church. The bishop goes to the altar, then kisses it and incenses it. After the incensing, he stands before the altar and with a suitable invitation introduces the Lord's Prayer, which all then sing or recite. The bishop continues immediately with the pertinent prayer provided in The Roman Ritual. The usual blessing and dismissal of the people follow.

CHAPTER 21

PROCESSIONS

1093 Public, sacred processions are a form of solemn supplication, deriving from the practice of our ancestors in the faith, in which the faithful, under the leadership of the clergy, pass in an orderly manner from one holy place to another as they recite prayers and sing sacred songs. The Catholic Church has adopted this practice to stir up the devotion of the faithful, to commemorate and give thanks for divine favors, or to implore God's aid. Such processions should, then, be celebrated with great reverence, since they represent great divine mysteries and since those devoutly taking part in them receive from God the salutary benefits of their Christian devotion. Pastors are therefore to accept the responsibility of preparing the faithful beforehand by instructing them on the meaning of religious processions.[390]

1094 Ordinary processions are those that take place on set days in the liturgical year in keeping with the provisions of the liturgical books or the customs of the local Church. Extraordinary processions are those that are scheduled on certain days by reason of some public cause or need.[391]

1095 The chief ordinary processions are those that commemorate mysteries of the Lord, namely, those held on the feast of the Presentation of the Lord, Palm Sunday, and the Easter Vigil; also the procession of the blessed sacrament following Mass on the solemnity of the Body and Blood of Christ (Corpus Christi).

1096 Extraordinary processions are those scheduled by the conference of bishops, for example, processions for the rogation days; or those scheduled by the local Ordinary, for example, processions held in the case of some public crisis or such processions as those with relics or images.

1097 Processions with the blessed sacrament follow Mass when the host to be carried in the procession is to be consecrated at that Mass. Other processions usually take place before the celebration of Mass, unless the local Ordinary, for some serious reason, decides otherwise.

1098 Processions, and especially those through public streets, should be arranged and formed in such a way that they are an edification to all. They should be adapted to the culture of the people and to the character of the country and of the area.

---

[390] See *Rituale Romanum*, ed. 1952, tit. X, cap. 1, no. 14.
[391] See *Rituale Romanum*, ed. 1952, tit. X, cap. 1, nos. 8, 9.

1099   The arrangement of processions should follow the order indicated for them in this *Ceremonial*[392] and in the various liturgical books. At the head of every procession there is to be a crossbearer between two ministers carrying lighted candles and, if incense is used, preceded by the censerbearer carrying censer with burning incense, except in processions of the blessed sacrament.

1100   When the bishop takes part in a procession of the blessed sacrament, of the wood of the cross, or of relics or images, it is always fitting that, wearing a cope, he preside by carrying the blessed sacrament or the sacred object.

When the bishop does not carry the blessed sacrament or the sacred object but is vested in a cope, he walks before the one who does. But if he is vested in choir dress, the bishop walks behind the blessed sacrament or the sacred object.

If other bishops should take part in a procession and they are vested in choir dress, they walk behind the blessed sacrament or sacred object, in such a way that those of higher rank walk nearer the blessed sacrament. But when they are wearing a cope, they walk ahead of the bishop, in such a way that the higher in rank are always nearer the blessed sacrament or the sacred object.

1101   Except in a procession of the blessed sacrament or of a relic of the true cross, the bishop wears a miter if he is wearing sacred vestments. He also carries the pastoral staff, unless he must hold some other object in his hand—a candle or a palm branch, for example. If the bishop himself does not carry the pastoral staff, it is carried before him by a minister.

---

[392] See, for example, in this *Ceremonial* nos. 246, 270, 343, 391; see also nos. 128 and 193.

CHAPTER 22

EUCHARISTIC EXPOSITION AND BENEDICTION

INTRODUCTION

1102   Exposition of the holy eucharist leads us to acknowledge Christ's marvelous presence in the sacrament and invites us to the spiritual union with him that culminates in sacramental communion. In such exposition care must therefore be taken that everything brings out the meaning of eucharistic worship in correlation with the Mass.[393]

1103   Genuflection in the presence of the blessed sacrament exposed for public adoration is on one knee.[394]

1104   For exposition of the blessed sacrament with a monstrance, the following are to be prepared:
    a. *Upon the altar or, in accord with the particular situation, near it*:
        — monstrance and, as circumstances require, a corporal;
        — four or six candles;
        — flowers, as circumstances suggest;
        — *Holy Communion and Worship of the Eucharist outside Mass*;
        — humeral veil;
        — for the bishop and ministers, chairs and kneelers, when and where they are needed.
    b. *In the vesting room (sacristy)*:
        — censer and incense boat with spoon;
        — the following vestments, white or of some other festive color:
        — for the bishop: alb, pectoral cross, stole, cope, miter, and pastoral staff;
        — for deacons: albs, stoles, and, as circumstances suggest, dalmatics;
        — for other ministers: albs or other lawfully approved vesture.

I. LENGTHY EXPOSITION

Exposition

1105   In the case of more solemn and lengthy exposition, the host should be consecrated in the Mass which immediately precedes the exposition and after communion should be placed in the monstrance upon the al-

---

[393] See HCWE, no. 82: DOL 279, no. 2208.
[394] See HCWE, no. 84: DOL 279, no. 2210.

tar. The Mass ends with the prayer after communion, and the concluding rites are omitted. Before the bishop leaves, he incenses the blessed sacrament, using the rite described in no. 1109.[395]

1106 If exposition takes place outside Mass, and the bishop presides, he is received in the manner already described in no. 79. In the vesting room (sacristy) or some other convenient place, he puts on an alb, pectoral cross, stole, and cope of appropriate color and, as a rule, uses the miter and pastoral staff. The bishop is assisted by two deacons, or at least by one, wearing diaconal vestments. In the absence of a deacon, the bishop is assisted by presbyters, vested in cope.

1107 When he reaches the altar, the bishop hands the pastoral staff to a minister and puts aside the miter. Together with the deacons assisting him he makes a deep bow to the altar or genuflects before the blessed sacrament if it is reserved in the sanctuary (chancel), and he remains kneeling before the altar.

1108 A deacon immediately puts on the humeral veil and, escorted by acolytes carrying lighted candles, brings the blessed sacrament from its place of reservation. The deacon puts the blessed sacrament into a monstrance and sets the monstrance upon the altar table, which is covered with an altar cloth and, as circumstances suggest, a corporal.[396] He then genuflects and returns to his place beside the bishop.

When the altar of exposition is also the place of reservation of the blessed sacrament, the deacon goes up to the altar, opens the tabernacle, genuflects, and places the sacrament into the monstrance on the table of the altar.

1109 The bishop rises, the censerbearer goes to him, and, as the deacon holds the incense boat before him, the bishop puts incense into the censer and blesses it. Kneeling, the bishop takes the censer from the deacon, bows together with the ministers assisting him, then incenses the blessed sacrament. After again bowing to the blessed sacrament, he returns the censer to the deacon.

1110 If the exposition is to be lengthy, the bishop may then withdraw.[397] But if he remains, he may take his place at the chair or at some other convenient place in the sanctuary (chancel).

---

[395] HCWE, no. 94.

[396] See HCWE, no. 93.

[397] HCWE, no. 93.

Adoration

1111   During the exposition there should be prayers, songs, and readings to direct the attention of the faithful to the worship of Christ the Lord.

To encourage a prayerful spirit, there should be readings from Sacred Scripture with a homily or brief exhortations to develop a better understanding of the eucharistic mystery. It is also desirable for the people to respond to the word of God by singing and to spend some periods of time in sacred silence.

Part of the liturgy of the hours, especially the principal hours, may be celebrated before the blessed sacrament when there is a lengthy period of exposition. The liturgy extends the praise and thanksgiving offered to God in the eucharistic celebration to the several hours of the day; it directs the prayers of the Church to Christ, and through him to the Father, in the name of the whole world.[398]

Benediction

1112   Toward the end of the exposition, the bishop goes to the altar.[399] But if this is the first time that he is present at the exposition, the provisions of no. 1107 are followed. When he reaches the altar, he hands the pastoral staff to a minister and puts aside the miter.

1113   With the deacons assisting him, the bishop genuflects, then remains kneeling before the altar.

During this time the *Tantum ergo Sacramentum* or some other eucharistic song is sung. After placing incense into the censer and blessing it, in the manner described in no. 1109, the bishop, kneeling, incenses the blessed sacrament, in the manner also described in no. 1109.

Then he rises and says, Let us pray. After a brief period of silence, the bishop, with hands outstretched, continues with the prayer Lord Jesus Christ or another of the prayers provided in *Holy Communion and Worship of the Eucharist outside Mass.*

1114   After the prayer, the bishop puts on the humeral veil, goes up to the altar, and genuflects. With the help of the deacon, he takes the monstrance, which, with both hands covered by the veil, he holds in a raised position; he then turns toward the people and makes the sign of the cross over them with the monstrance, in silence.[400]

---

[398] HCWE, nos. 95-96.
[399] See HCWE, no. 97.
[400] See HCWE, no. 99.

After the blessing, the deacon takes the monstrance from the hands of the bishop and places it on the altar. The bishop and the deacon genuflect. While the bishop removes the humeral veil and remains kneeling before the altar, the deacon reverently transfers the blessed sacrament to the place of reservation, where he returns it to the tabernacle, genuflects, and closes the tabernacle.

Meanwhile, the people may sing or recite an acclamation.[401]

The return to the vesting room (sacristy) takes place in the usual way.

II. Brief Period of Exposition

1115   When there is to be a short period of exposition with the ciborium at which the bishop presides, the following are to be prepared:

— at least two candles;
— censer and incense boat, as circumstances suggest;
— for the bishop: alb, pectoral cross, stole, cope;
— for a deacon or presbyter: alb and stole;
— for other ministers: albs or other lawfully approved vesture.

When he reaches the altar, the bishop makes the prescribed reverence and remains kneeling before the altar. The deacon or presbyter assisting him exposes the blessed sacrament.

If incense is to be used, the provisions of nos. 1109 and 1113 are followed.

Toward the end of the period of adoration the *Tantum ergo Sacramentum* or some other eucharistic song is sung. The bishop then rises and says, Let us pray. Afer a brief period of silent prayer, the bishop, with hands outstretched, says one of the prayers provided in *Holy Communion and Worship of the Eucharist outside Mass*.

Then he puts on the humeral veil, goes up to the altar, genuflects, and takes the ciborium with both hands, covered by the veil. He turns toward the people and makes the sign of the cross over them, in silence. He then places the ciborium back on the altar, genuflects, and, after taking off the humeral veil, remains kneeling before the altar until the deacon or presbyter assisting him has replaced the blessed sacrament in the tabernacle.

After the prescribed reverence to the altar, all return to the vesting room (sacristy).

---

[401] See HCWE, no. 100.

CHAPTER 23

BLESSINGS IMPARTED BY THE BISHOP

INTRODUCTION

1116 The ministry of blessing involves a particular exercise of the priest-hood of Christ, in keeping with the place and office within the people of God that belong to each person. In this understanding it belongs pre-eminently to the bishop to preside at celebrations that involve the entire diocesan community. The bishop may accordingly reserve such bless-ings to himself; but he may also delegate a presbyter to preside in his name.

It is also the responsibility of the bishop to teach the people the proper meaning of the rites and prayers employed by the Church in im-parting blessings, to forestall the intrusion into the celebration of any-thing that might replace genuine faith with superstition or a shallow credulity.[402]

1117 The typical celebration of a blessing as found in liturgical books consists of two parts: first, the proclamation of the word of God, and, second, the praise of God's goodness and the petition for his help. But, provided the structure of the celebration and the order of its parts are respected, options are granted in the various orders of blessing that fa-vor the primary criterion for the celebration, namely, active, conscious, and full participation. Therefore, even if certain things are to be blessed with a simple sign of the cross, the utmost attention must be given to the proclamation of the word of salvation, to sharing in fruitful faith, to praising God, and to petitioning God's help.[403]

I. ORDINARY BLESSING

1118 At the end of a stational Mass the bishop gives the blessing in the way already indicated in no. 169.

1119 In other Masses and liturgical services (for example, evening prayer or morning prayer, the end of a procession in which the blessed sacra-ment is not carried, etc.) or even outside a liturgical service, the bishop may impart the blessing by use of either of the two following formularies.

---

[402] See The Roman Ritual, *Book of Blessings*, General Introduction, nos. 18-19.
[403] See *Book of Blessings*, General Introduction, nos. 20-24, 27.

First form

1120 If he is using the miter, he puts it on and, with hands outstretched, greets the people, saying, The Lord be with you, and all reply, And also with you. With hands outstretched over the people, the bishop continues, May the peace of God, which is beyond all understanding, keep your hearts and minds in the knowledge and love of God and of his Son, our Lord Jesus Christ. All reply, Amen.

If he is using the pastoral staff, the bishop takes it and says, May almighty God bless you, and, as he makes the sign of the cross three times over the people, he adds, ✠ the Father, ✠ and the Son, ✠ and the Holy Spirit.

Second form

1121 After greeting the people in the manner already indicated in no. 1120, the bishop says, Blessed be the name of the Lord, and all reply, Now and for ever. The bishop then says, Our help is in the name of the Lord, and all reply, Who made heaven and earth. Then the bishop says the words of blessing, May almighty God, given in no. 1120.

II. Apostolic Blessing

1122 The diocesan bishop in his own diocese may bestow the papal blessing with a plenary indulgence, using the proper formulary, three times a year on solemn feasts, which he will designate, and even if he only assists at the Mass.

Other prelates equivalent in law to a diocesan bishop, even though not of episcopal rank, may, from the outset of their pastoral office, bestow within their own territories the papal blessing with the same plenary indulgence three times a year on solemn feasts, which they will designate.[404]

The blessing is given at the end of Mass in place of the usual final blessing.[405]

1123 In his introduction to the penitential rite of the Mass, the bishop should advise the faithful of the papal blessing with plenary indulgence that he will bestow at the end of Mass, and he should invite them to repent of their sins and dispose themselves to share in this indulgence.

---

[404] See *Enchiridion indulgentiarum*, no. 11, §2: DOL 390, no. 3203.

[405] See PR, nos. 33-36: AAS 60 (1968), pp. 406-412; DOL 550, nos. 4493-4496.

In place of the usual formulary that concludes the penitential rite, the following one is used:

May blessed Mary, ever virgin,
the holy apostles Peter and Paul,
and all the saints
assist you with their merits and prayers.

May the almighty and merciful Lord forgive you
and free you from all your sins.

May he help you persevere in fruitful penance,
good example, and sincere charity,
and lead you to everlasting life.

R. Amen.

1124 The general intercessions are to include the intention for the Church, and a special intention for the Roman Pontiff is to be added.

1125 After the prayer after communion, the bishop puts on the miter, and the deacon announces the blessing in the following or similar words:

The Most Reverend Father, N., by the grace of God and the Apostolic See, Bishop of this holy Church of N., will give the (apostolic) blessing with a plenary indulgence, in the name of the Roman Pontiff, to all present who are truly penitent and have confessed their sins and received Holy Communion.

Pray to God for our Most Holy Father, Pope N., our Bishop, N., and for holy Mother Church and strive, by holiness of life, to walk in full communion with it.

1126 The bishop, with the miter, then stands and, with hands outstretched over the people, greets them, The Lord be with you, and all reply, And also with you. The deacon then may say the words of invitation, Bow your heads and pray for God's blessing, or something similar. The bishop, with hands outstretched over the people, pronounces the formulary for the proper solemn blessing provided in *The Roman Missal* (*Sacramentary*). Then he takes the pastoral staff and concludes the blessing with the following formulary:

Through the intercession of the blessed apostles Peter and Paul, may almighty God bless you,
✠ the Father, ✠ and the Son, and ✠ the Holy Spirit.

R. Amen.

As he says the final words he makes the sign of the cross three times over the people.

III. Other Blessings

1127 Whenever a blessing is to be celebrated by the bishop with a large group of the faithful as a community, the rite is to be arranged in the manner prescribed in the *Book of Blessings* or in some other liturgical book. The bishop wears an alb, pectoral cross, stole, and a cope of appropriate color; he also uses the miter and pastoral staff.

1128 The bishop should properly be assisted by a deacon in alb, stole, and, as circumstances suggest, dalmatic, or by a presbyter in alb, or cassock and surplice, and stole, and by other ministers, in albs or other lawfully approved vesture.

   As a rule, in such a celebration the bishop reserves to himself: the greeting; brief homily on the biblical readings and the meaning of the blessing being celebrated; prayer of blessing, which he says standing and without miter; the introduction and concluding prayer of the intercessions, the inclusion of which is recommended; and, before the dismissal, the final blessing, which he imparts in the usual way.

PART VII

SPECIAL DAYS IN THE LIFE OF A BISHOP

CHAPTER 1

ELECTION OF THE BISHOP

1129   When the local Church is first informed that the canonical provision has been made, the administrator of the diocese announces a liturgical service of thanksgiving and prayer for the bishop-elect to be celebrated on a convenient date in the cathedral church.

1130   The bishop-elect must attend to the following as soon as possible:

a.   If he is present in Rome at the time of his election, he must go in person to the pope, or if he is not in Rome, send a letter, in order to express his communion with and reverence toward the pope, as well as to commend his Church to the pope.

b.   He must make a profession of faith and take an oath of loyalty to the Apostolic See. If he is in Rome, he does this in the presence of a cardinal appointed for this purpose; if he is not in Rome, before someone delegated by the Apostolic See.[1]

c.   He must visit the metropolitan or the senior bishop of his ecclesiastical province, in order to receive a report on the state of his own diocese, and, when applicable, to decide with that bishop on the day of his own episcopal ordination.

d.   He must resign any offices he holds so that by devoting himself to prayer and meditation he may prepare for his new ministry.

e.   If he is entitled to wear the pallium, he must request one from the pope.[2]

1131   Within the time prescribed by law, the bishop-elect must receive episcopal ordination and take canonical possession of his diocese, as these are described in nos. 1133-1140.

1132   The bishop-elect is entitled to use episcopal vesture and insignia, in keeping with liturgical norms, only from the moment of his ordination.

---

[1] See CIC, can. 380 and 833, 3°.
[2] See CIC, can. 437, §1.

CHAPTER 2

ORDINATION OF THE BISHOP

1133 Unless there is a delay because of some lawful impediment, a bishop-elect is required to receive episcopal ordination within three months of the date he receives the apostolic letter of election and before he takes possession of his office.[3]

1134 The ordination of a bishop is celebrated within Mass and follows the rite and the norms provided in *The Roman Pontifical* (see nos. 563-597 of this *Ceremonial*).

1135 It is most fitting that the bishop-elect's ordination take place in his cathedral church. In this case he takes possession of the diocese through the very rite of ordination, in which the apostolic letter is shown and read and the newly ordained bishop is installed in his chair (cathedra), as indicated already in nos. 573 and 589.

1136 In order to express episcopal collegiality, the very ancient practice of the Church calls for at least three concelebrating bishops to ordain the bishop-elect, unless the Apostolic See has dispensed from this requirement. But it is fitting for all the bishops present to ordain the bishop-elect.[4]

1137 As a rule, the principal consecrator of a suffragan bishop is the metropolitan; of an auxiliary bishop, the diocesan bishop, unless in the bull of nomination the pope has made some other provision.

---

[3] See CIC, can. 379.
[4] See OB, Introduction, no. 2.

CHAPTER 3

TAKING POSSESSION OF THE DIOCESE

1138 Unless he is held back by a legitimate impediment, a person promoted to the office of diocesan bishop must take canonical possession of his diocese within four months from the reception of the apostolic letter if he has not yet been ordained a bishop, or within two months if he has already been ordained.[5]

1139 If the bishop-elect is ordained in his own cathedral church, he takes possession of the diocese through the very rite of ordination, in which the apostolic letter is shown and read and the newly ordained bishop is installed in his chair (cathedra), as indicated already in nos. 573 and 589.

1140 If the bishop-elect has been transferred from another Church or if he has not received ordination in his own cathedral church, he takes possession of the diocese in accord with the provisions of law as stipulated in the rite of reception, to be described in nos. 1141-1144.

In such cases, the bishop-elect may take possession of the diocese by proxy, but it is preferable that he do so in person.[6]

---

[5] See CIC, can. 382, §2.
[6] See CIC, can. 382, §§3 and 4.

CHAPTER 4

RECEPTION OF THE BISHOP IN HIS CATHEDRAL CHURCH

1141 If the bishop-elect has been transferred from another Church or if he has not received ordination in his own cathedral church, he is received by the gathered community of the diocese and with the celebration of a stational Mass when he comes to his cathedral church for the first time.

1142 The bishop is received at the doors of the church by a minister dressed in cope, who is either the ranking member of the cathedral chapter or, where there is no chapter, the rector of the cathedral church. He offers the bishop a crucifix to be kissed, then a sprinkler of holy water, with which the bishop sprinkles himself and those present. The bishop may then be escorted to the blessed sacrament chapel, where he kneels for a moment in adoration, then to the vesting room (sacristy). There the bishop and the concelebrating presbyters, the deacons, and other ministers put on the vestments for Mass, which is celebrated in the form of a stational Mass.

1143 After reverencing the altar, the bishop goes to the chair (cathedra) and there, upon completion of the entrance song, greets the people. He then sits and puts on the miter. One of the deacons or concelebrating presbyters first shows the bishop's apostolic letter to the college of consultors, in the presence of the chancellor of the diocesan curia, so that he may record the matter in the acts of the curia. Then at the ambo the deacon or presbyter reads the apostolic letter, to which all listen, then respond with the acclamation Thanks be to God or with some other suitable acclamation. But in a newly erected diocese the apostolic letter is communicated to the clergy and people present in the cathedral church, and a senior presbyter among them records the matter in the acts of the curia.

After the reading of the apostolic letter, a bishop who is entitled to the pallium is invested with it, by use of the rite described in nos. 1149-1155.

The bishop is then customarily greeted by the ranking member of the chapter or, where there is no chapter, by the rector of the cathedral church.

In a manner in keeping with local custom, the cathedral chapter, some members at least of the diocesan clergy, members of the faithful, and, as circumstances suggest, representatives of the civil authority go to their bishop and offer some sign of obedience and reverence.

The penitential rite of the Mass is omitted, and also, as circumstances suggest, the *Kyrie*, and the bishop, putting aside the miter, rises, and, in keeping with the rubrics, the *Gloria* is sung.

1144   In the homily after the gospel reading, the bishop addresses his people for the first time.

The Mass continues in the usual way.

1145   But the metropolitan may introduce the bishop into the cathedral church. In this case, at the doors of the church the metropolitan presents the bishop to the ranking member of the chapter and presides in the entrance procession. At the chair (cathedra) he greets the people and bids the apostolic letter to be shown and read to him. After this reading and the acclamation of the people, the metropolitan invites the bishop to sit in the chair (cathedra). Then the bishop rises, and, in keeping with the rubrics, the *Gloria* is sung.

1146   If for some good reason the bishop takes possession of his see by proxy, the rite of reception is carried out in the manner just described, but the showing and reading of the apostolic letter are omitted.

1147   From the day the bishop takes possession of his diocese, his name is mentioned in the eucharistic prayer by all presbyters who celebrate Mass within the diocese, even in the churches and oratories of exempt religious.

1148   It is proper that an auxiliary or coadjutor bishop who has been ordained elsewhere than in the cathedral church of the diocese be introduced by the residential bishop to the people during some liturgical service.

Chapter 5

INVESTITURE WITH THE PALLIUM

1149 Whenever possible, the investiture with the pallium should take place within the rite of ordination, immediately after the presentation of the bishop's ring and before the investiture with the miter. The principal consecrator invests the bishop with the pallium while reciting the formulary To the glory of almighty God, provided in no. 1154.

When the investiture cannot take place within the rite of ordination, it may be carried out in conjunction with the bishop's reception into his cathedral church. The investiture takes place within a celebration of the eucharist, either in the bishop's cathedral or in another suitable church of his diocese, and is carried out by a bishop appointed for this by the Apostolic See, who uses the rite described in this chapter.

1150 The Mass is celebrated in the form of a stational Mass. A deacon carries the pallium in the entrance procession and places it on the altar.

1151 A chair is placed at a convenient place in the sanctuary (chancel) for the bishop appointed by the Apostolic See to present the pallium.

This bishop is the presiding bishop until the investiture has taken place.

1152 After the entrance song, the presiding bishop greets the people in the usual way and in a few words explains the meaning of the rite. When the investiture with the pallium coincides with the reception of the bishop into his cathedral church, a deacon goes to the ambo and reads the apostolic mandate, during which all sit and listen and at the end respond with the acclamation Thanks be to God or some other suitable acclamation that may be more in keeping with local custom.

1153 After the reading of the apostolic mandate or, if the investiture does not coincide with the bishop's first reception into his cathedral church, after the introductory words of the presiding bishop, the bishop-elect goes to the presiding bishop, who, with the miter, is seated. The bishop-elect kneels and makes the profession of faith and the oath of loyalty according to the form indicated by his apostolic letter.

1154 After the profession of faith and the oath, the presiding bishop takes the pallium from the deacon and places it on the shoulders of the bishop-elect, as he says the following formulary.

To the glory of almighty God
and the praise of the Blessed Virgin Mary
and of the apostles Peter and Paul,
in the name of Pope N., Bishop of Rome,
and of the holy Roman Church,
for the honor of the Church of N.,
which has been placed in your care,
and as a symbol of your authority as metropolitan archbishop:
we confer on you the pallium, taken from the tomb of Peter
to wear within the limits of your ecclesiastical province.

May this pallium be a symbol of unity
and a sign of your communion with the Apostolic See,
a bond of love, and an incentive to courage.
On the day of the coming and manifestation
   of our great God and chief shepherd, Jesus Christ,
may you and the flock entrusted to you
be clothed with immortality and glory.
In the name of the Father, and of the Son, and of the Holy Spirit.

R. Amen.

1155 The penitential rite of the Mass is omitted, and also, as circumstances suggest, the *Kyrie*, and the archbishop who has received the pallium begins the *Gloria*, if it is to be said.
The Mass then proceeds in the usual way.

CHAPTER 6

TRANSLATION OF THE BISHOP TO ANOTHER SEE OR RESIGNATION OF THE BISHOP

1156   When a bishop is transferred to another see or his resignation is accepted by the Roman Pontiff, it is proper that he gather his people at a liturgical service. In this way he can bid them farewell and with them give thanks for the blessings received from God during his episcopate.

CHAPTER 7

DEATH AND FUNERAL OF THE BISHOP

1157 When suffering from infirmity and illness, the bishop shows his people good example by receiving the sacraments of reconciliation and eucharist, and when seriously ill, the sacrament of the anointing of the sick.

1158 When he is informed that he is near death, the bishop should ask for and receive viaticum, according to the rite provided in *Pastoral Care of the Sick*.[7]

1159 The presbyterate of the diocese and especially the college of diocesan consultors or the cathedral chapter should conscientiously seek to assist the bishop in his last agony, being particularly concerned to recite in his presence the prayers of commendation of the dying[8] and to have the faithful pray for him.

1160 Upon the death of the bishop, the prayers provided in *Pastoral Care of the Sick* are to be said.[9] Then the body is to be dressed in the violet vesture and with the insignia prescribed for a stational Mass, including the pallium, if the bishop had the right to wear it, but not the pastoral staff. If the bishop had been transferred from another see or from other sees and had received several pallia, these are to be placed in the coffin, unless he had instructed otherwise before his death. After these arrangements and until the time of transferral to the cathedral church for the funeral, the bishop's body is to lie in state in a place suitable for visitation and prayer by the faithful. A vigil service (see OCF, nos. 54-97) or the Office for the Dead (see OCF, nos. 348-396) is to be celebrated at the bier or in the cathedral church.

1161 At a convenient day and time the clergy and people of the diocese are gathered to celebrate the bishop's funeral. The president of the conference of bishops or the metropolitan presides; other bishops and the presbyters of the diocese concelebrate with him.

1162 The funeral is celebrated in the manner indicated already in nos. 821-838.

---

[7] See PCS, nos. 189-196, 197-211.

[8] See PCS, nos. 217-222.

[9] See PCS, no. 221.

1163 The bishop who is the principal celebrant presides alone at the rite of final commendation and farewell.

1164 The body of a deceased diocesan bishop is buried in a church, and as a rule in the cathedral church of his diocese. A retired bishop is buried in the cathedral church of his last see, unless he has made other arrangements.

1165 All the communities of the diocese are to offer prayers for the deceased bishop, whether by celebrating Mass or the Office for the Dead or in some other way of their choosing.

CHAPTER 8

VACANT EPISCOPAL SEE

1166 When a see becomes vacant, the diocesan administrator should ask the clergy and people to offer their prayers that the pastor chosen will be one who can meet the needs of the local Church. In all churches of the diocese the Mass for the election of a pope or a bishop (RM, Masses and Prayers for Various Needs and Occasions, I. For the Church, 4. For the Election of a Pope or Bishop) should be celebrated at least once, except on the days listed in nos. 1-4 of the table of liturgical days.[10]

---

[10] See Appendix II of this *Ceremonial*.

CHAPTER 9

CELEBRATION OF VARIOUS ANNIVERSARIES

1167   Each year in the cathedral church and in all the churches and communities of the diocese there is to be a celebration of the anniversary of the bishop's episcopal ordination. The Mass for the bishop (RM, Masses and Prayers for Various Needs and Occasions, I. For the Church, 3. For the Bishop) is celebrated, except on the days listed in nos. 1-6 of the table of liturgical days.[11]

It is recommended that on this day the bishop of the place preside at a stational Mass in the cathedral church.

1168   There is also a longstanding tradition that each year the anniversary of the last deceased bishop be observed, unless he had been transferred to another diocese. The occasion is marked by the celebration of Mass, and it is recommended that the bishop of the place preside in the cathedral church. The faithful and particularly priests are to be instructed that in the Lord they should remember their leaders, those who spoke the word of God to them.[12]

---

[11] See Appendix II of this *Ceremonial*.
[12] See Hebrews 13:7.

Part VIII

LITURGICAL CELEBRATIONS
IN CONNECTION WITH OFFICIAL ACTS
PERTAINING TO THE GOVERNMENT
OF A DIOCESE

CHAPTER 1

PLENARY OR PROVINCIAL COUNCIL AND DIOCESAN SYNOD

1169 From the longstanding practice of the Church, a council or a diocesan synod includes liturgical services, modeled on the celebrations that are recorded in Acts 15:6-29. The governance of the Church is never to be looked upon as a mere administrative act; under the influence of the Holy Spirit, its governing assemblies are gathered in the name of God and for God's glory, and they therefore are an expression of the unity of the Mystical Body of Christ, which shines with greatest clarity in the liturgy. It is right that those who bear the one responsibility together also share in the one prayer together.

1170 These assemblies should all begin with the celebration of a Mass, to which the people are invited and which all the members of the council or synod rightly concelebrate with the president of the assembly. Those who do not concelebrate may receive communion under both kinds. Except on the days listed in nos. 1-4 of the table of liturgical days,[1] the Mass for a council or synod (RM, Masses and Prayers for Various Needs and Occasions, I. For the Church, 5. For a Council or Synod) is celebrated; red vestments are used.

1171 When before the Mass, in keeping with local circumstances and the occasion, there is a procession, the antiphon Hear us, O Lord or some other suitable song may be sung at the gathering place. After the singing, the president of the assembly greets the people and, after brief introductory remarks by the president or by one of the concelebrants or deacons, the president says one of the prayers for pastoral or spiritual meetings or for the local Church (RM, Masses and Prayers for Various Needs and Occasions, I. For the Church, 16. For Pastoral or Spiritual Meetings, or 1. For the Universal Church, particularly prayer E, For the Local Church). Incense is then placed in the censer and, as circumstances suggest, the deacon says, Let us go forth in peace, and the procession is formed. In the procession a deacon reverently carries the Book of the Gospels, and as the procession makes its way to the church, the Litany of the Saints is sung, with this addition before the final invocation: Visit and bless this assembly.

In their proper place invocations of the patron saint of the local Church, of its founder, and of its saints may be added. When the procession reaches the church, the concelebrants reverence the altar, then take

---

[1] See Appendix II of this *Ceremonial*.

their assigned places; the president of the assembly also reverences the altar and incenses it. He then goes to the chair (cathedra) and there says the opening prayer; the introductory rites of the Mass are omitted.

1172 When there is no procession, the Mass begins in the manner usual for a stational Mass. After the gospel reading, the open Book of the Gospels is placed on a suitable stand in the center of the sanctuary (chancel).

1173 After the president has given the homily, the profession of faith is always sung or recited; the oath is then taken by the members and the president of the council or synod.

When the prayer after communion has been said, the president gives the final blessing, and the deacon dismisses the people. The president then begins and all join in the following or some other prayer:

> We stand before you, Holy Spirit,
> conscious of our sinfulness,
> but aware that we gather in your name.
>
> Come to us, remain with us,
> and enlighten our hearts.
>
> Give us light and strength
> to know your will,
> to make it our own
> and to live it in our lives.
>
> Guide us by your wisdom,
> support us by your power,
> for you are God,
> sharing the glory of Father and Son.
>
> You desire justice for all:
> enable us to uphold the rights of others;
> do not allow us to be misled by ignorance
> or corrupted by fear or favor.
> Unite us to yourself in the bond of love
> and keep us faithful to all that is true.
>
> As we gather in your name
> may we temper justice with love,
> so that all our decisions
> may be pleasing to you,
> and earn the reward
> promised to good and faithful servants.
> Amen.

1174 During the council or synod, it is fitting that each day's session be preceded by the celebration of Mass, the celebration of the hour of the liturgy of the hours corresponding to the time of day, or a celebration of the word of God.

When Mass is celebrated, the Book of the Gospels is carried reverently in the entrance procession and placed on the altar, as is done in a stational Mass. After the gospel reading, the open Book of the Gospels is placed on a suitable stand in the center of the sanctuary (chancel).

When an hour of the liturgy of the hours is celebrated, at the end the Book of the Gospels is carried reverently by the deacon, accompanied by acolytes carrying lighted candles; with the same rite as is used at Mass, an appropriate gospel reading is proclaimed. When the reading is finished, the deacon places the open Book of the Gospels on a suitable stand in the center of the sanctuary (chancel).

1175 At the conclusion of the final session, the hymn *Te Deum* is sung and is followed by the blessing by the president and the dismissal. If Mass is celebrated at the end, the *Te Deum* is sung before the prayer after communion. As circumstances suggest, the acclamations known as the *laudes regiae* or *carolinae** may be sung after the dismissal.

1176 These provisions for a council or a diocesan synod, which are solemn meetings, apply, with appropriate adaptation, also to other, more frequent meetings convoked for the ordinary government of the Church, for example, a meeting of the conference of bishops, priests' council, and the like.

---

* See *New Catholic Encyclopedia* (McGraw-Hill Book Company, New York, copyright © 1967), v. 1, p. 80, a.

CHAPTER 2

PASTORAL VISITATION

1177 The bishop in fulfilling the obligation to visit the parishes or local communities of his diocese should not appear to be satisfying a purely administrative duty. Rather the faithful should see in him the herald of the Gospel, the teacher, shepherd, and high priest of his flock.

1178 To ensure this happening, the visitation of the bishop should take place, if at all possible, on days that permit large numbers of the faithful to gather. Sufficient time should also be devoted to an apt, preparatory catechesis of the people by their presbyters. The visitation itself should be sufficiently long to enable the bishop to preside at celebrations of the liturgy and to evaluate, promote, encourage, and put into effect the apostolate of the clergy and laity and the works of charity.

1179 The bishop, in the vestments indicated in no. 63, should be received in a manner suited to the circumstances of the place and the situation. If this seems appropriate, the bishop may be solemnly received and greeted by the clergy at the door of the church. But the bishop may even be escorted to the church with festive song, when this is feasible and appropriate. A dignified solemnity in receiving the bishop is a sign of the love and devotion of the faithful toward their good shepherd.

1180 At the entrance of the church the parish priest (pastor), vested in cope, meets the bishop, offers him the crucifix to be kissed, and presents the sprinkler, with which the bishop sprinkles himself and those present. After a brief, silent prayer before the blessed sacrament, the bishop goes to the sanctuary (chancel); there the parish priest (pastor), standing before the altar, invites the faithful to join in prayer for the bishop and, after a brief pause for silent prayer, says the prayer God, eternal shepherd or God, our Father, our shepherd and guide, provided in *The Roman Missal (Sacramentary)*.[2]

The bishop then greets the people and announces his agenda for the visitation. He then says the collect for the titular of the church or the patron of the place, and, in the usual way, blesses the people. Then the parish priest (pastor) dismisses them.

---

[2] See RM, Masses and Prayers for Various Needs and Occasions, I. For the Church, 3. For the Bishop, A.

1181 But when Mass is to follow the reception of the bishop, immediately after the prayer for the bishop has been said, the bishop, at the chair, puts on the vestments for Mass. The presbyters charged with the pastoral care of the parish or presbyters living within the parish confines concelebrate the Mass with the bishop, and the faithful take an active part. Such participation is particularly to be sought in the more remote parts of the diocese where the people rarely or never have the opportunity to take part in a stational Mass celebrated by the bishop in their own area.

1182 It is recommended that during the pastoral visitation the bishop confer not only the sacrament of confirmation but other sacraments as well, particularly in his visits to the sick. In this way he will more clearly appear to the faithful as the chief steward of the mysteries of God and as the overseer and guardian of the entire liturgical life in the Church entrusted to his care.

1183 When there is a lengthy visitation, there should be a celebration of the liturgy of the hours in the church or a celebration of the word of God, with the homily by the bishop and with intercessions for the universal Church and for the local Church.

1184 As circumstances suggest, the bishop should also go to the cemetery with the people and there offer prayers for the dead and sprinkle the graves with holy water, in the manner described already in nos. 399-402.

CHAPTER 3

INTRODUCTION OF A NEW PARISH PRIEST (PASTOR)
INTO HIS PARISH

1185 Before being introduced into his parish or in the very act of taking possession of it, a new parish priest (pastor) is to make the profession of faith before the local Ordinary or his delegate.

1186 The introduction of a new parish priest (pastor) into his parish is carried out by the bishop himself or by his delegate on a convenient day and at a convenient time, in the presence of the assembly of the faithful. The introduction may be done in a way suited to local custom or, quite fittingly, in the way described in this chapter.

1187 It is appropriate that the introduction take place in conjunction with a Mass, which, depending on the rubrics, will be either the Mass of the day or a votive Mass of the titular of the church or of the Holy Spirit. The bishop should preside, and the new parish priest (pastor) as well as other presbyters of the parish or of the district should concelebrate with him.

1188 But if, for good reason, the bishop is present but does not celebrate the Mass, then, as has been said already in nos. 175-185, it is proper that he at least preside during the liturgy of the word and bless the people at the end of Mass.

1189 Local customs should be observed. Otherwise, as circumstances suggest, the rites to be described here may be used in whole or in part.

1190 Where the circumstances permit, the bishop and the new parish priest (pastor) may be met at the parish boundary and escorted in procession to the doors of the church. There the bishop briefly introduces the new parish priest (pastor) and hands him the keys of the church. The introduction may also take place at the beginning of Mass, after the greeting, and particularly when at the beginning of Mass, after the bishop's greeting, the parish priest's (pastor's) letter of appointment is read and, in keeping with the provisions of the law, he makes the profession of faith.

1191 It is fitting that the new parish priest (pastor) proclaim the gospel reading; beforehand he goes to the bishop and from him receives the Book of the Gospels and asks for a blessing.

1192   In the homily the bishop explains to the faithful the office of a parish priest (pastor) and the meaning of the rites that will take place immediately after the homily.

1193   After the homily, it is recommended that the parish priest (pastor) renew the promises he made at his ordination, as the bishop puts the following questions to him.

> My dear brother, in the presence of the people whom you are about to receive into your care, I ask you to renew the promises you made at your ordination.
>
> Are you resolved that under the guidance of the Holy Spirit you will without fail live up to your responsibility to be the faithful co-worker of the order of bishops in shepherding the flock of the Lord?
>
> R. I am.
>
> Are you resolved that in praise of God and for the sanctification of the Christian people you will celebrate the mysteries of Christ devoutly and faithfully, and in accord with the tradition of the Church?
>
> R. I am.
>
> Are you resolved that in preaching the Gospel and teaching the Catholic faith you will worthily and wisely fulfill the ministry of God's word?
>
> R. I am.
>
> Are you resolved that you will bind yourself ever more closely to Christ, the high priest who for us offered himself to the Father as a spotless victim, and that with Christ you will consecrate yourself to God for the salvation of your brothers and sisters?
>
> R. I am.
>
> Do you promise respect and obedience to me and to my successors?
>
> R. I do.
>
> May God who has begun this good work in you bring it to fulfillment.

1194   As circumstances suggest, a procession with censerbearer, crossbearer, candlebearers, and other ministers may then be formed, so that the bishop may lead the parish priest (pastor) around the church and entrust to him the various places that will be the sacred sites of his ministry: presidential chair, the chapel of the blessed sacrament, the baptistery, the confessional. The bishop may also invite the parish priest (pastor) to open the tabernacle door and incense the blessed sacrament. He may also incense the baptistery. If this can be done conveniently, the bishop may also invite the parish priest (pastor) to ring the church bells.

Depending on the circumstances, all these things may be done before Mass.

1195 In the general intercessions there is a special intention for the bishop and for the parish priest (pastor).

1196 For the rite of peace the parish priest (pastor) may himself exchange the sign of peace with some of the people as representatives of the parish.

1197 After the prayer after communion, the bishop invites the parish priest (pastor) to speak briefly to the community.

1198 It is recommended that the parish priest (pastor) go with the bishop and the people to the cemetery and there offer prayers for the dead and, as circumstances suggest, sprinkle the graves with holy water, in the manner described already in nos. 399-402.

APPENDIXES

APPENDIX I

VESTURE OF PRELATES*

I. VESTURE OF BISHOPS

Choir dress

1199 The bishop always wears the ring, the symbol of his fidelity to and nuptial bond with the Church, his spouse (see no. 58).

This is the choir dress of the bishop both inside and outside his diocese: purple cassock; purple silk sash, with silk fringes at both ends (but without tassels); rochet of linen or some similar material; purple mozzetta (without hood); over the mozzetta the pectoral cross with cord of green interwoven with gold strands; purple skullcap; purple biretta with tassel. Purple stockings are also worn.

1200 The purple *cappa magna*, without ermine, may be worn only within the diocese and for the most solemn feasts.

1201 The bishop wears ordinary black shoes, without buckles.

1202 The bishop wears the dress just described whenever he goes publicly to or from church, when he is present at a liturgical service but does not preside, and in other instances indicated in this *Ceremonial*.

Vesture of the bishop for solemn but nonliturgical occasions

1203 This is the vesture of the bishop for solemn but nonliturgical occasions: black cassock with piping and red-silk stitching, red buttonholes and buttons, but without the oversleeves; the elbow-length cape, trimmed in the same manner as the cassock, may be worn over it; purple silk sash, with silk fringes at both ends; pectoral cross, hanging from a chain; purple skullcap and *collare* (rabat).

Use of purple stockings is optional. The black plush hat may, if necessary, be adorned with a green cord. Use of the purple watered-silk cloak is reserved for more solemn occasions.

Over these a decent black cloak, even with hood, may be worn.

---

* These paragraphs follow the provisions of the Instruction of the Secretariat of State *Ut sive solli-cite*, on the dress, titles, and insignia of cardinals, bishops, and lesser prelates, 31 March 1969: AAS 61 (1969), pp. 334-340; DOL 551, nos. 4497-4532; and the Circular Letter of the Sacred Congregation for Clergy *Per Instructionem*, on the reform of choir dress, 30 October 1970: AAS 63 (1971), pp. 314-315; DOL 552, nos. 4533-4537.

Vesture for ordinary, daily wear

1204 The vesture for ordinary or everyday use may be the plain black cassock with purple sash. Bishops from religious orders may wear the habit of their institute. With the black cassock black stockings are worn; the purple *collare* (rabat), skullcap, and sash may be worn. The pectoral cross hangs from a chain. The ring is always worn.

II. VESTURE OF CARDINALS

1205 All that has been said about the vesture of bishops applies to that of cardinals, with the following exceptions:

a. whatever is purple in the case of a bishop is red in the case of a cardinal;

b. the red sash, skullcap, and cloak are of watered silk;

c. the cord for the pectoral cross and the cords and tassels of the plush hat are of red interwoven with gold strands;

d. the biretta of red watered-silk is to be worn only with choir dress, not as an everyday head covering.

III. VESTURE OF OTHER PRELATES

1206 Prelates who are equal in law to a diocesan bishop but have not been raised to the episcopate may wear the same vesture as bishops.

1207 The higher ranking prelates of the offices of the Roman Curia who do not have episcopal rank, the auditors of the Rota, the promoter general of justice, and the defender of the bond of the Apostolic Signatura, apostolic protonotaries *de numero,* papal chamberlains, and domestic prelates wear the following vesture:

a. as choir dress: the purple cassock with purple sash and fringes of silk at the two ends, rochet, purple mantelletta, black biretta with red tuft;

b. on solemn but nonliturgical occasions: black cassock with red piping and other ornaments, but without cape; purple sash and fringes of silk at both ends; purple silk cloak (optional); black stockings and ordinary shoes, without buckles.

1208 Supernumerary apostolic protonotaries and honorary prelates of His Holiness wear the following vesture:

a. as choir dress: the purple cassock and purple silk sash with fringes, unpleated surplice, black biretta with black tuft;

b. on solemn but nonliturgical occasions: black cassock with red piping and other ornaments, but without cape; purple sash and fringes of silk at both ends; the purple silk cloak, although not obligatory, is retained for supernumerary apostolic protonotaries, but not for honorary prelates of His Holiness.

1209 As choir dress and on solemn but nonliturgical occasions the chaplains of His Holiness wear the purple-trimmed black cassock with purple sash and other ornaments. As choir dress they wear a surplice over the cassock.

III. Vesture of Canons

1210 As choir dress in liturgical celebrations, canons who are not bishops wear over the cassock proper to their rank only a surplice and a black or gray mozzetta with purple trim. Clerics holding benefices wear over the cassock proper to them only a surplice and a black or gray mozzetta.

Outside liturgical celebrations they wear the vesture proper to their status.

TABLE OF LITURGICAL DAYS
(ACCORDING TO THEIR ORDER OF PRECEDENCE)

I

1. Easter Triduum of the Lord's passion and resurrection.

2. Christmas, Epiphany, Ascension, and Pentecost.
   Sundays of Advent, Lent, and the Easter season.
   Ash Wednesday.
   Weekdays of Holy Week from Monday to Thursday inclusive.
   Days within the octave of Easter.

3. Solemnities of the Lord, the Blessed Virgin Mary, and saints listed in the General Calendar.
   All Souls.

4. Proper solemnities, namely:
   a. solemnity of the principal patron of the place, that is, the city or state;
   b. solemnity of the dedication of a particular church and the anniversary;
   c. solemnity of the title of a particular church;
   d. solemnity of the title or of the founder or of the principal patron of a religious order or congregation.

II

5. Feasts of the Lord in the General Calendar.

6. Sundays of the Christmas season and Sundays in Ordinary Time.

7. Feasts of the Blessed Virgin Mary and of the saints in the General Calendar.

8. Proper feasts, namely:
   a. feast of the principal patron of the diocese;
   b. feast of the anniversary of the dedication of the cathedral;
   c. feast of the principal patron of a region or province or a country or of a wider territory;
   d. feast of the title, founder, or principal patron of an order or congregation and of a religious province, without prejudice to the directives in no. 4;

e. other feasts proper to an individual church;

f. other feasts listed in the calendar of a diocese or of a religious order or congregation.

9. Weekdays of Advent from 17 December to 24 December inclusive. Days within the octave of Christmas. Weekdays of Lent.

III

10. Obligatory memorials in the General Calendar.

11. Proper obligatory memorials, namely:

a. memorial of a secondary patron of the place, diocese, region, or province, country or wider territory, or of an order or congregation and of a religious province;

b. obligatory memorials listed in the calendar of a diocese, or of an order or congregation.

TABLE OF RUBRICS GOVERNING RITUAL MASSES, MASSES FOR VARIOUS NEEDS AND OCCASIONS, AND MASSES FOR THE DEAD

Sigla

V1 = Ritual Masses (General Instruction of the Roman Missal, no. 330).

Masses for various needs and occasions and votive Masses, in cases of serious need or pastoral advantage, at the direction of the local Ordinary or with his permission (GIRM, no. 332).

V2 = Masses for various needs and occasions and votive Masses, in cases of serious need or pastoral advantage, at the discretion of the rector of the church or the priest celebrant (GIRM, no. 333).

V3 = Masses for various needs and occasions and votive Masses chosen by the priest celebrant in favor of the devotion of the people (GIRM, no. 329, b and c).

D1 = Funeral Mass (GIRM, no. 336).

D2 = Mass on the occasion of news of a death, final burial, or the first anniversary (GIRM, no. 337).

D3 = Daily Mass for the dead (GIRM). When D1 and D2 are not permitted, neither is D3.

+ = permitted.

− = not permitted.

1. Solemnities of precept	V1 – D1 –		
2. Sundays of Advent, Lent, and the Easter season	V1 – D1 –		
3. Holy Thursday, Easter Triduum	V1 – D1 –		
4. Solemnities not of precept, All Souls	V1 – D1 +		
5. Ash Wednesday, weekdays of Holy Week	V1 – D1 +		
6. Days in the Easter octave	V1 – D1 +		
7. Sundays of Christmas, and in Ordinary Time	V1 + D1 +	V2 – D2 –	
8. Feasts	V1 + D1 +	V2 – D2 –	
9. Weekdays 17–24 December	V1 + D1 +	V2 – D2 +	
10. Days in the Christmas octave	V1 + D1 +	V2 – D2 +	
11. Weekdays of Lent	V1 + D1 +	V2 – D2 +	
12. Obligatory memorials	V1 + D1 +	V2 + D2 +	
13. Weekdays of Advent to 16 December	V1 + D1 +	V2 + D2 +	
14. Weekdays of Christmas from 2 January	V1 + D1 +	V2 + D2 +	
15. Weekdays of the Easter season	V1 + D1 +	V2 + D2 +	
16. Weekdays in Ordinary Time	V1 + D1 +	V2 + D2 +	V3 + D3 +

Appendix IV

ABBREVIATIONS AND SIGLA

I. DOCUMENTS OF VATICAN II

CD Decree on the Pastoral Office of Bishops *Christus Dominus*, 28 Oct 1965
LG Dogmatic Constitution on the Church *Lumen gentium*, 21 Nov 1964
SC Constitution on the Liturgy *Sacrosanctum Concilium*, 4 Dec 1963

II. RITES AND RITUAL BOOKS

AC Admission to Candidacy for Ordination as Deacons and Priests, *The Roman Pontifical*, English ed., 1978, ch. 7

BA Blessing of an Altar, The Roman Pontifical, *Dedication of a Church and an Altar*, English ed., 1978, ch. 6

BC Blessing of a Church, The Roman Pontifical, *Dedication of a Church and an Altar*, English ed., 1978, ch. 5

BCP Blessing of a Chalice and Paten, The Roman Pontifical, *Dedication of a Church and an Altar*, English ed., 1978, ch. 7

BAb Blessing of an Abbot, *The Roman Pontifical*, English ed., 1978, ch. 14

BAbs Blessing of an Abbess, *The Roman Pontifical*, English ed., 1978, ch. 15

BOCC *Rite of Blessing of Oils and Rite of Consecrating the Chrism*, The Roman Pontifical, English ed., 1972

CIBVM *Order of Crowning an Image of the Blessed Virgin Mary*, English ed., 1985

CLV Consecration to a Life of Virginity, *The Roman Pontifical*, English ed., 1978, ch. 16

DA Dedication of an Altar, The Roman Pontifical, *Dedication of a Church and an Altar*, English ed., 1978, ch. 4

DC Dedication of a Church, The Roman Pontifical, *Dedication of a Church and an Altar*, English ed., 1978, ch. 2

HCWE *Holy Communion and Worship of the Eucharist outside Mass*, The Roman Ritual, English ed., 1974

IA Institution of Acolytes, *The Roman Pontifical*, English ed., 1978, ch. 6

IR Institution of Readers, *The Roman Pontifical*, English ed., 1978, ch. 5

LFS Laying of a Foundation Stone or Commencement of Work on the Building of a Church, The Roman Pontifical, *Dedication of a Church and an Altar*, English ed., 1978, ch. 1

LH *The Liturgy of the Hours*, English ed., 1974

LM *Lectionary for Mass*, 2nd English ed., 1981

OB Ordination of a Bishop, *The Roman Pontifical*, English ed., 1978, ch. 12

OBB Order for the Blessing of Bells, The Roman Ritual, *Book of Blessings*, English ed., 1987, ch. 30

OBBF Order for the Blessing of a Baptistery or of a New Baptismal Font, The Roman Ritual, *Book of Blessings*, English ed., 1987, ch. 25

OBC Order for the Blessing of a Cemetery, The Roman Ritual, *Book of Blessings*, English ed., 1987, ch. 35

OBNC Order for the Blessing of a New Cross for Public Veneration, The Roman Ritual, *Book of Blessings*, English ed., 1987, ch. 28

OCF *Order of Christian Funerals*, The Roman Ritual, English ed., 1985

OD Ordination of Deacons, *The Roman Pontifical*, English ed., 1978, ch. 8

ODP Ordination of Deacons and Priests in the Same Celebration, *The Roman Pontifical*, English ed., 1978, Appendix III

OP Ordination of Priests, *The Roman Pontifical*, English ed., 1978, ch. 10

PCS *Pastoral Care of the Sick: Rites of Anointing and Viaticum*, The Roman Ritual, English ed., 1982

RBC *Rite of Baptism for Children*, The Roman Ritual, English ed., 1969

RC Rite of Confirmation, *The Roman Pontifical*, English ed., 1978, ch. 3

RCIA *Rite of Christian Initiation of Adults*, The Roman Ritual, English ed., 1985

RF *Rite of Funerals*, The Roman Ritual, English ed., 1970

RM *The Roman Missal (Sacramentary)*, 2nd English ed., 1985

RMar *Rite of Marriage*, The Roman Ritual, English ed., 1969

RPen *Rite of Penance*, The Roman Ritual, English ed., 1974

RPM Rite of Religious Profession for Men, The Roman Ritual, *Rite of Religious Profession*, English ed., 1975, Part I

RPW Rite of Religious Profession for Women, The Roman Ritual, *Rite of Religious Profession*, English ed., 1975, Part II

III. General Abbreviations

AAS *Acta Apostolicae Sedis*. Commentarium officiale (Vatican City, 1909–)

can. canon

CCL *Corpus Christianorum, Series latina* (Turnhout, Belgium, 1953–)

ch. chapter

CIC *Codex Iuris Canonici (Code of Canon Law)*, 1983

DOL ICEL, *Documents on the Liturgy; 1963-1979: Conciliar, Papal, and Curial Texts* (The Liturgical Press, Collegeville, Minn., 1982)

EV Easter Vigil

GF Good Friday, Celebration of the Lord's Passion

GILH General Instruction of the Liturgy of the Hours, SC Worship, 22 Feb 1971: DOL 426

GIRM General Instruction of the Roman Missal, 4th ed., SC Worship, 27 Mar 1975: DOL 442

GNLYC General Norms for the Liturgical Year and Calendar, Congregation of Rites, 21 Mar 1969: DOL 442

HT Holy Thursday, Mass of the Lord's Supper

ICEL International Commission on English in the Liturgy

MQ Motu Proprio *Ministeria quaedam*, on first tonsure, minor orders, and the subdiaconate, Paul VI, 15 Aug 1972: DOL 340

MS Instruction *Musicam sacram*, Congregation of Rites, 5 Mar 1967: DOL 508

no. number

nos. numbers

p. page

PG *Patrologiae cursus completus: Series graeca*, J.P. Migne, ed., 161 v. (Paris, 1857-1866)

PL *Patrologiae cursus completus: Series latina*, J.P. Migne, ed., 222 v. (Paris, 1844-1855)

pp. pages

PR Instruction *Pontificales ritus*, on simplification of pontifical rites and insignia, Congregation of Rites, 21 June 1968: DOL 550

SC Worship Sacred Congregation for Divine Worship

SC Rites Sacred Congregation of Rites